Megaproject Development
and Decision Making

Megaproject Development and Decision Making

Strategies for Successful Projects and Investments

Akin Oni, PMP, CCP, DTM

BUSINESS EXPERT PRESS

Leader in applied, concise business books

Megaproject Development and Decision Making:
Strategies for Successful Projects and Investments

Cover design by Akin Oni

Interior design by S4Carlisle Publishing Services, Chennai, India

First published in 2026 by
Business Expert Press, LLC
222 East 46th Street, New York, NY 10017
www.businessexpertpress.com

ISBN-13: 978-1-63742-938-9 (paperback)
ISBN-13: 978-1-63742-939-6 (e-book)

Portfolio and Project Management Collection

First edition: 2026

10 9 8 7 6 5 4 3 2 1

EU SAFETY REPRESENTATIVE
Mare Nostrum Group B.V.
Mauritskade 21D
1091 GC Amsterdam
The Netherlands
gpsr@mare-nostrum.co.uk

Dedication

To every project professional across the globe who imagines boldly, evaluates wisely, and delivers with excellence—this book is dedicated to you and your pursuit of The Best Projects.

Description

Why do so many billion-dollar megaprojects—designed to power economies and transform societies—fail, and what can be done to change the story?

Megaproject Development and Decision Making: Strategies for Successful Projects and Investments answers this urgent question by focusing on the most overlooked stage of every large venture: the period before the first shovel hits the ground. Drawing on more than three decades of global project leadership in energy, mining, refining, and infrastructure across six continents, Akin Oni demonstrates that the fate of megaprojects is rarely sealed in execution; it is determined in the early stages of development, evaluation, and strategic decision making.

This book dismantles the myths that complexity, politics, or market volatility are the primary culprits of failure. Instead, it reveals how weak governance, unclear goals, flawed evaluations, and poor risk discipline doom projects long before approval. With clarity and conviction, Oni equips leaders with the frameworks, tools, and foresight to prevent these costly missteps.

Far from a theoretical treatise, this is a practical, field-tested guide for project managers, executives, investors, and policymakers. Readers will find:

- Proven evaluation and decision-making frameworks tailored to high-stakes projects
- Early warning signals and diagnostic tools to spot problems before they escalate
- Templates and case-based insights from global projects across sectors
- Guidance on embedding ethics, sustainability, and stakeholder alignment into every stage

Both a practitioner's manual and a leadership call to action, the book reframes megaprojects as more than technical or financial feats: they are ethical commitments, legacies of trust, and opportunities to shape a better future.

If you are entrusted with stewarding capital-intensive projects, this book will not only inform you—it will challenge you to lead differently.

Contents

x   CONTENTS

List of Figures and Tables

Figures

Tables

Acknowledgments

I begin by giving all honor to God Almighty—the well of wisdom from which I continually draw, and the source of life, strength, and clarity that has guided me every step of the way.

To my wife, Flora Oni, and to our children—Daniel, Bernice, and Arlen—you are my deepest joy and my surest foundation. Thank you for your unwavering love, patience, and encouragement. You have walked with me through the long nights of writing and the endless days of projects, reminding me of what truly matters.

I remain profoundly grateful to those who first opened my eyes to the discipline and beauty of project management. At the university, Professors Kam Jugdev and Janice Thomas planted the seeds of knowledge and curiosity that continue to grow in me. In the workplace, my earlier years at NETCO (NNPC/Bechtel JV) and BHP Billiton became living classrooms where theory met reality, and where I was shaped by the wisdom, challenges, and camaraderie of remarkable colleagues.

A special word of thanks to my heavy-pen readers and reviewers—Professor Kam Jugdev, Graciela Garcia de Duva, Iwona Wilson, and Austin Wilson. Your careful feedback, honest critique, and encouragement refined both the message and the delivery of this work.

And finally, to the countless professionals, colleagues, leaders, and friends I have met on this journey—across companies, projects, organizations, and professional associations worldwide—you are too many to list by name, but your influence is deeply imprinted on these pages. Your dedication, insights, and inspiration not only shaped my career but also compelled me to write this book.

This is, in truth, a collective work—born out of shared experiences, challenges, and victories in the pursuit of delivering *The Best Projects*. For that, I thank you all.

Foreword

It is rare to encounter a book that speaks with both the authority of lived experience and the clarity of structured insight. *Megaproject Development and Decision Making: Strategies for Successful Projects and Investments* is such a book.

For decades, I have researched and been a part of the complexities of energy industry project management, especially the forces that shape success and failure at the largest scales. The sobering truth is that too many megaprojects—despite talent, technology, and ambition—still fail to deliver on their promises. Most books and frameworks focus on execution. Yet, as Akin Oni powerfully demonstrates, the fate of megaprojects is sealed long before execution begins.

This book fills a critical gap. With three decades of global leadership in energy, mining, and infrastructure, Akin distills the lessons that practitioners, executives, and policymakers urgently need. He does not present theory in isolation. Instead, he weaves practical tools, early warning signals, and case-driven insights into a guide that challenges us to rethink how we evaluate, decide, and lead.

What I value most in this book is its balance: between vision and discipline, between ambition and accountability, between the technical and the human. It is uplifting because it believes megaprojects can succeed. It is challenging because it insists we take responsibility for the decisions that shape billions of dollars—and millions of lives.

To anyone entrusted with stewarding capital projects, this book is not optional reading. It is a compass for decision making under uncertainty and a reminder that our projects are more than assets: They are legacies.

I commend Akin for contributing a work that will stand as both a practitioner's manual and a leadership call to action. It is my esteemed honor and privilege to introduce this timely and much-needed book.

Leye Owolabi, PhD (*Penn State*), MBA (*University of Delaware*)
Industry Executive, Scholar, and Project Practitioner

Epigraph

"Make big plans; aim high in hope and work, remembering that a noble, logical diagram once recorded will never die."—Daniel H. Burnham

"Megaprojects are where vision meets risk, and decisions become destiny. To lead them is to balance strategy with discipline, and courage with wisdom."—Akin Oni

CHAPTER 1

Introduction

Learning Outcomes

After reading this chapter, you will be able to:

1. Understand the purpose and practical relevance of this book in addressing front-end megaproject challenges.
2. Describe the foundational reasons why megaprojects often fail before execution begins.
3. Recognize the importance of early-stage strategic alignment, stakeholder engagement, and risk identification.
4. Explain the concept of megaprojects as a bridge between strategy and operational delivery.
5. Identify the distinct characteristics and life cycle stages of megaprojects in the energy, metals, and mining sectors.

It was during the final stretch of my executive MBA in project management degree between 2007 and 2008 in Canada. My thesis research was meant to be empirical, structured, and focused. However, through the "shoot for excellence" challenge thrown at me by my thesis (i.e., applied project) professor, Kam Jugdev, it became something else—a personal reckoning.

I immersed myself in data and case studies on global megaprojects—dozens across industries and continents. And what I found was both predictable and shocking. Megaprojects—those capital-intensive endeavors designed to redefine industries—were failing often and consistently. Overruns. Delays. Lawsuits. Community unrest. Reputation damage. But the trustworthy source of the failures? That's where the insight struck like lightning.

Most megaprojects fail long before construction even begins. This observation is consistent with global trends where megaprojects face cost overruns and benefit shortfalls due to poor front-end planning (Ika et al. 2024; Cottafava et al. 2024).

More than a decade of hands-on project leadership in energy, mining, and infrastructure has taught me a different truth: megaprojects deserve not to fail. Early project life cycle activities fail because strategies are unclear, assumptions are unverified, and warning signs are missed or ignored.

This book calls for changing directions, capturing the attention of people and institutions around investment decisions in megaprojects at the front end, where risks, time, and available capital are shaped, and successful projects are launched for sustainable delivery.

The Mission Behind This Book: What, How, and Why

This book is for anyone committed to understanding what drives successful megaprojects and how this approach differs from traditional thinking.

There are no easy projects anymore!

Today, we face increasing regulatory oversight, Environmental, Social, and Governance (ESG) scrutiny, digital disruption, and a rapidly evolving definition of stakeholder value. Yet megaprojects are still being greenlit based on wishful thinking, slide decks, and boardroom politics rather than informed decision making. Governance gaps and misaligned policy often contribute to these decisions (Locatelli et al. 2017; Brookes and Locatelli 2015).

Many decision makers assume that a project with a good technical team and a budget will somehow "figure itself out." When it doesn't, they throw people and money at it to deliver at all costs.

Too many project managers confuse Gantt charts with strategy, and many governance frameworks are mere theater.

This is neither a theoretical textbook nor a postmortem on failed megaprojects. It is a practical guide crafted for business leaders, investors, lenders, project professionals, and decision makers who are responsible for setting up capital projects for long-term success. It is grounded in the belief that successful execution begins before the first site mobilization.

The journey to write this book is not just a professional endeavor but a personal mission to transform the landscape of megaproject management. By sharing stories of failed and successful megaprojects, I aim to illustrate the emotional and professional catalysts behind this book, blending reflective, motivational, and narrative tones to resonate with readers.

Instead of examining what goes wrong after a project breaks ground, this book focuses on the front end of the megaproject life cycle, the critical planning, framing, alignment, and evaluation activities that decide whether a project will survive or die. The pages are brimming with kernels of real-world experience, templates, and decision-making frameworks drawn from work across continents and cultures in the energy, metals, and mining sectors.

While the basics of execution are briefly discussed, this book's primary goal is to equip readers with the foresight, tools, and knowledge they need, starting from opportunity framing and stakeholder engagement through concept definition, risk planning, case framing, optimization, evaluation, execution planning, and decision support packages—all before arriving at the Final Investment Decision (FID).

I wrote this book to say: **Enough**!

Enough with:

- Treating evaluation as a tick-box exercise
- Confusing motion with progress
- Delegating risk thinking until it's too late
- Believing that being "on time and budget" alone equals success

This book offers a better way to craft from the crucible of experience. It's not a textbook or an academic treatise. It's a practical field manual for those who want to challenge how megaprojects are imagined, developed, evaluated, and greenlit.

Whether you're a business executive aiming to sharpen alignment, understand what the project will deliver, and reduce risk, or a project manager/director responsible for delivering a multibillion-dollar venture, or an investor or lender wanting to "put your money where your mouth is," this guide offers a practical, repeatable roadmap to help ensure your project doesn't just start strong—it finishes strong.

How Megaprojects Take Shape

Finally, nothing about project outcomes, success or failure, happens accidentally. The result arises from the combination of people, planning, and performance in a specific manner. When projects succeed, it's often due to thoughtful preparation and informed leadership. Poor communication, poor ownership, lack of direction, or lack of information sometimes set a project on the course to failure. In the megaproject world—enormous, complex projects face chronic issues in most sectors, and the energy, metals, and mining sectors are no exception.

Megaprojects are not simply large in scale. They are high-risk ventures with billions of dollars at stake, oftentimes with emerging or untested technologies. These compete within the same supply chain ecosystem across international markets, and have a high impact on society and the environment. They are the size and complexity of the ones for which government, investors, local community, and media are, oftentimes, interested. This is because on such projects, timelines may be delayed, with cost overruns and possible safety issues—causing significant reputational damage within a short period.

With global markets further evolving and increased pressure from regulation, competition, social-political pressures, and climate change concerns, the demand for successful megaprojects only grows. Consequently, these projects should be planned, endorsed, developed, evaluated, approved and executed with long-term value in mind. This also involves ensuring capital is allocated appropriately, risks are actively managed, benefits are clearly defined and delivered, and governance is strong from day one. Except when implemented intentionally and with discipline, such projects are prone to derailing, even before the ground is broken.

If megaprojects fail, most fail not only in execution but in the development and evaluation stages of the project's life cycle. A project can start destroying its value before it is built: factors such as skipping steps, unclear goals, poor stakeholder engagement, being efficient on ineffective solutions, late user involvement, or weak risk planning can doom a project before the whistle blows. Other common drivers of failure are the lack of a single point of accountability, lack of team alignment on the project's objectives, and making decisions without fully understanding the context. The book's core message starts here since it describes everything that occurs before the FID. This is because, once we get that part right, we could maximize every effort to give the project its best chance for success.

Additionally, some organizations do not regard project management as a strategic asset. Such organizations treat project management as an operational function, with minimal visibility by the decision makers. This poor executive-level visibility can be fatal. A megaproject's development needs to tap into strategic goals and be championed by the executive leadership rather than technical and operation crews. In the case of strategic alignment, the earlier it is defined and bought into by all relevant stakeholders, the higher the likelihood that the project outcomes will create real business value.

This book is written with practical relevance for professionals and executives in asset-intensive sectors. Rather than focusing on theoretical frameworks, it offers real-world cases, tools, templates, forms, models, and insights that can easily be applied by project managers, business executives, practitioners, and, in some cases, the investing public. The chapters are written in the natural megaproject life cycle **from opportunity assessment to the FID, that is, just before the start of execution**. Through a focus on the critical development and evaluation stages, deliverables, activities, and tasks, this book allows readers to make better investment decisions and execute projects in a manner that drives repeatable, predictable success.

While the core framework presented in this book is globally applicable, many examples and references are drawn from U.S. and international projects in the energy and resources sectors. This reflects the author's professional experience and the global relevance of capital project challenges across jurisdictions.

The Energy, Metals, and Mining Sectors Megaprojects Transactions and Construction

The sectors featured in this book—energy, metals, and mining—have several things in common regarding megaprojects. These are not industries where change happens quietly or in isolation. Instead, these industries are characterized by a considerable delivery timeline, capital expenditure

(CAPEX), rigorous regulatory scrutiny, and complex engineering and operational requirements.

These sectors are particularly challenging and characterized by:

- Large-scale plants and infrastructure construction projects prevalent in facilities such as offshore–onshore oil and gas production facilities, refineries, power plants, pipelines, and mines. They are capital-intensive ventures with long timelines and high complexity.
- Volatility in commodity prices, political conditions, and market dynamics can be massive, with significant impacts on the projects. Cycles of boom and bust are something that decision makers have to always prepare to go through.
- High upfront CAPEX and/or more extended payback periods. If such projects are delayed and/or a budget overrun occurs, they may significantly impact profitability.
- Stringent regulatory requirements, such as environmental permits and safety standards, where noncompliance can result in severe delays or shutdowns. Permitting a mine development project alone can last over a decade in the Western world.

These factors, combined, make planning, evaluating, and firm governance of megaprojects in these sectors very difficult. A slight misjudgment in the first few Stages—especially predevelopment assessment, concept framing and selection, and optimization—can lead to a cascade of expensive failures later on. For this reason, the early Stages are when the project team and the sponsoring organizations have the best chance of setting the project up for long-term success. Early-Stage options definition and assessment include, per option, the strategic alignment, key people/skills, key risks, delivery timelines, preliminary CAPEX and OPEX (operating expenditure) estimates, constructability, maintainability, reliability, and so on. Such failures are often tied to unclear governance mechanisms and underdeveloped systems thinking (Alqershy et al. 2024; Hosseini and Farid 2025).

Megaprojects in these sectors can be either transactions (e.g., mergers, acquisitions, and divestitures) or construction (developing a resources extraction facility; drilling and completion; a new processing plant; constructing pipelines, compressors, and meter stations; mine development; and so on). These projects can be different in nature, expectations, planning needs, evaluation models, execution methodology, and so on. For example, a mega transaction project might entail much due diligence and a strategic fit, whereas concept, engineering design, and contracting and execution strategies might be the primary focus areas of a mega construction project.

Understanding these nuances is critical. Without that context, it can be more difficult than necessary to estimate what success should look like or plan the best way to achieve it. This book provides a lens specifically designed for these sectors and, based on real-world experiences and examples, makes the concept of success tangible for the readers. To acknowledge the similarities and differences of megaproject types, it is expected that each project's team's skillset, project management approach, location, tools, and evaluation methods, among others, be aligned to the particular project's needs.

Project as the Bridge

In most organizations, strategy, operations, and project execution are headed by different executive leaders. The strategy team finds new opportunities for fit. The operations team runs day-to-day plant activities, and the output remains standard. The project team sits between these two groups, and its one clear mission is to turn strategy into operational reality. This explains why each of the teams should not, and cannot successfully, work in isolation and why the project execution teams are referred to as change or transformation agents, and rightfully so. While it is best practice for each to understand their lanes in the decision-making process, each team should also have an equal voice during business strategy sessions and in the boardrooms, especially when seeking alignment on the Go/No-Go decision and drivers of any investment.

A project is the bridge between strategic ideas and their real-world deployment. A business' decision could be that it wants to enter into a new market, use new technologies, and so on. These are just ideas until they permeate into a defined project. Without projects, strategic ideas and operational realities never become visible.

Then, the project team matures these ideas into actionable steps. Once the idea has passed strategic fit tests through cross-functional opportunity or predevelopment assessment, the next steps (not necessarily in the sequential order stated here) are to conduct concept and/or feasibility studies, select the preferred development option, evaluate the risks, optimize the selected option, design the system, schedule the overall scope, estimate the costs, bring the stakeholders on board, evaluate the economics based on the business approved models and hurdle rates, develop execution plan and the decision support package (DSP), and set the stage for the execution. Once FID is taken, the project team delivers what is approved (or better) in line with the approved key performance indicators (KPIs) and the overarching company goals, meets the needs of the stakeholders (internal and external), and then transition (often called "handover") the completed project to the Operations team. A matured capital investment organization will normally conduct an independent post investment review about 18 months into the operations Stage. This is meant to test whether or not the facility is delivering on its promised value, and to document the learnings from that review.

This 'bridge role' is even more critical in megaprojects, especially because most megaprojects are as large as, if not larger than, many businesses. Consequently, the project team cannot be a bunch of technical experts alone; they need to be good at communication, negotiation, commercial management, leadership, and so on. In fact, the director of a project, especially a megaproject, should be experienced enough to know that they must focus on delivering the "business of the project or investment" and not managing the discipline through which they became the project director. This is vital. It is the secret weapon for successfully translating vision into tangible designs, executable plans, and operable facilities.

In addition, teams that are successful in projects act as integrators. They are helping to knit together different actors across geographies, functions, and organizations. Such integration under uncertainty requires adaptive decision-making models and systems thinking (Malekpour et al. 2020). They ensure that financial models remain realistic and aligned with business goals; that procurement strategies are grounded in sound contractual terms and conditions and well-thought-out logistics; and that sociocultural, environmental, and community interests are not forgotten.

The value of great project teams lies in the fact that they can see the big strategy picture and yet are able to take care of the details needed to deliver a successful project.

This bridge function also assists organizations in building internal and external trust. Strong project teams demonstrate confidence that the company will handle complexity and successfully deliver value when the project is completed. At the same time, it provides an opportunity for future investment and growth potential.

This connection between the two is revisited throughout this book and made the basis of exploring how well successful megaprojects are built and executed and how seeing the project as the bridge remains central to the overall project success (i.e., project management success and product success). A project led by a weak project team has the potential for scope creep, missed objectives, stakeholder dissatisfaction, business failures, career challenges, and so on. However, strong project teams give momentum, spur innovation, transform ambitious ideas into reality, and help organizations achieve their business goals. *The bridge between every corporate plan and concrete operational results is a megaproject. Without that bridge, strategy remains a vision, and operations stay static.*

What Is a Megaproject?

Projects are authorized to increase asset value, enhance shareholder return, control additional market share, meet socioeconomic needs, enter new markets, gain competitive advantage, and so on. Megaprojects in the energy, metals, and mining sectors are no exception.

Megaprojects are definite endeavors characterized by relatively large investment size, high profile risks (country and/or reputational), complexity, new and unproven technology, and/or major effects on the society. They are transformative ventures that could change the nature of markets, shape the regional development path, and build targeted legacies.

In many ways, megaprojects manifest an organization's motivation. They often represent leaps into new markets, capabilities, or technologies. But with ambition comes risk. That is where the need to understand megaprojects at a deeper level is found, including what they are, how they come together, and why some fail and others succeed.

Examples of megaprojects include:

- The Interstate H-3 in Hawaii, proposed in 1960 and completed in 1997, faced significant delays and cost overruns from an initial estimate of $250 million to $1.3 billion due to environmental and cultural concerns.
- Ciudad Real Central Airport in Spain, opened in 2008 and closed in 2012, which failed due to its remote location, receiving flights from only two airlines.
- Naypyidaw in Myanmar, the new capital city featuring 20-lane highways and costing over $4 billion, which remains almost empty.
- Forest City in Malaysia is a city built on four man-made islands intended to house 700,000 residents by 2035, which remains largely uninhabited due to political issues.
- The Yucca Mountain Nuclear Waste Repository in Nevada, the United States, has been put on indefinite hold due to environmental and health concerns.
- A multibillion-dollar infrastructure project in Asia—spanning five years of planning and political alignment—was approved based on economic forecasts that were outdated by the time the ink dried on the contract. Yet no one paused to reassess. The result? A white elephant used at less than 20 percent of its intended capacity. The board celebrated its on-time delivery. But to the country and its citizens, it was a national embarrassment.
- A high-profile liquefied natural gas (LNG) project in North America was developed at speed to catch a market window. The project team had raised concerns—about unproven technologies, rushed regulatory submissions, and unrealistic schedule assumptions. But the financial backers were in a hurry. "We'll fix it in execution," they said. They never did. The overruns reached billions. Lawsuits followed. Careers ended.
- By contrast, a mining megaproject in South America took three years to be conceptualized, framed, defined, and planned—painfully, meticulously. Stakeholders were embedded early, plus

the right project team members, in the right number, at the right time. Indigenous communities were consulted—not just informed. Operational readiness was tracked from day one. That project hit full production 90 days ahead of schedule and returned value ahead of expectations. It is not perfect, but it is a powerful proof that front-end rigor works.

Most of these are the stories that no glossy investor deck will show. But they are the real heartbeat behind this book.

Figure 1.1 shows how a typical megaproject, or any project at all, is broken down into Stages of development from cradle to grave—i.e., from being an opportunity put forward for assessment until being

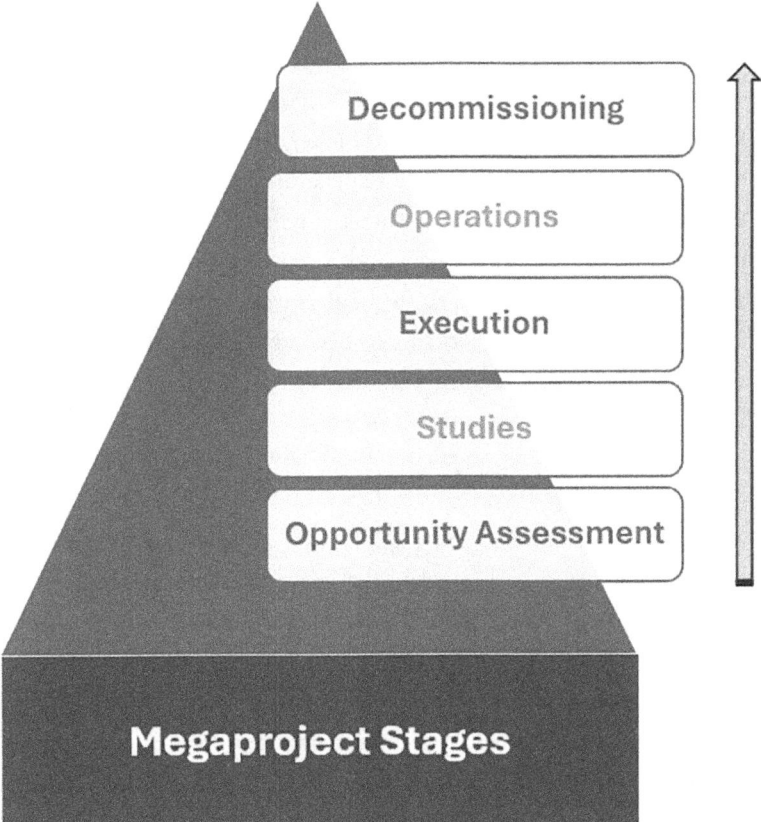

Figure 1.1 The five core Stages of megaproject development

decommissioned at the end of its useful life. Each level represents a progressive shift from optionality to realization, reflecting the structured journey from early vision to full implementation.

Megaproject Success

Just finishing on time and/or within budget doesn't count as megaproject success anymore. Simply defined, **megaproject success** is a combination of **project management success** (scope, quality, and within budget (schedule and cost)) and **product success** (i.e., an asset that performs as expected, delivers value, and meets or exceeds the business case set during the definition and planning Stage).

Let me ask you—how much of the product success criteria are/were you familiar with on your current or past projects, irrespective of the size? As a business executive, project manager or an investor, the more familiar you are with the criteria, the more likely it is for those criteria to be delivered, as-defined or better.

Most projects are a hit on one of these goals but miss on the other. For example, a project may meet all operational goals but suffer budget overruns, or it may be delivered under time and cost budgets but fall short of performance expectations. Both dimensions must be achieved and aligned for the megaproject to be deemed a success. This explains why fully owning megaproject success beyond project management success is a recipe for maximizing project success.

Megaproject Development and Planning

Megaproject development and planning are all activities, studies, and processes that take place prior to project approval for execution. They are basic steps that translate a vision into a concrete, stable plan. They define the scope and quality, assess feasibility, identify risks, outline the schedule, estimate costs, and allocate resources for the entire project.

Front-End Loading (FEL) is the systematic process of progressively developing project definition to reduce risk and improve predictability before major capital investments are committed. Recent research underscores how structured FEL improves project predictability and capital alignment (The Future of Megaproject Management 2024).

In the energy and mining sectors, FEL can be broadly broken down into the following distinct stage gates:

FEL-1 (Concept/Opportunity Identification)

- Establishes business case and technical viability
- Identifies key risks and constraints
- Defines scope at a high level
- Provides order-of-magnitude cost estimates (± 50 percent)
- Framing (Opportunity/Case)
- Evaluates multiple concepts
- Select the preferred technical solution

FEL-2 (Option Optimization)

- Refines scope definition
- Develops a preliminary execution plan
- Improves schedule and cost estimates (± 30 percent)
- Conducts preliminary hazard analysis

FEL-3 (Detailed Scope Definition and Planning)

- Finalizes engineering deliverables needed for execution
- Completes detailed scope definition
- Conducts detailed risk analysis and mitigation
- Refines and finalizes execution plan, but keep it a living document
- Firms up execution strategy and schedule
- Produces definitive cost estimate (± 10 to 15 percent)
- Develops a DSP

The primary value of FEL is that investment in early planning drastically reduces scope changes, schedule delays, and cost overruns during execution. It also positions the project to deliver on its promised product success criteria or KPIs. Each Stage gate requires formal approval before proceeding, ensuring alignment between business objectives and project execution.

Most megaprojects suffer from scope creep, budget overruns, and stakeholder conflict during the execution Stage if poorly developed and/or planned. Robust development and planning mean that the project has the right team, a clear roadmap, all significant risks have been identified and accounted for, and both the KPIs and the risks are aligned.

Typically, the following are the more common components of the development and planning stages:

1. ***Opportunity (and Case) framing:*** Why is there a need for the project? If it is solving a business problem or opportunity, what is it? What are the expected benefits? Essentially, it is a way to achieve clarity and alignment between the key stakeholders and decision makers on what the opportunity is, and its various shapes, the draft strategy table, and, eventually, the right solution. Whereas Opportunity Framing defines the why and what of investment, Case Framing defines the how and with what approach. Combined, they are the backbone of front-end excellence; and when done very well, they de-risk investment, align stakeholders, and enhance value realization.

2. ***Stakeholder map and engagement:*** What/who will the project impact, and with whom do I need to develop expectations, and interests?

3. ***Implementation potential:*** Determining whether the project, with its current capabilities and technologies, can be implemented.

4. ***Project footprint*** with local communities, regulators, and environmental bodies for Environmental and Social Impact Assessments (ESIA) and other third-party studies.

5. ***Preliminary timelines, budgets*** and buffers for risks, uncertainties, and so on.

6. ***Risks and control action(s):*** Risk management framework.

7. ***Decision Rights:*** Who will make decisions and manage different types of decisions, who will make diagnostic decisions, under what conditions, and how will information flow?

The integrated master plan aspect of the parameter will contain the above elements and be proposed to the executive sponsor(s), the investment committees, and the board for decision making.

This book provides tools and templates for performing stakeholder assessments, structuring risk matrixes, writing a business case, and preparing for the various gate reviews for each of these components. Many of the megaproject success drivers will be discussed in the development and planning chapters.

Project Evaluation and Investment Decision Making

Prior to the FID, a mega opportunity, transaction, or project goes through a series of stages or gates with each stage requiring studies, engineering, techno-commercial evaluation, and "gate approval."

Different businesses do this differently depending on their transactions and construction project development maturity, risk appetite, lessons learned, market environment, available competencies, and so on. This book will recommend a few ideas that help the sponsoring organization(s) deploy a fit for purpose evaluation methodology that results in quality decisions over the long term.

Every project is at a critical decision point after the development and planning Stages are complete. At this point, executive leadership must decide if the project is ready to proceed to execution. This is referred to as the FID Gate. However, choosing whether to proceed or not is not easy. The decision drivers relate to confirming the underlying techno-commercial assumptions and judging whether the project's returns exceed these risks and uncertainties.

Project evaluation is the formal process of reviewing the project's strategic alignment, people, scope, quality requirements, risks, schedule, costs, and so on to ascertain the desirability or otherwise of proceeding with the investment. It usually entails the involvement of various internal and external subject matter experts (SMEs) who have no emotional attachment to the project. It also aims to validate the assumptions in the project's business case while testing the robustness of the plan (scope, time, and costs).

Questions usually addressed in evaluation include:

- Is the project what the organization needs to do over the long term? Why invest, and why now?
- Have all critical risks been identified, and are the mitigation plans real?
- Are the timelines and cost estimates from actual data done on a solid track record of underlying methods?
- What is the expected internal rate of return (IRR), Net Present Value (NPV), and Capital Efficiency (CE) compared to other opportunities?
- Has due diligence been conducted? Are adequate governance and decision-making protocols in place?

It is often gated, and every Stage of the project development is reviewed and approved before the next Stage begins. When done well, it guarantees discipline and rigor and helps ascertain continuous commitment to resources—labor and nonlabor.

Key Tools in Evaluation:

- **Stage-Gate Models:** These allow work progress assessment and visualization at the end of each development Stage.
- **DSPs** are comprehensive packages that provide all of the critical project information in one document. Disciplined use of DSPs helps prevent investment bias (Cottafava et al. 2024; Ika et al. 2024).
- **Scenario Planning:** Exploring best-case, worst-case, and most likely outcomes, including a set of underlying assumptions per case.
- **Independent Peer Reviews:** for the assessment of the project's assumptions and methods—team composition, work processes, methods employed, models built, studies conducted, and the final reports.

The Project Definition Package integrates technical, financial, social, and environmental dimensions into a cohesive framework. FID approval is only granted once all components are aligned, ensuring a balanced, well-evaluated project proposal (Figure 1.2).

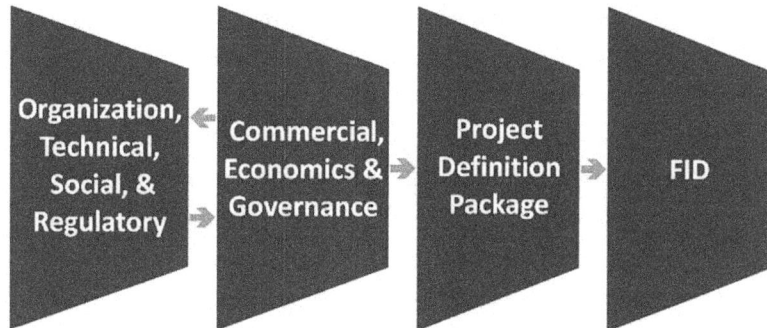

Figure 1.2 Project definition package alignment before FID

Effective project evaluation is not just a checkpoint; it is a safeguard against long-term organizational risk. Many high-profile megaproject failures could have been prevented through more disciplined evaluation and decision frameworks. Similarly, many success stories owe their achievements to thorough preparation during the development and planning Stages.

In the following chapters, we introduce practical steps that enhance disciplined deliverables compilation, evaluation rigor, robust risk assessment and reviews, compelling business case, gate review preparation guides, and competent decision board. These are established to improve transparency, strengthen governance, and align projects more closely with strategic organizational goals.

Beyond traditional evaluation methods, the book also explores how emerging technologies, such as predictive analytics, real-time scenario modeling, and digital twin simulations are reshaping how investment decisions are made on megaprojects. Future-ready organizations will be those that embed both foundational discipline and innovative techniques into their project evaluation culture. The future isn't waiting—the future is here. Technology won't replace leadership; but leaders who leverage technology will replace those who don't.

Typical Megaproject Life Cycles: Transactions Versus Construction

By understanding the timeframe of a megaproject, we can appreciate how one of these colossal undertakings will move from idea to implementation. This also enables us to differentiate between two broad categories of megaprojects in the energy, metals, and mining sectors—mega transactions and mega construction projects. Although both types follow structured sequences, the internal dynamics (with respect to stakeholders, risks, and deliverables) differ.

A megaproject life cycle helps you understand the road mapped out for a project from creation through the planning Stages until its execution and the entire closing process. It is a roadmap to aid project teams, executives, and investors by predicting milestones, allocating resources, watching for risks, and tracking progress against predetermined KPIs.

Figures 1.3 and 1.4 are not mere templates. They represent how disciplined thinking and a structured phasing will help ensure that each element of people, scope/quality, risks, schedule, and cost is adequately addressed before committing large capital to long-term projects. Life cycle governance frameworks must adapt across transaction and construction models (Alqershy et al. 2024; Li et al. 2024).

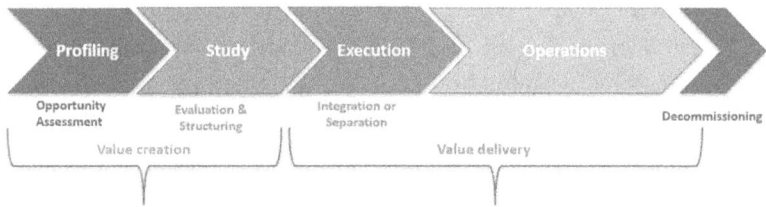

Figure 1.3 Typical mega transactions life cycle

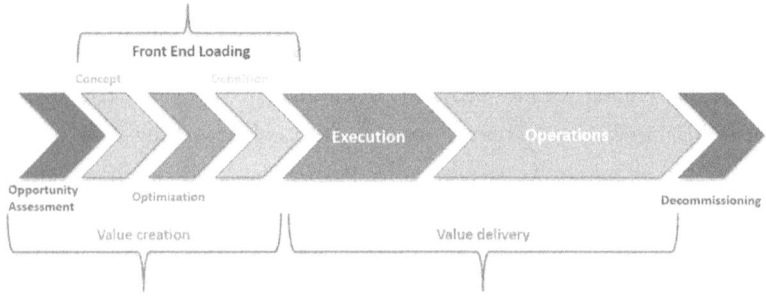

Figure 1.4 Typical mega asset development life cycle

The chart in Figure 1.3 illustrates the sequence of typical transactional projects, from opportunity identification through concept framing to evaluation and structuring and subsequent integration or separation.

These stages help determine commercial and strategic value, perform due diligence, and create decision-support packages to support a potential acquisition or divestment.

The chart in Figure 1.4 shows the construction life cycle stages, including additional technical and engineering-focused stages like optimization, definition, and detailed design. These are steps needed to improve scope, schedule, cost, and design integrity before any shovel hits the ground.

Each Stage of the life cycle categories will be explored in more detail with the understanding that, in real life, transaction and construction projects can sometimes overlap under one megaproject description. This is because certain mega transactions have the potential to metamorphose into a mega construction project once the transaction deal has closed.

A mega transaction is usually an acquisition, divestment, or merger of significant assets, such as a mining operation, an oil block, a gas infrastructure portfolio, or a water or power infrastructure portfolio. These initiatives are motivated by strategic business imperatives such as entering emerging markets, entering new countries, securing a sustainable supply, portfolio diversification, or consolidation to realize synergy.

Profiling/Screening: Typically, in the initial Stage of a mega transaction's life cycle, an opportunity to acquire, merge, or divest asset(s) is profiled or screened through identification and analysis for strategic fit, value, asset performance, market conditions, risk profile, and executability, at the very least. After this initial work, preliminary due diligence is performed to validate assumptions and screen for most show-stopping issues. At this point, business objectives and next Stage (i.e., Study) workplan and objectives are developed for executives' approval.

Study (Evaluation and Screening): After determining a viable route, the work moves to full-scale due diligence. During this Stage, develop transaction processes, including the diligence execution approach and deal structure. In the energy and mining sectors, this typically involves the disciplines of strategy, marketing, land, legal, technical (exploration, geosciences, reservoir, drilling and completions, facilities, etc.), environmental, financial, regulatory, project management, project services (project controls and contracts), and economics. Subject matter experts review asset conditions (technical, commercial, financial, reputational, etc.), validate reserves (if applicable) and licenses, and evaluate possible future major capital developments, ongoing liabilities and forecast future project performance. Valuation model and reports, transaction's expected deal value, risk profile, draft offer letters, announcement materials, and shareholder approval packages are drawn up at the same time.

This stage ends when the investment committee reviews the final investment recommendation and, ultimately, the board-level decision to acquire or divest is taken.

Execution/Implementation (Integration/Separation): After FID, the transaction proceeds to the final negotiation and closing stage, including the finalization of the contract, regulatory filing, and the execution of commercial agreements. Here, asset integration or separation occurs (depending on whether it is an acquisition or a divestment). Document and obtain approvals for all changes in execution; then develop transactions closeout report, including learnings.

Operation: Operate the entity, if a merger or an acquisition, and conduct post investment review 18 months into operating the new entity.

On the other hand, and as shown in the following paragraphs, mega construction projects start with opportunity assessment, then the development and planning stages, leading to the FID. These projects are generally physical developments with significant engineering, procurement, and construction (EPC) activities, as well as possible additional studies. Examples include refineries, offshore rigs, onshore/offshore production facilities, liquefied natural gas/natural gas liquids (LNG/NGL) plants, transmission pipelines, metallurgical plants, minerals and metals processing plants, and so on. These undertakings involve many civil, mechanical, electrical, architectural, and environmental engineering disciplines and often require global coordination, with multilocation execution strategies.

Opportunity/Predevelopment Assessment: The mega construction projects life cycle starts with an opportunity framework, where strategic priorities are articulated in a business requirements document.

Concept: During conceptual engineering, broad scope and technologies are defined. The project's commercial and technical logic is tested during feasibility studies. Early buy-in from key stakeholders such as regulatory agencies and community groups, among others, is obtained to ensure comments and existing concerns are flagged, addressed, and, if possible, closed early. This stage consists of the identification and articulation of development options, and the selection of a preferred alternative. Option selection is not typical across businesses in this stage. Some businesses take the different options into the next stage before selecting and optimizing the preferred alternative. Deliverables at the end of this stage could include study reports, independent review reports, valuation model and reports, key value drivers, and executive approval request package.

Optimization: This is more commonly referred to as Pre-Front End Engineering Design (Pre-FEED) stage. It is when the selected development option is optimized through further engineering work, scoping, and refinement of the technical and commercial deliverables. Deliverables at the end of this stage could include study reports, Level 2 and Class 3, respectively, of schedule and cost estimates, independent review reports, valuation model and reports, key value drivers, and board approval request package, and so on.

Definition: A more detailed definition follows as the project gains momentum. The project team further defines the scope, chooses technology providers, refines schedules, and commences developing a detailed cost estimate that would metamorphose into budgeting once FID is taken. Also part of this stage is the detailed risk assessments and the development of the execution strategies and plan. Deliverables at the end of this stage could include study reports, Level 3 and Class 2, respectively, of schedule and cost estimates, schedule and cost risk analysis, procurement plan, independent review reports, valuation model and reports, key value drivers, and board approval request package, announcement materials, possible Q&As, and so on.

The project development and planning are complete when the project is ready to proceed to execution, that is, after FID is taken. Until then, and irrespective of the value of pre-FID execution scope (aka precommitment) being implemented, the project is not in execution yet.

Execution: It begins with the contract award and subsequent mobilization of contractors, detailed engineering progress, the implementation of the procurement strategies and plan, and the commencement of the preliminary site work. Plans developed are mainly used to direct the works through governance frameworks such as safety, quality, control schedule (for baselining), control budget, and stakeholder alignment. Performance metrics and project control/cost engineering systems are used to monitor progress. Toward the end of execution, the project goes into commissioning and start-up. It is tested, validated, and transitioned to the operations and maintenance team. In parallel, a project wide closeout report is developed, including the documentation of execution learnings, and fed into the organizational knowledge systems.

Operation: Operate the facility and conduct post investment review 18 months into operations.

Decommissioning/Abandonment: Facility decommissioning and abandonment in the energy, metals and mining sectors is a critical phase in the asset life cycle. It involves the safe retirement of infrastructure such as wells, platforms, pipelines, plants, and mining operations. The primary objectives are to eliminate safety and environmental risks, comply with regulatory obligations, and restore the site for future use or natural recovery.

Successful decommissioning requires cross-functional coordination, engineering, robust project controls, and proactive risk management. Key success factors include early planning, transparent stakeholder engagement, and integration of environmental, safety, and financial performance metrics. When executed effectively, decommissioning not only fulfills legal and environmental responsibilities but also enhances corporate reputation and supports long-term sustainability goals.

Despite differences between the two life cycle types, standard anchors exist between them: planning (scope, risks, time and costs), studies, execution, and operation. Irrespective of what the implementation strategy is concerning acquiring a gas field or building a processing facility, ultimately, success is driven not just by execution and operations brilliance but also by the quality of decisions made during the development and planning stages.

The organizations that develop and execute megaprojects are not just living by theoretical charts; they are living the reality of megaproject life cycles. Improvements are derived from each stage regarding team formation, budgeting, stakeholder engagement, strategic control, and gate approvals. It gives stakeholders a clear reference point for where the project stands in its life cycle to keep people from getting carried away by the emotion of the situation or possible common pitfalls and stay aligned with business goals.

Additionally, there is no equivalence in how each organization's life cycle stages are structured. While a specific naming convention for "Concept," "Pre-Feasibility," and other such processes may vary from company to company, they all have a similar purpose behind each stage: *to bring clarity, order, discipline, and insight to a highly intricate process.*

To allow business leaders to understand what is happening in the life cycle stages, ensure the following:

- Always set adequate expectations at every gate review, especially deliverables and review requirements.
- Define and communicate how the evaluation will take place, including responsibilities and accountabilities.
- Anticipate future resource needs and governance requirements.
- Be certain that strategic assumptions are valid as the project develops.
- Develop an independent peer review Terms of Reference (ToR) template.
- Develop a robust project wide communication plan that drives transparent reporting.

As you advance through this book, there will be an expansion, on a stage-by-stage basis, of the requirements, trade-offs in development, the execution framework (including detail design, contracting, procurement, project controls, quality assurance, and control, regulatory compliance, construction, commissioning, transition [handover] to operations, close-out report, post investment review, etc.), the early warning signs framework, and the learning environment to create so that future megaprojects will garner valuable insights from the experience of this project team.

Although the focus is slightly different, both paths eventually amount to turning strategic opportunities into value-generating assets through a planned series of studies, decisions, evaluations, and implementation actions.

Megaprojects are among the most ambitious and high-stakes capital-development ventures globally. They have a high investment threshold, massive scale, cross-functionality, and low frequency and are usually launched to achieve strategic imperatives of market share expansion, shareholder return, socioeconomic development, or sector change. Megaprojects are a common way to achieve transformative growth, particularly in asset-intensive sectors such as energy, metals, and mining.

Consequently, if you're a project executive, a board member, an investor, a planner, or a young professional on your first transaction or capital project—this book was written for you.

And because every megaproject we greenlight tells a story about who we are as professional project managers, let's make sure our next megaproject ... is a story worth telling, through our activities and the decisions we make.

Let's get it right ... before the first dollar is spent.

And yes, we can—and sustainably, too!

As will be discussed in later chapters, megaprojects of the future will be shaped not only by capital and policy but by how effectively organizations learn, adapt, and make strategic decisions using data, AI, and behavioral insight. We begin the next chapter by unmasking megaproject (transactions and construction) development and why it is foundational in setting the stage for the eventual asset's long-term value.

Reflection Questions

1. Why do so many megaprojects fail before construction begins, and how can early planning mitigate these risks?
2. In what ways do megaprojects act as a bridge between corporate strategy and operational activities?
3. How do the characteristics of energy, metals, and mining sectors amplify the complexity of megaprojects?

CHAPTER 2

Development

Learning Outcomes

After reading this chapter, you will be able to:

1. Distinguish between megaproject development and execution, with a focus on front-end planning.
2. Analyze key activities required to prepare a megaproject for FID.
3. Understand the interplay between corporate governance and project-level decision making in large capital projects.
4. Evaluate the role of internal organizational alignment in increasing project readiness and stakeholder confidence.
5. Identify success factors that enhance decision quality during megaproject development stages.

Overview

The quest for megaprojects delivery success is not new; neither are instances of megaproject failures. In fact, the history of large-scale industrial ventures across the globe is replete with both inspirational success stories and cautionary tales of massive overruns and reputational damage. The distinction between the two outcomes almost always lies in the rigor and discipline exercised during the development phase. The opportunity assessment Stage determines whether an idea can be matured into a viable megaproject (Denicol et al. 2023).

Megaprojects development is the foundational process that sets the tone and trajectory for a project's entire life cycle. It encompasses the early framing, scoping, economic validation, stakeholder engagement, and strategic alignment required to convert an initial opportunity into a bankable, executable investment. Unlike smaller-scale projects where flexibility is greater, megaprojects demand intensive scrutiny and deliberate planning to avoid costly errors down the line.

An optimum development of any megaproject requires that costs be minimized while maximizing other economic parameters such as IRR, NPV, payback period, and capital efficiency. However, economic metrics alone are insufficient if the foundational assumptions and project configurations are not grounded in reality. As such, a successful development effort must also prioritize alignment with corporate strategy, environmental and social obligations, technological feasibility, and operational viability.

Additionally, megaproject development is not a one-size-fits-all process. It is heavily influenced by the sector in question, whether energy, mining, or industrial infrastructure, as well as by the geographic, political, and regulatory environments in which it is situated. Development plans must account for jurisdictional risks, community dynamics, environmental regulations, and labor market realities.

The development phase is where ideas meet reality. A project that appears viable on paper can rapidly become unfeasible if preliminary groundwork is not conducted with the thoroughness and diligence that megaprojects demand. The flip side of this is that, when the preliminary groundwork is conducted with the thoroughness and diligence that megaprojects demand, a project that appears good on paper can look bad, either to be discontinued or for it to be reconfigured differently before it may be investable. Unlike smaller-scale projects, where adjustments can often be made with minimal impact, megaprojects possess a level of scale and complexity that magnifies the consequences of early missteps. That is why the development phase is often referred to as the "make-or-break" stage of any major capital investment.

Moreover, the development phase must incorporate a long-term vision that spans the entire life cycle of the asset, from concept to decommissioning. This vision must be supported by robust scenario planning, where the project is tested against various economic, environmental, and social conditions to assess its resilience and adaptability. Tools such as Monte Carlo simulations, sensitivity analyses, and stakeholder mapping are often utilized at this stage to ensure that every aspect of the project is stress-tested before a single shovel hits the ground.

Governance plays a critical role in megaproject development. Effective governance ensures that roles and responsibilities are clearly defined, that decision-making processes are transparent, and that there is accountability at every stage. It also facilitates the engagement of stakeholders, ranging from government regulators and community leaders to investors and internal business units, who must be aligned to ensure the project's ultimate success.

Stakeholder management is particularly crucial during development. Unlike execution or operations, the development phase involves articulating the project's purpose, gathering stakeholder input, and addressing concerns before they solidify into opposition. Community engagement, environmental assessments, and stakeholder feedback loops must be built into the development cycle to derisk the project from reputational and social backlash.

Another indispensable element of successful development is FEL, which refers to the practice of spending more time and resources at the front end of a project to define and refine its scope, schedule, cost, and risks. Projects with strong FEL are statistically more likely to succeed, and the cost of this additional effort is usually far outweighed by the savings generated through fewer revisions and changes during execution.

The development phase should also integrate digital tools and methodologies to enhance efficiency and decision quality. Digital platforms can significantly improve integration (Liu et al. 2023). Digital twins, building information modeling (BIM), geospatial analytics, and advanced project simulation platforms can provide powerful insights and predictive capabilities that were previously unavailable. These technologies help project teams visualize outcomes, optimize designs, and simulate performance under various operating conditions, allowing for better planning and mitigation strategies.

Another emerging best practice is the use of integrated project delivery (IPD) approaches during development. IPD involves the early collaboration of all stakeholders—including owners, designers, contractors, and suppliers—to codevelop the project strategy and execution plan. This approach reduces misalignment, improves communication, and encourages innovation and shared accountability.

In addition, megaproject development cannot be isolated from global trends and external pressures. Issues such as climate change, evolving regulatory standards, supply chain disruptions, and technological advancements must be anticipated and embedded into development planning. Projects that fail to consider these externalities may find themselves obsolete or noncompliant even before construction begins.

Risk management is not a one-time task during development; it is a continuous process that evolves with the project. Effective development requires a risk culture that is proactive rather than reactive. This includes creating a comprehensive risk register, conducting scenario planning, and continuously updating risk assessments as more data becomes available. Risks should be categorized by likelihood and impact, and mitigation plans should be robust, actionable, and regularly tested.

Furthermore, development must be viewed through a sustainability lens. ESG considerations are now integral to capital allocation decisions, and megaprojects that ignore these factors risk losing investor confidence and community support. Sustainable development practices not only ensure regulatory compliance but can also improve project economics by reducing life cycle costs and enhancing asset value.

Finally, a successful development process ends with the preparation of a comprehensive DSP. This package consolidates all the critical information gathered during development business case, engineering designs, risk analysis, stakeholder input, economic evaluations, and regulatory compliance and presents it to decision makers in a structured format. The DSP serves as the final gatekeeper before a project advances to the FID, and ultimately the execution stage.

In conclusion, the development phase is the cornerstone of megaproject success. It demands a rigorous, multidisciplinary approach that combines strategic vision, technical excellence, stakeholder alignment, and operational pragmatism. A well-developed project not only sets the stage for smooth execution but also ensures that the investment delivers lasting value across its life cycle.

Megaproject Development Stages

The life cycle of a megaproject is generally structured into a series of sequential stages. This division allows for better control over the scope, risks, resources, and alignment with the strategic objectives of the sponsoring organization. As the project progresses, each stage contributes to a clearer understanding of the megaproject's feasibility, implementation requirements, and long-term value. This progressive approach enables organizations to make informed decisions and effectively manage uncertainties.

Each stage of development consists of specific activities and tangible deliverables. Activities typically include defining the megaproject's objectives, assessing potential risks, preparing work plans, establishing detailed schedules, estimating costs, and identifying required contingencies. These efforts are designed to shape and refine the megaproject's scope and approach. In parallel, the process yields critical deliverables such as concept studies, environmental and impact assessment reports, comprehensive scope, schedule and cost estimate documents, and economic analyses including IRR and NPV. These deliverables are verifiable work products that serve as the foundation for key decisions and stakeholder engagement.

To ensure discipline and accountability throughout the development process, each stage concludes with a structured review. These reviews, commonly referred to as stage gates, tollgates, or phase gates, serve as formal checkpoints where project performance, planning adequacy, and risk management are evaluated. During these gate reviews, decision makers assess whether the scope of the current stage has been satisfactorily completed, whether planning for the upcoming stage is sufficiently mature, and whether risks are clearly understood and appropriately addressed. Only when these criteria are met does the project receive authorization to proceed.

Following the initial opportunity identification and predevelopment assessment, the megaproject typically advances through four core Stages. The first is the concept Stage, where potential technical and commercial pathways are identified, initial feasibility is established, and alignment with organizational strategy is examined. This Stage provides the first structured opportunity to determine whether the identified opportunity is viable and worth pursuing further.

The next Stage is optimization, which focuses on refining the selected concept to enhance capital efficiency and life cycle value. During this stage, multiple cases and scenarios are framed and analyzed, assumptions are validated, and trade-offs are considered to determine the most effective path forward. The aim is to produce an optimized development solution that meets business, technical, and regulatory expectations.

Once the concept has been optimized, the definition Stage begins. This Stage involves detailed front-end engineering and scope finalization for the selected concept and case. Teams prepare the full package of documentation required to support the FID, including finalized scope, risks register and mitigation plans, schedules, cost estimates, execution strategies, and contractual frameworks. The clarity achieved in this stage lays the groundwork for successful implementation during the execution Stage.

The execution Stage, which includes turnover to operations and project closeout, lies technically beyond the FID boundary. When FEL is fully implemented, the FID becomes a simple and robust decision (The Future of Megaproject Management 2024). However, its success is largely dependent on the strength and completeness of the previous development stages. Execution involves the physical construction and realization of the project, commissioning activities, and the formal transfer of responsibility to the operations team.

An effective development life cycle for megaprojects is not only about moving through a series of steps but about building the foundation for sustainable success. The entire process should be designed to support repeatable, high-value investments that enhance shareholder wealth, bolster organizational reputation, and reinforce strategic positioning. When structured effectively, the development stages serve as a disciplined roadmap that enables project managers and executives to navigate complexity with confidence, ensuring that decisions are grounded in evidence and aligned with long-term goals.

Opportunity and Predevelopment Assessment

The Strategic Origin of Megaprojects

As in all sectors, megaprojects in the energy, metals, and mining sectors rarely emerge by chance. Instead, they originate from strategic planning exercises or market-driven initiatives undertaken by organizations seeking to grow, diversify, or reposition themselves competitively. These opportunities may arise from a deliberate search aligned with long-term business strategy, or they may be identified as responses to evolving external conditions, such as market shifts, regulatory changes, geopolitical developments, and technological advancements.

Each organization typically maintains a portfolio of potential opportunities often referred to as the opportunity "hopper." These are reviewed systematically and compared against each other based on a defined set of investment criteria. The goal is to identify those that warrant deeper examination and resource commitment. Opportunities at this stage are not yet projects; they are prospects that require shaping, filtering, and refinement before entering formal development.

Typology of Opportunities

Opportunities can be categorized based on their origin and nature. They may be either organic or inorganic. Organic opportunities are those initiated internally, often driven by innovation, research and development, or internal capability exploration. Inorganic opportunities, in contrast, emerge from acquisitions, joint ventures, partnerships, or asset divestitures—essentially strategic moves that bring external ideas or assets into the business.

Additionally, opportunities may be classified as proactive or reactive. Proactive opportunities result from intentional exploration and are integrated into the regular planning cycles of the organization. Reactive opportunities arise in response to external prompts, such as unsolicited proposals, policy shifts, or competitor activity. Regardless of how an opportunity is sourced, it undergoes an evaluation process to determine its alignment with the organization's vision, goals, and capital allocation strategy.

Opportunity Screening and Initial Assessment

The initial Stage of assessment is typically referred to as screening. This involves applying a predefined set of strategic, technical, and financial criteria to determine whether an opportunity merits further analysis. Screening helps to quickly eliminate ideas that are misaligned or unfeasible, ensuring that limited resources are only allocated to promising candidates.

Following screening, a more detailed scoping exercise begins. This includes high-level feasibility checks, consideration of technical barriers, an overview of regulatory implications, initial stakeholder mapping, and a basic understanding of market dynamics. At this stage, senior leadership is engaged to validate the strategic importance of the opportunity and assess its fit within the company's portfolio.

Comprehensive Opportunity Study

For opportunities that pass the initial screening, a more in-depth study stage follows. This stage is crucial in transitioning the opportunity from an abstract idea into a viable investment case. The opportunity study includes a broad range of assessments, such as legal and regulatory due diligence, anti-corruption compliance checks, stakeholder engagement plans, confidentiality and communication strategies, and high-level technical and economic modeling.

A particularly important element at this point is the risk assessment. Projects in the energy, metals, and mining sectors are frequently exposed to complex geopolitical, environmental, and operational risks. A multidisciplinary team evaluates these risks and outlines potential mitigation strategies. Similarly, the opportunity's economic viability is modeled, taking into account resource characteristics, market pricing forecasts, and estimated capital and operational expenditures.

Deliverables at this stage may include a business objective statement, a formal opportunity framing report, case framing summaries, stakeholder assessments, risk and scope assumptions, marketing strategies, initial field layouts, schedule benchmarks, and economic evaluation outputs. For transactions, additional deliverables include due diligence reports and integration or exit plans. Functional review meetings are held to consolidate findings and determine whether the opportunity is ready for capture.

Capture and Approval for Advancement

The capture stage represents the point at which the organization formally decides to commit resources to pursue the opportunity. This is not yet an execution commitment, but rather an authorization to advance the opportunity into detailed planning or transactional negotiation. Key decision makers must be satisfied that all critical assessments have been completed and that the opportunity offers a compelling case for further investment.

If all conditions are met, such as technical feasibility, strategic alignment, economic viability, and acceptable risk profile, then funding is allocated to progress the opportunity. A closeout report of the opportunity study is finalized, and for transactions, integration or separation plans are activated. For construction-focused megaprojects, the next step is entry into the Concept Stage. Regardless of the path forward, documentation is critical at this stage to ensure institutional memory and future reference.

Sector-Specific Control Processes

In the energy and mining sectors, opportunity and predevelopment assessments often include additional layers of industry-specific technical control processes. These include the exploration process, which is a comprehensive evaluation of subsurface and aboveground conditions. Activities include basin and reservoir assessments, geological modeling, well planning and execution, and commercial potential evaluations.

In parallel, control elements such as resource threshold validation, well investment justifications, post-well analyses, and exit strategies are embedded within the process. These sector-specific workflows ensure that technical and geological risks are fully integrated into the early decision-making framework, thereby enhancing the quality and credibility of the opportunity assessment.

Functional Reviews and Gate 0 Approval

A significant milestone in the opportunity and predevelopment assessment is Gate 0, often referred to as the point of entry into formal project development. Before a megaproject is allowed to transition into the Concept Stage, a functional review must be conducted. This involves a thorough examination by subject matter experts across key business functions, including strategy, marketing, finance, legal, engineering, project controls, procurement, risk management, and economics.

The review evaluates the completeness and robustness of the opportunity assessment, the alignment with strategic goals, certain level of scope understanding or clarity, and the adequacy of proposed plans for the Concept Stage. Gate 0 approval signifies that the opportunity is now deemed worthy of further evaluation and full concept development.

Cross-Functional Collaboration

Opportunity and predevelopment assessments are inherently cross-functional. They are often led by the Strategy and Business Development teams in collaboration with Exploration, Operations, Facilities/Projects, Commercial, and Legal departments, at the very least. As the opportunity matures, additional input may be required from the ESG teams, Health and Safety experts, and external advisers (Turner and Kalidindi 2021).

This collaborative structure ensures that multiple dimensions; technical, economic, regulatory, and reputational are taken into account. It also allows for robust debate, challenge, and refinement of the opportunity before any irreversible commitments are made. Cross-functional collaboration minimizes blind spots and promotes a culture of accountability and shared ownership.

Summary of Key Deliverables

Deliverables during this stage are designed to enable informed decisions and reduce uncertainty. These typically include opportunity framing reports, business objectives documentation, stakeholder engagement plans, preliminary field layouts, scope and risk assumptions, schedule and cost benchmarks, and early-stage economic models. Additional documents, such as due diligence reports, confidentiality agreements, and marketing strategies, may be required based on the opportunity type.

For construction projects, a specific set of input deliverables is prepared to support the transition into the Concept Stage. For transactions, the opportunity may progress directly into post transaction integration planning or exit/separation implementation. In both cases, a post investment review process is initiated typically within 18 months to assess the outcome and capture lessons learned.

Bridging Strategy to Execution: Why This Stage Matters Most

Industry experience consistently shows that many megaproject failures originate not from technical challenges during execution, but from deficiencies in the early stages, particularly in opportunity identification, framing, and assessment. Common failure factors include inadequate stakeholder assessment, unclear project goals, insufficient scope definition, poor technology selection, unrealistic economic assumptions, and the absence of a single point of accountability.

These factors can all be addressed during the Opportunity and Predevelopment Stage. Doing so not only reduces risk but dramatically increases the probability of megaproject success. By devoting adequate time, resources, and governance to this stage, organizations can build a strong foundation for execution and long-term operational excellence. In particular, projects are more likely to be successful when the governance model is adaptable (Zhang and Chen 2023).

The Strategic Imperative of Gate Discipline

The importance of structured, disciplined, and transparent decision making cannot be overstated. Gate 0 is more than a procedural milestone, it is a cultural and strategic checkpoint that reflects the organization's commitment to responsible resources (people, funds, etc.) deployment. Effective gate discipline fosters internal trust, enables external accountability, and supports the consistent delivery of business value.

Organizations that rigorously apply stage-gating principles during the Opportunity and Predevelopment Stage are better equipped to navigate complexity, manage change, and adapt to dynamic market conditions.

Conversely, those that rush through or skip this stage often pay the price in the form of delays, budget overruns, reputational damage, and suboptimal outcomes.

Conclusion

The Opportunity and Predevelopment Assessment Stage is the essential entry point into the megaproject development life cycle. It serves as a rigorous, evidence-based process for transforming ideas into viable investments. By identifying strategic fits, testing assumptions, modeling scenarios, and managing risks early, this stage sets the tone for all subsequent stages.

In the context of energy, metals, and mining megaprojects, this stage is particularly vital due to the capital intensity, long lead times, and exposure to external volatility inherent in these sectors. The lessons captured and decisions made during opportunity assessment not only define the direction of a single project but often influence broader portfolio strategies and corporate performance.

As such, this book devotes significant attention to this pre-FID period. It is here long before the first contract is signed or the first piece of equipment is mobilized that the seeds of success or failure are planted. And it is here that project managers, business leaders, and technical professionals must collaborate to ensure that every megaproject starts on a firm, deliberate, and strategically sound footing.

Concept

The Concept Stage represents the formal beginning of the megaproject development life cycle. It is the first structured stage following the opportunity and predevelopment assessment and marks the point where an idea transitions from possibility to potential. At this stage, the sponsoring organization begins to assign preliminary resources, define objectives, and shape the scope of the project in a way that supports strategic alignment and long-term business goals. The key purpose of the Concept Stage is to explore the feasibility of the opportunity in greater depth, evaluate alternative development paths, and establish a credible basis for selecting a preferred investment option.

Defining the Strategic Fit

A core activity in the Concept Stage is determining and/or reconfirming the strategic fit of the opportunity. This includes aligning the project with the overarching corporate vision, growth aspirations, and asset portfolio strategy. Strategic fit is not only about financial returns but also about how well the project supports long-term business positioning. It considers geopolitical exposure, environmental obligations, market demand, and competitive advantages.

To achieve this alignment, the Concept Stage kicks off with a formal funding application, often referred to as the Concept Stage Implementation Plan. This document outlines the scope of work for the Stage, defines roles and responsibilities, and provides a high-level roadmap for deliverables, decision gates, and resource requirements. It includes project objectives, business drivers, a summary of the opportunity's origin, and a justification for investment.

Establishing Project Objectives and Business Case

At this stage, the megaproject's foundational objectives are clearly articulated. These objectives include what the project intends to achieve, such as increasing production capacity, entering a new market, reducing operational costs, enhancing sustainability compliance, or meeting regulatory mandates. The objectives are accompanied by a rationale as to why the organization should pursue the project now, and what business benefits are anticipated if the project is successfully delivered.

The business case is developed as a living document that evolves throughout the project's life cycle. In the Concept Stage, it typically includes strategic justifications, expected returns (IRR, NPV), estimated timing and CAPEX, OPEX, revenue projections, and high-level assessments of project risks and sensitivities. It also begins to quantify intangible benefits, such as brand enhancement, political goodwill, and technological innovation leadership.

Stakeholder Identification and Engagement Plan

Another essential output of the Concept Stage is the stakeholder analysis plan. Megaprojects often operate within complex ecosystems involving government agencies, regulatory bodies, local communities, financial institutions, joint venture partners, and internal corporate sponsors. Early identification of these stakeholders and their influence on project success is crucial (Smith and Lee 2025).

A stakeholder map is developed to assess interest, power, and potential impact. Engagement strategies are formulated based on this analysis, ensuring that communication is tailored and responsive. Proactively managing expectations at this stage helps reduce the risk of opposition or delay later in the life cycle (van Marrewijk and Smits 2024).

Technical and Commercial Evaluation

The Concept Stage serves as the technical and commercial feasibility gateway. Several key assessments are initiated, including geological, geotechnical, environmental, and market studies. These assessments help validate the project's viability from both a technical and business perspective. For instance, in the energy sector, early reservoir simulation or drilling studies may be conducted, while in the mining sector, ore grade and recoverability evaluations may be prioritized.

This Stage may also include high-level constructability assessments, logistics planning, and supply chain strategy development. These activities identify major constraints or cost drivers early on. Additionally, this is when licensing requirements and permitting pathways begin to be reviewed and documented.

Concept Options Development and Comparison

One of the most valuable components of the Concept Stage is the structured development and comparison of multiple investment alternatives. Rather than prematurely locking into a single path, organizations should develop a range of technically and economically viable options that meet the same business objectives.

Each option is evaluated for schedule implications, capital intensity, risk exposure, and stakeholder acceptance. Sensitivity analyses are performed to identify the "breaking points" of each option under different market or operational scenarios. These comparisons enable executive leadership to select a preferred path based not only on value but also on resilience and strategic alignment.

Deliverables and Documentation

The Concept Stage culminates in the production of a number of key deliverables. These documents provide the foundation for entering the Optimization Stage and enable senior leadership to make informed go/no-go decisions. Typical deliverables include:

- A preliminary development plan, outlining the project strategy, design intent, and high-level implementation roadmap.
- A Concept Study Report, which includes updated assessments of resource availability, market environment, technical feasibility, risk profile, preliminary CAPEX and OPEX, and a proposed execution strategy.
- A structured business case that quantifies economic metrics and aligns them with the broader strategic vision.
- Stakeholder engagement and regulatory plans.
- Options evaluated and the rationale for selecting the preferred option.
- A resource plan for the next Stage and a list of key questions to be answered in Optimization.

All deliverables are subjected to internal peer review and functional endorsement. This provides confidence that the work completed is sound and that the decision to proceed further is based on solid analysis and reasoning.

Governance and Gate Reviews

At the conclusion of the concept Stage, a gate 1 review is held. This is a formal governance checkpoint where internal reviewers and senior decision makers assess the completeness and quality of the concept Stage work. The review also validates whether the project meets the criteria for entry into the optimization Stage. These criteria typically include a confirmed strategic fit, a well-defined business case, viable technical solutions, acceptable risk exposure, and a clear plan for advancing the project. Effective governance and gate review processes are essential (National Audit Office 2025).

The gate review process not only ensures accountability but also provides an opportunity to identify any unresolved issues or critical gaps. If significant concerns are raised, the project may be asked to return to the Concept Stage for additional work before being allowed to advance (Escaping the Governance Trap 2025).

Benefits of a Strong Concept Stage

Investing adequate time and resources into the Concept Stage has long-term benefits. It helps prevent costly rework in later Stages, reduces the likelihood of delays during execution, and increases the probability that the project will meet its performance targets. It also allows the organization to make smart investment decisions, based on comparative analysis of options, rigorous feasibility testing, and clear-eyed understanding of risk.

Furthermore, a robust Concept Stage enhances organizational confidence. It provides evidence to sponsors, partners, regulators, and even external stakeholders that the project is grounded in logic, discipline, and due process. In many organizations, a well-run Concept Stage becomes a model for future projects, embedding a culture of excellence and accountability in project delivery.

Summary and Transition to Optimization

In summary, the Concept Stage of a megaproject's life cycle is focused on identifying, framing, and comparing investment alternatives in order to select a preferred option that best meets the business and strategic objectives of the organization. This Stage may involve moderate expenditure and time, but the payoff is significant clarity, confidence, and direction.

While **some organizations choose to delay option selection into the Optimization or even the Definition Stage**, this often results in increased front-end costs, unresolved uncertainties, and missed opportunities for stakeholder alignment. Early commitment, when done correctly, empowers the team to develop deeper, more actionable plans and better manage downstream risks.

With a selected development path in place, and with endorsement from the Gate 1 (i.e., end of Concept Stage) review, the megaproject is now ready to transition into the Optimization Stage. Here, the project's technical and commercial frameworks will be refined further, risks will be more fully understood, and a comprehensive case will be built for an eventual successful FID.

Optimization

The Optimization Stage is the second major step in the megaproject development life cycle, following *the selection of a preferred investment concept*. While the Concept Stage is concerned with the identification and comparison of development alternatives, the Optimization Stage is focused entirely on enhancing the value, feasibility, and readiness of the selected path. It aims to refine the strategic, technical, commercial, and operational assumptions made in the earlier Stage in order to unlock the full potential of the investment. This is where the project begins to take form as a viable, efficient, and executable asset.

Purpose and Position of the Optimization Stage

Once a preferred concept has been endorsed, the Optimization Stage seeks to challenge and improve it from every angle. The goal is not simply to validate the selection but to interrogate every component of the proposal scope, execution plan, risk posture, cost, stakeholder alignment, environmental footprint, and life cycle performance. The objective is to ensure that what was initially a promising option now emerges as a robust, optimized business case that will stand up to rigorous internal and external scrutiny.

This Stage also serves as the foundation for successful execution planning. It bridges the conceptual strategy developed earlier with the practical implementation that will follow. By the end of the Optimization Stage, there must be clarity and confidence that the project is technically feasible, financially sound, organizationally supported, and executable under current or reasonably forecasted conditions.

Scope of Optimization Activities

Optimization encompasses a wide range of activities and disciplines. It is a cross-functional, iterative, and detail-intensive process that seeks to add value and reduce risk. At its core, the Stage addresses the following areas:

- Finalizing case framing and scope configuration by challenging baseline assumptions and applying lessons learned from similar projects
- Revisiting technical design alternatives to improve constructability, operability, maintainability, and safety performance
- Refining resource estimates, schedules, and budgets based on additional data, updated benchmarks, and input from specialists
- Exploring contracting and procurement strategies to leverage market conditions, improve delivery certainty, and reduce costs
- Deepening stakeholder engagement, particularly in jurisdictions where approvals, land access, or community consent are complex or sensitive
- Advancing regulatory and permitting activities to preempt delays in the execution stage
- Strengthening the business case by testing it against multiple scenarios, including downside, upside, and base-case market conditions

By the end of the stage, the project must evolve from a promising idea into a thoroughly vetted and compelling investment proposition.

Refining the Plan of Development

One of the most significant deliverables in the Optimization Stage is the updated Plan of Development. This document captures all modifications made to the original concept, justifies these changes, and outlines how the project will be delivered in practice. The Plan of Development now includes greater detail about scope, design standards, operating philosophy, and technical specifications.

The refinement process often involves multiple design iterations, consultations with engineering and operations experts, interface analysis, and early contractor involvement. Depending on the sector, it may include integrated reservoir modeling, metallurgical testing, site layout reconfiguration, or utility and logistics integration.

Capital and Operational Efficiency

Cost optimization is a central theme of this Stage. Teams work collaboratively to identify design simplifications, eliminate unnecessary redundancies, and evaluate modularization opportunities. Scope compression, vendor input, and value engineering sessions are common strategies to reduce CAPEX without sacrificing performance or safety.

Operational efficiency is also addressed by evaluating maintenance plans, energy consumption, material handling systems, and automation strategies. By reducing OPEX and enhancing throughput, the project becomes more competitive and resilient across market cycles.

These changes must be quantified and clearly reflected in updated economic models. The optimization team develops multiple financial scenarios, performs sensitivity analyses, and applies risk-adjusted performance metrics to support sound investment decision making.

Constructability, Operability, and Maintainability Reviews

The Optimization Stage is the ideal time to conduct formal Constructability, Operability, and Maintainability (COM) reviews. These multidisciplinary assessments test the feasibility of the project from a practical delivery and operations standpoint. Constructability reviews verify that the project can be built using available techniques, labor, and logistics. Operability reviews ensure the design supports efficient and safe operations. Maintainability reviews confirm that the plant or facility can be sustained with reasonable maintenance cycles, spare parts access, and minimal disruption.

These reviews are not academic exercises they often reveal design flaws, schedule vulnerabilities, or integration gaps that could compromise downstream performance. COM assessments often result in redesigns, technology substitutions, or procurement changes that lead to improved life cycle value.

Updated Technical and Economic Study Report

The Optimization Stage produces a comprehensive study report that reflects the current technical and economic status of the project. This includes refined resource assessments (e.g., oil in place, ore reserves), updated schedules, cost breakdowns, critical path activities, and risk registers. Where applicable, third-party validation of reserves or engineering assumptions may be included to increase stakeholder confidence.

This study also outlines the organizational structure proposed for the execution Stage, identifying key roles, resource requirements, and leadership positions. It addresses potential execution risks and includes updated mitigation strategies. The report concludes with an assessment of the project's readiness to advance to the Definition Stage.

Stakeholder and Regulatory Advancement

Engagement with key stakeholders intensifies during this Stage. By now, project plans are mature enough to be shared for consultation with regulatory agencies, community leaders, and potential partners. Environmental Impact Assessments (EIAs) may be initiated or advanced, and necessary documentation for permits and licenses is prepared. Strategic communications are developed to manage stakeholder perceptions and enhance support.

This engagement must be proactive, transparent, and responsive to feedback. Projects that ignore or underestimate stakeholder concerns during Optimization often face resistance and reputational damage in later stages.

Functional Inputs and Integration

At this stage, a wide range of functional teams contribute to the optimization process. Engineering, finance, commercial, legal, procurement, and operations all provide subject matter expertise. Their input ensures that the optimized project is not only well-designed but also legally sound, commercially feasible, and organizationally supported.

Integration workshops, interface control sessions, and joint planning meetings are conducted to align the various work streams and eliminate silos. The goal is to produce a unified project definition that reflects consensus and buy-in across the business.

Deliverables for Gate 2 Review

The Optimization Stage culminates in the Gate 2 review. This is a formal decision point where leadership determines whether the project is ready to proceed to the Definition Stage—the start of CAPEX. To support this decision, the following deliverables are submitted:

- An updated Plan of Development, reflecting all optimizations made
- A comprehensive Optimization Study Report, including refined technical, commercial, and financial evaluations
- A clear recommendation on the project's readiness for Definition
- A risk-adjusted economic model with scenario and sensitivity analysis
- A high-level execution and contracting strategy
- A summary of stakeholder engagement outcomes and regulatory progress
- A draft resourcing and team structure for the next Stage

The Gate 2 review ensures that all modifications are sound, justified, and beneficial, and that the project is advancing in accordance with governance protocols and strategic expectations.

Strategic Importance of Optimization

The Optimization Stage is critical because it is the last chance to influence major project outcomes before entering the costly and detailed planning work of the Definition Stage. Errors, omissions, or assumptions that persist beyond this point become significantly more expensive and complex to resolve. Optimization allows organizations to "get it right" before investing heavily in engineering, procurement, and execution planning.

More importantly, this Stage represents a cultural inflection point. It encourages humility, curiosity, and collaboration. The willingness to challenge assumptions, seek better alternatives, and involve diverse voices helps embed a mindset of continuous improvement and adaptive thinking.

Transition to the Definition Stage

Following a successful Gate 2 review, the project transitions into the Definition Stage, where front-end engineering, procurement planning, and execution readiness activities take place. The groundwork laid during Optimization provides a strong foundation, ensuring that the next Stage is efficient, focused, and aligned with broader business expectations. A project may not transition into the Definition Stage if there is evidence of major unfinished deliverables during the Optimization Stage.

Definition

The Definition Stage is the final and most detailed stage in the megaproject development process prior to the FID. It represents the culmination of all preceding efforts; opportunity identification, conceptualization, and optimization and serves to finalize the project scope, plan, and execution strategy in comprehensive detail. This Stage validates the project's readiness for delivery, tests its robustness under multiple operational and economic conditions, and ensures that it meets all the strategic, financial, technical, and operational requirements of the sponsoring organization.

A project that enters the Definition Stage without adequate preparation risks facing delays, cost overruns, or scope misalignment during execution. Conversely, a well-run Definition Stage positions the project for predictable and high-confidence delivery, with minimized uncertainty and full organizational alignment.

Purpose and Strategic Role

The core purpose of the Definition Stage is to refine and finalize the selected development option so that it is fully executable. This includes confirming scope, completing front-end engineering design (FEED), detailing the execution strategy, solidifying contracting and procurement plans, finalizing schedule and cost baselines, and validating the risk management framework.

This Stage also focuses on demonstrating execution readiness. The project must now be able to show that it has all the elements in place to transition seamlessly into the construction and implementation stages. Execution readiness does not mean having everything built or purchased, it means having a fully developed, fully resourced, and fully validated plan that has been scrutinized from all critical angles and has the endorsement of both internal governance structures and external stakeholders where required.

Scope Refinement and Front-End Engineering Design

FEED is the centerpiece of the Definition Stage. Building on conceptual and optimized designs, the project team develops a sufficient design package that includes preliminary process flow diagrams, technical specifications, major equipment sizing, general arrangement drawings, and interface boundaries. At this stage, the design shifts from conceptual intent to a disciplined and structured framework that provides the basis for execution planning and investment decisions.

Scope refinement during FEED involves the development of comprehensive breakdown structures, including the work breakdown structure (WBS), cost breakdown structure (CBS), and organizational breakdown structure (OBS). These frameworks support alignment between technical, commercial, and project controls teams. Engineering deliverables are identified and scheduled, and quantities are defined to a level sufficient for Class 2 cost estimates and preliminary procurement planning.

This Stage also includes the finalization of key technology choices, operability assumptions, redundancy requirements, and systems integration strategies. For brownfield projects, special attention is given to tie-in planning, shutdown sequencing, and alignment with existing operations, often in collaboration with the asset owner or operations team.

By the end of FEED, the project should be execution-ready in terms of definition, and a robust business case should be in place to support the FID. Importantly, Detailed Engineering, which involves full construction-level drawings and vendor-specific detailing, remains outside the scope of the Definition Stage and is performed after FID approval during the Execution Stage, except in situations where certain Execution Stage scope elements are part of the Early Works that the team and the sponsoring organization(s) agreed to start prior to FID for a variety of reasons.

Schedule and Cost Baselines

A critical outcome of this Stage is the development of a Level 3 schedule and Class 2 cost estimate. These will become the baselines against which project duration and cost performance will be measured during execution.

The schedule must be integrated, resource-loaded, and aligned with procurement and construction sequences. It must include a clear critical path, milestone definition, and float calculations. Key risks to schedule, such as permitting, access, weather, and labor availability must be explicitly modeled, and mitigation plans developed.

The cost estimate must reflect the most current and complete understanding of scope, Material Take-Offs (MTOs), market conditions, execution strategy, and commercial terms. It must account for allowances, contingencies, and forward escalation to project completion. Ideally, it is supported by internal and/or third-party benchmarks and validated through internal review and assurance processes. This Stage also determines the project's capital efficiency, life cycle cost profile, and alignment with corporate cost expectations.

Risk and Contingency Planning

By the Definition Stage, risk management must evolve from identification to integration. Risks are not only documented—they are analyzed, monetized, and built into the schedule and cost baselines. For each major risk, there must be a defined owner, a mitigation strategy, and a monitoring plan.

Contingency Planning and Monte Carlo Simulations

Contingencies are developed based on quantified risk exposure. These are not arbitrary percentages, but rather are grounded in statistical analyses and probabilistic modeling to ensure a more accurate and defendable representation of potential project outcomes. One of the most effective tools in this regard is the Monte Carlo simulation, which allows the project team to evaluate a wide range of possible scenarios by assigning probability distributions to key risk variables.

The Monte Carlo simulation process begins with the identification of critical schedule and cost drivers, which are then modeled using statistical distributions based on historical data, expert judgment, and quantitative risk assessments. Variables such as material prices, labor productivity, weather delays, and regulatory approval times are often included. Instead of using single-point estimates, the simulation runs thousands of iterations to generate a spectrum of outcomes. The result is a probability distribution curve for both schedule and cost, typically highlighting the P50 (most likely), P80 (80 percent confidence), and P90 (high-confidence) thresholds.

The benefit of using Monte Carlo simulation is that it provides a risk-adjusted view of the total project estimate, helping decision makers understand not just the most likely outcome but also the range and likelihood of exceeding the baseline schedule or budget. This insight is invaluable when setting appropriate contingency reserves, preparing board presentations, and engaging with external stakeholders such as joint venture partners, regulators, or financiers, who increasingly demand transparency in risk quantification.

Monte Carlo simulations also aid in sensitivity analysis, identifying which variables have the most significant impact on project outcomes. This, in turn, enables focused mitigation efforts and more effective allocation of contingency budgets. Once simulations are complete, the project team can integrate the findings into the overall project control system, thereby enhancing the robustness of financial forecasts and execution planning.

Risk reviews during this stage are conducted cross-functionally, involving technical, commercial, legal, regulatory, and operational stakeholders, as well as key contractors and advisers. Where possible, independent review teams or external risk consultants may validate the assumptions and methodology to further increase confidence in the derived contingencies, especially since megaprojects are inherently complex (Policy and Society 2023).

Change Management

Change is an unavoidable reality in the life cycle of a megaproject, and its effective management is critical to ensuring project success. Given the size, duration, and complexity of such endeavors, changes may arise from evolving stakeholder needs, regulatory updates, technical design improvements, or unforeseen external disruptions. These changes can impact scope, schedule, cost, or quality, and must therefore be evaluated with care. A formal change control process should be in place, including structured protocols for submitting, reviewing, approving, and documenting change requests. Each request should be analyzed not only for its technical implications but also for commercial, contractual, and operational impact, including safety. Decisions must be made transparently, based on consistent evaluation criteria, and aligned with the overall project objectives.

Change management also plays an integral role in risk and contract governance. Approved changes must be reflected in the project's risk register, highlighting any new exposures or mitigation strategies. Commercially, all changes should align with contract terms, and any agreed variations must be supported by formal documentation to avoid future disputes. A centralized change log should be maintained to track origin, status, and impact, ensuring accountability and auditability. These protocols must strike a balance and robust enough to prevent uncontrolled scope growth, yet flexible enough to accommodate necessary adaptations during the project's evolution.

Execution Strategy and Contracting Plan

Execution planning becomes fully operational during the Definition Stage. This includes defining the project delivery model EPC, EPCM (Engineering, Procurement, and Construction Management), alliance, integrated team, or owner-managed and identifying the contracting strategy for each major work package.

Procurement strategies are finalized, including long-lead items, critical path materials, and local content obligations. The logistics plan is detailed, particularly for remote or offshore locations. Construction methodology is locked in, including sequencing, modularization, preassembly, and site setup requirements.

Quality assurance and quality control (QA/QC) plans are also developed, including inspection regimes, compliance protocols, and vendor surveillance. Project control systems are configured to support schedule monitoring, cost tracking, and performance reporting.

In parallel, the project team structure is finalized. Roles, responsibilities, reporting lines, interfaces, and authority levels are agreed upon. This organizational clarity is vital for execution speed, accountability, and decision making.

Final Business Case and Investment Justification

All aspects of the Definition Stage converge in the final business case. This comprehensive document presents the fully validated justification for investment. It incorporates final schedule and cost estimates, updated economic modeling, risk-adjusted financials, and strategic alignment narratives.

The business case must stand up to scrutiny from internal investment committees, boards of directors, joint venture partners, lenders, and external regulators. It must clearly articulate value, risk, alignment, and readiness. Supporting appendixes include engineering packages, procurement strategies, stakeholder engagement summaries, and legal and regulatory compliance documentation.

Sensitivity analysis and downside scenarios are included to test resilience. Recommendations must be firm, actionable, and backed by multidisciplinary consensus.

Execution Readiness Reviews and Gate 3

Before the project can proceed to execution, it must pass a formal execution readiness review, often referred to as Gate 3. This review is conducted by an independent assurance team and involves a thorough examination of all Definition Stage deliverables.

The Gate 3 review assesses whether the project has the maturity, clarity, and robustness to proceed into execution. This includes checks on scope stability, engineering completeness, procurement status, permitting progress, risk mitigation, stakeholder alignment, and team readiness. It also evaluates contingency adequacy, change control procedures, and alignment with corporate governance requirements.

Only when the project satisfies all Gate 3 criteria is it presented for the FID. This decision authorizes full funding, contract awards, and the mobilization of resources for implementation.

Deliverables of the Definition Stage

The Definition Stage results in a comprehensive set of deliverables that collectively demonstrate the project's readiness for execution. These include:

- Final Plan of Development and execution strategy
- FEED packages
- Final schedule and cost baselines, including risk-adjusted scenarios
- Contracting and procurement strategies
- Project Execution Plan (PEP; covering project controls, engineering, procurement, construction, commissioning, QA/QC, safety, and integration)
- Final business case and investment recommendation
- Updated stakeholder and regulatory documentation
- Risk registers, contingency plans, and change control protocols
- Finalized organizational structure and resourcing plan
- Execution readiness review report and Gate 3 approval documentation

These deliverables become the foundation for all subsequent execution activities and are typically archived in the project management system as formal records of design intent and decision-making rationale.

The Strategic Value of a Well-Run Definition Stage

The Definition Stage often determines the difference between a successful project and one plagued by delays, budget overruns, and performance issues. It is the last opportunity to ensure that every element of the megaproject is understood, owned, and aligned. This is not a Stage to be rushed. Investing sufficient time, talent, and attention at this stage protects the company's reputation, capital, and long-term value.

A well-executed Definition Stage promotes clarity, discipline, and confidence. It minimizes the need for firefighting during execution and positions the project team to manage change effectively, execute with precision, and deliver on the project's strategic promise.

Connecting the Megaproject Development Dots

Whether a megaproject is structured as a transaction or a capital construction initiative, the principles that guide its development remain largely consistent. These projects are massive in scale, complexity, and risk. Therefore, understanding how to connect the different elements, both across and within Stages is not a luxury but a necessity. Success depends not only on how well each Stage is executed individually but on how coherently the project evolves as a continuous, interconnected journey.

The Integration Imperative

Megaproject development cannot be seen as a series of stand-alone tasks or documents. Each Stage: opportunity assessment, concept, optimization, and definition must transition seamlessly into the next, carrying forward the knowledge, assumptions, data, and decisions that have already been vetted. When integration is poor, megaprojects suffer from knowledge silos, duplicated effort, stakeholder misalignment, and ultimately, strategic and financial underperformance.

To avoid these outcomes, all critical components must be treated as interconnected: people, process, tools, SHSEC (security, health, safety, environment, and community), scope, risk management, stakeholder engagement, Stage planning, FEL, schedule and cost controls, change management, contracting strategy, reviews and approvals, due diligence, value engineering, economics, metrics, reporting, and lessons learned. These elements work together like a finely tuned engine—each one influences the others, and failure in one area often triggers a cascade of issues elsewhere.

Right People, Right Time, Right Roles

Perhaps the most overlooked yet crucial element is human capital. Megaprojects require the right blend of talent—engineers, scientists, planners, cost estimators, risk managers, cost controllers, contract specialists, constructors, economists, and stakeholder engagement experts deployed at the right time. Engaging key personnel too late leads to misaligned decisions and missed opportunities, while overstaffing too early can bloat costs and create inefficiencies.

Functional involvement must be deliberate and timely. For example, operations personnel should be involved during definition to influence maintainability; commercial and procurement teams must shape the contracting strategy during optimization, not post-FID. Without synchronized human resources, even the most sophisticated process architecture will collapse under its own weight.

Process Maturity and Alignment

Processes provide the governance backbone of megaproject development. But process maturity is not about rigid bureaucracy; it is about clarity, accountability, and decision-making discipline. Clear Stage definitions, well-articulated deliverable expectations, and structured gate reviews create confidence in execution and transparency in leadership (Bakke and Johansen 2025).

However, these processes must be aligned with the actual risk, size, and complexity of the project. A "one-size-fits-all" template designed for a past project may be ill-suited to a new opportunity in a different geography, commodity, or regulatory environment. Adaptability without compromising quality is critical.

Tools, Systems, and Digital Enablement

Today's megaprojects demand real-time data visibility, seamless collaboration, and digital integration across locations and disciplines. Tools such as cloud-based project management suites, shared engineering platforms, AI-assisted scheduling engines, and digital twins help break down silos and accelerate coordination.

These tools, however, are only as good as the data they rely on and the people who use them. Selecting the right tools early, ensuring they are fit for purpose, and training teams to use them effectively are prerequisites to maximizing their value. Moreover, system integration, linking scheduling, cost control, risk management, and engineering databases provides unified reporting and better decision making.

Front-End Loading and Progressive Maturity

The principle of FEL remains central to effective megaproject development. By investing effort and discipline upfront in the earliest Stages, the organization minimizes downstream risks. Each Stage should progressively mature the project: scope becomes clearer, risks are better understood, schedule and cost estimates are refined, and organizational alignment is strengthened.

FEL is not about doing everything early; it's about doing the right things, in the right sequence, and to the right level of detail. Misapplication of FEL can lead to bloated teams, excessive studies, or analysis paralysis. But done well, it provides the single greatest opportunity to influence project success and cost outcomes. FEL is used in the development of capital projects (Merrow and Pillay 2025).

Stage Continuity and Institutional Memory

One of the biggest threats to integration is personnel turnover or lack of continuity between Stages. A project team that develops the concept but is replaced before optimization may lose critical context. Similarly, if the optimization team is not engaged during opportunity framing, it may inherit flawed assumptions.

To maintain institutional memory, documentation must be structured and accessible. Lessons learned from previous megaprojects, both successes and failures must be captured and applied. Knowledge management systems, standardized templates, and peer reviews across functions are critical tools to reduce institutional amnesia.

Stakeholder Engagement as a Thread

Stakeholder management should not be confined to a single Stage. It is a thread that runs across the entire development process. Government relations, local community engagement, partner alignment, and internal sponsor management must be treated as living, evolving dimensions of the project. Early neglect or poor communication cannot be reversed easily once resistance sets in.

Each Stage should include updated stakeholder maps, engagement records, and alignment metrics. Communications should shift from informing to collaborating, especially with communities and regulators. When stakeholder engagement is consistently managed across Stages, approvals accelerate, resistance diminishes, and project credibility improves.

Metrics, Reporting, and Decision Readiness

Too often, project metrics are tracked in isolation—schedule without resources, cost without scope, or risk without mitigation progress. Integrating the metrics framework ensures that each development Stage provides actionable insights, not just status updates. KPIs must be aligned to business outcomes, and reporting tools must serve decision making, not just compliance.

Decision readiness is not just a function of having completed the deliverables for a gate. It is about having a coherent, traceable, and defendable narrative that demonstrates how the project has matured, how it aligns with the strategy, and why it is ready for investment.

Learning Loops and Continuous Improvement

The final piece in connecting the development dots is learning, both during and after each project. Megaprojects are inherently high-stakes, but they also offer unmatched learning opportunities. Teams must be empowered to record, review, and share lessons systematically. These insights must then be accessible, structured, and reapplied on future initiatives.

Organizational learning is not accidental. It must be built into processes, incentivized through culture, and sustained by leadership. Post-Stage reviews, third-party audits, and embedded feedback loops enhance collective intelligence and protect against repeating mistakes.

In summary, the development of a megaproject is not a series of isolated actions but a continuous, interlinked process where early decisions shape long-term outcomes. Success hinges on the disciplined application of structured stages; opportunity identification and assessment, concept framing, optimization, and definition executed with the right people, tools, governance, and mindset. When these elements are connected with clarity and purpose, megaprojects can evolve from complex undertakings into well-positioned, high-value investments.

Successful megaprojects don't begin with execution, they begin with clarity of purpose, alignment of vision, and strategic opportunity framing. The groundwork laid in the early Stages determines whether a project is positioned for long-term value or destined for missteps. But identifying opportunity is only part of the equation. The next essential step is rigorous evaluation: testing assumptions, analyzing feasibility, and determining whether the vision can withstand financial, technical, and operational scrutiny. In the following chapter, we explore how evaluation becomes the gateway to informed decision making and resilient project outcomes. follow the journey.

Reflection Questions

1. What are the critical differences between project development and execution phases in megaprojects?
2. How can strong internal alignment influence the outcome of FIDs?
3. What role does corporate governance play in shaping the development of capital-intensive projects?

CHAPTER 3

Evaluation

Learning Outcomes

After reading this chapter, you will be able to:

1. Understand the key reasons why megaproject evaluations often fall short of supporting sound investment decisions.
2. Differentiate between evaluation methods used for mega transactions (e.g., M&A, divestitures) and mega construction projects.
3. Identify critical gaps in traditional evaluation processes, including overreliance on financial metrics and lack of stakeholder alignment.
4. Apply a broader evaluation lens that includes strategic fit, risk-adjusted performance, and decision readiness.
5. Recognize how poor evaluations contribute to megaproject failure and how more robust evaluation can mitigate this risk.

Evaluation is the gateway through which capital-intensive decisions are tested for strategic fit, technical feasibility, commercial viability, and execution readiness. In this chapter, we examine two critical domains of evaluation: **mega mergers and acquisitions (M&A)** and **mega engineering–procurement–construction (EPC)** project delivery. M&A evaluations focus on strategic alignment, risk exposure, and integration planning, while EPC evaluations assess project design maturity, stakeholder alignment, and financial robustness. Together, these perspectives provide a comprehensive framework for assessing whether a project or an acquisition is truly ready to proceed.

This chapter begins with the evaluation of mega M&As where strategic alignment, due diligence, and integration planning are foundational to value capture. It then transitions into evaluating the technical, commercial, and stakeholder readiness of projects being developed or executed under traditional EPC models. This chapter is divided into three parts:

- Part 1: Mega M&A Evaluation
- Part 2: EPC Project Readiness Evaluation
- Part 3: Megaproject Evaluation Framework

PART 1

Mega M&A Evaluation

Steps and Practical Realities Behind the Deal Curtain

Megaproject M&As, and divestitures represent one of the most strategically complex areas in the capital projects ecosystem, where technical depth intersects with financial ambition, and where the implications of integration extend far beyond numbers. These transactions often involve multibillion-dollar assets such as LNG terminals, pipelines, refineries, mining operations, and integrated infrastructure systems. As such, evaluating them demands more than standard financial diligence. It requires a cross-functional, future-back approach grounded in engineering realities, risk discipline, and stakeholder alignment.

This section outlines the key dimensions and practical steps for evaluating a mega M&A in the context of complex, capital-intensive projects.

Step 1: Strategic Fit and Intent Clarification

Every successful transaction begins with clarity of purpose. Evaluation must first validate the **core intent** of the acquisition: is it a move toward market expansion, offtake security, resource control, digital capability, or life cycle value enhancement?

Strategic fit must go beyond surface-level synergy claims. It requires alignment between the acquirer's development philosophy and the target's execution model, governance approach, and cultural DNA. In volatile environments, this also includes scenario validation against shifting energy transition mandates, ESG regulations, and macroeconomic headwinds (Kwak et al. 2024).

Evaluator's Lens: Purpose before pricing. Strategic misalignment often hides behind valuation disagreements.

Step 2: Comprehensive Technical Due Diligence

Megaproject M&A due diligence must scrutinize the **design, maturity, scalability, and resilience** of the asset portfolio. Evaluators should assess:

- The project's stage in its life cycle: FEED, FID-ready, under construction, or in early operations
- The integrity and relevance of the design basis
- Technology readiness, modularity, and risk of obsolescence
- The realism of schedule, CAPEX, and OPEX baselines, supported by independent benchmarks

Evaluator's Lens: Proforma pitch books often understate risk. Independent technical validation is nonnegotiable (Turner and Simister 2023).

Step 3: Risk and Liability Mapping

In megaprojects, risks are not linear, they are systemic. Evaluation must reveal legal, technical, commercial, and regulatory exposures through:

- Review of EPC, operations and maintenance (O&M), and long-term offtake agreements for embedded penalties (aka "Commercial Unpriced Terms and Conditions")
- Validation of permitting pathways and environmental/social licensing
- Investigation of legacy litigation, arbitration, or community grievances

Evaluator's Lens: Not all liabilities live in data rooms. Speak with project operators, community liaisons, and field-level engineers (Miller and Waller 2024).

Step 4: Financial Valuation Grounded in Project Reality

A mega M&A project's value is shaped not just by future cash flows but by execution risk and delivery capacity. DCF models should be tested against:

- Validated assumptions for throughput, commodity pricing, and life cycle cost
- Downside cases involving project slippage, FX volatility, and financing constraints
- Deal structures that incorporate milestone-based earnouts or contingent consideration (Patel and Davies 2023)

Evaluator's Lens: Models built in isolation from project teams often collapse under real-world scrutiny.

Step 5: Human Capital, Culture, and Organizational Capability

The people behind the projects often determine whether post deal integration succeeds. Evaluation must consider:

- Retention plans for technical leads, construction managers, and planners
- The execution culture: compliance-driven versus entrepreneurial, hierarchical versus agile
- Compatibility of systems and processes (Primavera, SAP, Aconex, governance frameworks)

Evaluator's Lens: Cultural friction silently erodes post-merger value. Integration starts with trust and continuity (Lindner and Schreyögg 2024).

Step 6: Stakeholder Landscape and Integration Mapping

In the megaproject world, power often resides outside the boardroom with regulators, host communities, and indigenous groups. Effective evaluation includes:

- Stakeholder mapping and influence analysis
- Identification of integration friction points: political, social, or operational
- Development of tailored communication strategies aligned to new ownership vision

Evaluator's Lens: Many M&A failures originate in town halls, not term sheets. Engagement must start early.

Step 7: Execution Readiness and Value Capture Planning

Evaluation must end with a forward-looking blueprint for execution. This includes:

- Day 1, day 90, and year 1 integration plans
- Reassessment of pending FIDs, risk registers, and procurement strategies under new ownership
- Identification of synergy levers capital rationalization, shared supply chains, centralized control towers

Evaluator's Lens: In megaprojects, synergy realization is operational, not just financial.

The evaluation model is represented diagrammatically in Figure 3.1.

From Target to Transformation

Evaluating a mega M&A deal is not just about acquiring physical assets; it is about absorbing an entire project identity one that must be reshaped

Figure 3.1 Seven-step mega M&A evaluation model

and reoriented to align with new strategic goals. The real value lies not in balance sheets, but in execution credibility, stakeholder alignment, early identification of the scale of the capital project within the asset to be acquired, and the readiness to deliver capital projects at scale.

PART 2

EPC Project Readiness Evaluation

Overview

> The most successful M&A deals are those where decision makers ask not only, "What are we buying?" but, "What must we become to make this succeed?"

Following the evaluation of mega M&A opportunities, it is equally critical to assess the readiness of capital projects being delivered through EPC models. Before any such project proceeds to execution, it must be thoroughly evaluated to determine whether the foundations for success are firmly in place. This evaluation, carried out prior to the FID, is the gateway through which a project transitions from concept and planning into tangible implementation. The integrity of this evaluation process directly influences the project's ability to achieve its quality, schedule, cost, and performance objectives.

Key project metrics provide a structured lens through which readiness is assessed. These metrics not only reflect the current state of the project but also serve as predictive indicators of future success. When reviewed, measured, validated systematically, they help reduce uncertainties, align stakeholders, and confirm the desirability or otherwise of moving the project forward. This section outlines the most critical pre-FID metrics that contribute to successful execution, each presented as a distinct but interconnected pillar of evaluation.

Front-End Engineering Design Completeness

One of the first indicators of megaproject readiness is the completeness of the FEED. The FEED represents the technical backbone of the project and forms the basis for schedules, cost estimates, procurement planning, and risk assessments. A comprehensive FEED demonstrates that the scope of work has been thoroughly defined, the major design challenges have been addressed, and the technical configuration aligns with strategic business objectives.

A project with a high degree of FEED completion offers confidence that all stakeholders understand what will be built, how it will be built, and what resources will be required. It reflects not only the quality of the engineering effort but also the extent to which constructability reviews, operational considerations and life cycle cost optimization have been incorporated. Incomplete or poorly developed FEED documentation is often a precursor to scope changes during execution, which inevitably lead to schedule delays, cost overruns, and increased risk exposure. Therefore, the FEED must be evaluated for both its technical content and its alignment with the broader project strategy (Chen and Zhang 2024).

Risk Assessment and Mitigation Plan

Megaprojects are inherently risky due to their scale, complexity, and external dependencies. The evaluation process must assess how well the project team has identified, quantified, and prepared for risks that could derail execution. This begins with a comprehensive risk register that captures technical, financial, environmental, and stakeholder-related risks.

Beyond identification, the focus must shift to the robustness of the mitigation strategy. Evaluation should determine whether mitigation actions are specific, measurable, and embedded into the project's execution plan. Quantitative risk assessments such as sensitivity analyses or Monte Carlo simulations can provide insight into potential deviations in schedule and cost and outcomes (Ghazali and Hassan 2023).

Risk ownership is another critical component. A mature risk management plan clearly assigns responsibilities, escalation paths, and trigger conditions. It also incorporates schedule and cost contingencies aligned with the level of risk retained by the project. Projects with effective and efficient risk management frameworks exhibit greater resilience, enabling them to adapt to emerging threats while maintaining control over performance indicators.

Schedule Definition and Maturity

The project schedule is a dynamic instrument that maps the journey from FID to completion. It establishes the sequence of activities, defines the critical path, allocates resources, and synchronizes interfaces across multiple work or contract packages and/or work streams. A well-developed schedule is not merely a list of tasks; it is a strategic planning tool that enables the team to visualize constraints, identify float, manage dependencies, visualize human resource requirements, and monitor progress.

The maturity of the schedule must be evaluated in the context of execution complexity. A mature schedule incorporates milestones, performance logic, and risk-adjusted durations. It integrates permitting, detail engineering, procurement, permitting, construction, and commissioning activities into a coherent whole. Evaluation must also consider whether the schedule reflects realistic productivity rates, considers site access and logistics, location-specific weather swings, and includes buffers or allowances for known uncertainties such as political terrain, labor market, and simultaneous operations (SIMOPS).

Projects with immature schedules often experience coordination/integration issues, misalignment among contractors, and with the owner's teams (project and operations), and underestimation of duration for critical activities. These shortcomings become particularly problematic when multiple parties are involved in simultaneous construction, commissioning, and transition to operation tasks. In contrast, a mature schedule serves as a foundation for successful execution by enhancing visibility, facilitating communication, and enabling effective decision making. A mature megaproject schedule (time estimate) must also be supported by a Basis of Schedule document (Marques and Monteiro 2024).

Refer to Appendix I for a sample template.

Cost Estimate Accuracy

Cost estimation is a defining aspect of project evaluation, as it provides a financial representation of the scope, risks, and schedule. An accurate and realistic cost estimate is essential for securing financing, managing stakeholder expectations, and structuring contracts. It also establishes the financial baseline against which project performance will be measured throughout execution. It is also the primary driver of the economics evaluation in a quest to determining the viability of the project.

During evaluation, the accuracy of the cost estimate must be assessed not only in terms of numerical precision but also in terms of transparency and reliability. This involves reviewing the assumptions, methodologies, and data sources used in the estimation process. Estimates that fall within the industry-accepted accuracy range typically ±10 percent for Class 2 estimates signal that the project has undergone a rigorous and disciplined development process.

A credible estimate should be supported by detailed quantity take-offs, vendor quotes, labor rates and productivity, indirect costs, escalation models, and contingencies. It must also incorporate insights from similar projects and reflect current market conditions. Overly optimistic estimates, often based on inadequate scope or flawed benchmarks, can mislead decision makers and erode credibility once execution begins. Therefore, cost estimate must be evaluated as a holistic process, one that combines data, experience, and sound judgment to produce a financially executable plan. A mature megaproject cost estimate must also be supported by a Basis of Cost Estimate (BoCE) document (Wong and Lee 2023). Refer to Appendix II for a sample template.

Stakeholder Alignment and Commitment

Stakeholder dynamics can significantly influence the trajectory of a megaproject. Evaluation must include whether the project has earned the support and commitment of internal and external stakeholders. This includes shareholders, government agencies, regulators, local communities, financial institutions, joint venture partners, and so on.

A strong indicator of stakeholder alignment is the existence of documented approvals, communication plan, memoranda of understanding, permits, or social licenses to operate. However, documentation alone is insufficient. The evaluation must also examine the depth of engagement, the extent to which stakeholder input was incorporated into project design, and whether unresolved concerns remain.

Effective and efficient stakeholder engagement builds trust, mitigates opposition, and facilitates smoother project execution. Conversely, weak or superficial engagement can result in legal challenges, protests, or reputational damage. Evaluators must scrutinize whether stakeholder strategies are proactive, inclusive, and sustained, rather than reactive or symbolic (Okafor and van der Merwe 2024).

Procurement Readiness

Procurement is a pivotal activity that bridges planning and execution. The evaluation must determine whether the procurement plan is sufficiently detailed, whether procurement packages are aligned with the schedule, and whether vendor engagement has begun in a timely manner. Projects that fail to secure long-lead items, specialized equipment, or critical services in advance often suffer from execution delays and cost escalation.

Procurement readiness includes clarity on sourcing strategies, market assessments, vendor qualifications, logistics constraint, and contract terms. Evaluation should also examine whether the procurement process incorporates lessons from similar projects, including strategies for local content, supply chain resilience, and inflation risk.

A well-prepared procurement strategy demonstrates that the project has a firm grip on its supply chain and can move seamlessly from planning into execution. It minimizes exposure to bottlenecks, enhances cost predictability, and improves integration between engineering, construction, and commissioning.

Contracting Strategy and Readiness

The structure of contracts defines the operating environment for project execution. Evaluation must review whether the contracting strategy aligns with the project's risk profile, delivery model, and governance expectations. It should also assess whether key contracts have been finalized or are nearing closure.

Contracting readiness encompasses the allocation of scope, responsibilities, and performance obligations. It reflects the level of trust and collaboration between the owner and contractors, the mechanisms for change management, and the incentives for quality, safety, and timeliness.

Poorly structured contracts often lead to claims, disputes, and delays. Conversely, clearly defined and negotiated agreements reduce ambiguity, enhance accountability, and streamline performance monitoring. Evaluation should also consider whether contracting documents reflect realistic schedules, resource availability, and escalation provisions. Figure 3.2 lists the contract types in three broad categories. There could be more variations to what is listed, but these are more common.

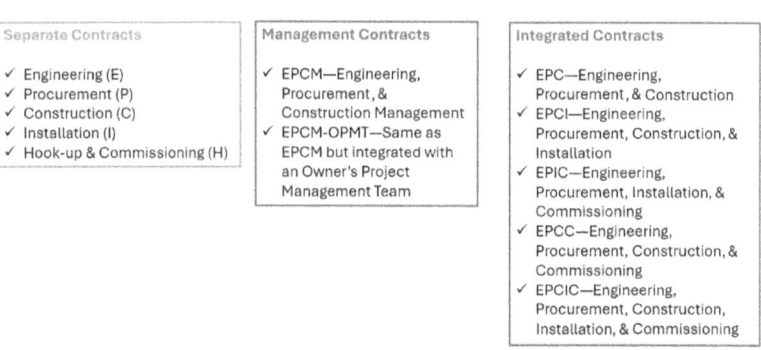

Figure 3.2 Contract types

As there are contract types so are pricing mechanisms and pricing matrix, as shown in Figures 3.3 and 3.4.

Pricing mechanisms should be tailored to each project, considering contract type, market conditions, owner's risk preferences, and contractor capabilities. The mechanism must reflect the degree of scope definition at contract award and the bidders' ability to price the work accurately. Most

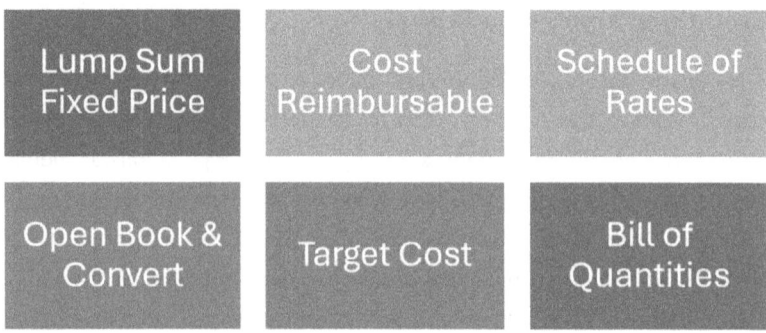

Figure 3.3 Pricing mechanisms

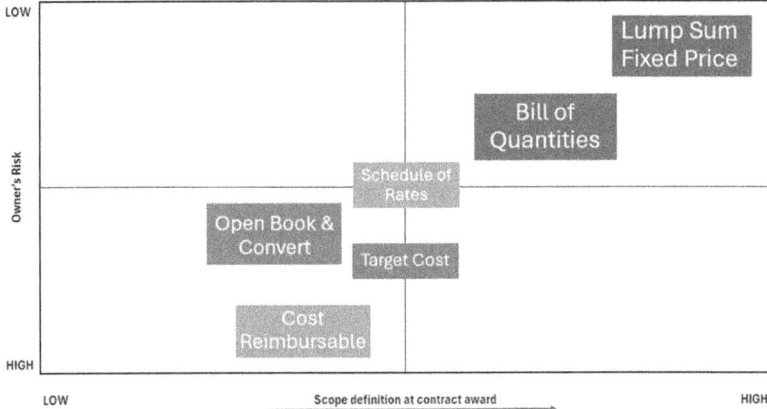

Figure 3.4 Pricing matrix

megaprojects adopt a hybrid model—blending lump sum fixed-price and cost-reimbursable elements—balanced according to project-specific risk, scope clarity, and market dynamics.

Environmental and Regulatory Compliance

Compliance with environmental and regulatory requirements is both a legal obligation and a measure of the project's social legitimacy. The evaluation process must verify whether the project has identified all necessary permits, conducted EIAs, and secured approvals from relevant authorities. These challenges highlight the growing need for sustainability-aware frameworks and safety-centered planning models (Li et al. 2024; Research on Safety Decision-Making Behavior 2024).

Evaluation should also assess the alignment of the project with international standards for environmental management, emissions control, biodiversity preservation, and waste management. It must review mitigation plans for environmental risks and examine whether these plans have been accepted by regulators and affected communities.

Failure to obtain or comply with environmental permits can result in project suspension, fines, or loss of public trust. Therefore, evaluation must confirm that compliance is not treated as a checklist but as an integrated function of project planning and design. A well-executed compliance strategy supports responsible project execution and reinforces stakeholder confidence.

Owner's Team Capability and Preparedness

The ability of the owner's team to oversee execution is a key success factor that cannot be overlooked. Evaluation must assess whether the organizational structure is fully defined, whether critical roles are staffed, and whether team members possess the necessary experience and training. Mobilization timing is key, as well. It is of minimal use bringing on the right people late in the cycle. Essentially, it is right people, right time, and right number.

Preparedness also involves clarity in roles and responsibilities, decision-making protocols, reporting lines, and communication strategies. Evaluation should consider whether the team has participated in similar projects and whether knowledge transfer mechanisms are in place.

An under resourced or inexperienced owner's team can lead to weak governance, delayed decisions, and poor contractor performance management. In contrast, a competent and cohesive team ensures that project objectives are met, changes are controlled, and value is delivered consistently.

Technology Readiness

The incorporation of advanced technologies can drive innovation and efficiency but also introduces new risks. Evaluation must determine whether critical technologies have reached a sufficient level of maturity and whether their integration into the project has been planned and validated.

Assessment of technology readiness includes performance history, scalability, interface requirements, and vendor support. It also considers the availability of spare parts, service contracts, training needs, and fallback options.

Projects that rely on unproven or incompatible technologies often experience costly disruptions and reputational damage. Evaluation should confirm that all technological elements are aligned with execution strategy and operational requirements and that contingency measures are in place.

Financial Structure and Financing Readiness

A sound financial structure is essential for the transition from planning to execution. Evaluation must review whether sufficient funds have been committed, whether financing terms are secured, and whether disbursement aligns with the project schedule.

The financial model must be tested for accuracy, assumptions, sensitivity to risk, and alignment with commercial objectives. Evaluation should also consider the robustness of cash flow planning, reserve strategies, and investor commitments.

Projects that advance without clear financing often face uncertainty, interruptions, or cost-cutting that undermines quality and performance. A robust financial structure supports smooth execution and signals credibility to stakeholders.

PART 3

Megaproject Evaluation Framework

The Strategic Rationale for an Independent Project Evaluation

Megaprojects, by their very nature, represent a significant commitment of resources and reputation. These initiatives often span multiple years, engage diverse stakeholders, and carry substantial financial implications. As a result, the decision to proceed from development to execution must be founded on more than internal confidence or managerial assertions. It must be grounded in verified readiness, objective insights, and sound governance. Independent project evaluation serves as a strategic instrument that fulfills this need (Baroudi and Jackson 2023). It bridges the gap between internal development efforts and executive decision making, offering a fresh, unbiased, and comprehensive assessment of whether the project is genuinely prepared to proceed to execution. This section explores the core strategic rationales for undertaking such evaluations, detailing the various dimensions through which independent reviews contribute to better project outcomes and organizational resilience. Refer to Appendix III for a sample Terms of Reference (ToR) template for independent evaluation.

Objective Performance Assessment

One of the primary justifications for independent project evaluation lies in the need for objectivity. As megaprojects evolve through various stages of planning and development, those closest to the work often develop emotional attachment and a sense of ownership that, while beneficial in terms of accountability, can inadvertently cloud judgment. Project teams immersed in technical challenges, stakeholder negotiations, and schedule coordination may lose sight of the broader picture. Their proximity to the project, coupled with internal pressure to demonstrate progress, can lead to confirmation bias, selective reporting, and underestimation of emerging risks. Independent evaluation counters this tendency by introducing a neutral perspective, uninfluenced by organizational dynamics or political considerations.

Independent evaluators assess project status through an analytical lens that emphasizes evidence over optimism. They examine documentation, performance data, stakeholder feedback, and execution planning outputs to determine whether progress aligns with strategic objectives and accepted benchmarks. This external perspective is not constrained by departmental agendas or internal narratives. Instead, it emphasizes integrity, verification, and transparency. In doing so, it provides decision makers with a more accurate picture of how the project is performing, or will perform, relative to its goals. This objectivity is essential in organizations where leadership is several layers removed from day-to-day project activities and requires validated information to support high-stakes investment decisions.

Beyond internal assurance, the objective nature of independent evaluation strengthens communication with external stakeholders. Investors, regulators, and financing partners often require evidence that project performance is being monitored impartially. An evaluation conducted by a credible, experienced third party provides that assurance. It signals that the sponsoring organization takes accountability seriously and is willing to subject itself to external scrutiny. This alone can enhance the project's credibility in the marketplace and with oversight bodies, reducing skepticism and increasing the likelihood of stakeholder cooperation.

Risk Mitigation

Risk is an omnipresent element in megaprojects. The scale and duration of these endeavors inherently increase exposure to volatility, whether through market fluctuations, policy changes, supply chain disruptions, or unforeseen technical complications. Managing such risk requires a proactive and structured approach. While internal teams often perform risk assessments as part of project development, independent evaluation adds an essential layer of rigor and independence to this process.

An external evaluation team brings fresh eyes and broad experience to the task of identifying risk. Drawing on lessons from other projects, sectors, and geographies, they are able to recognize patterns that may elude internal staff. For instance, they may detect early signs of schedule slippage that suggest deeper issues with scope definition or contractor performance. They may identify financial risks stemming from overly optimistic revenue projections or incomplete financing arrangements. They may uncover gaps in regulatory compliance that could result in costly delays or legal liabilities. The benefit of this external lens is that it is not limited by organizational familiarity or internal hierarchies. It allows for a more candid and comprehensive view of project vulnerabilities.

Moreover, independent evaluators do not stop at identification. Their role includes the development of practical, targeted mitigation strategies that can be implemented before execution begins. These strategies are often informed by precedent solutions that have worked in similar circumstances elsewhere. Whether through contract renegotiation, rescoping, schedule rebalancing, or contingency planning, these recommendations are aimed at reducing uncertainty and increasing the project's resilience. Importantly, because they are delivered before major capital is committed, the cost of mitigation is far lower than it would be post-FID, making this a highly cost-effective intervention point.

Enhanced Accountability

Accountability is at the core of any high-performance project environment. In megaprojects, where investments are often measured in billions of dollars and public scrutiny can be intense, the mechanisms for ensuring accountability must be especially robust. Internal reporting lines and governance frameworks, while necessary, are not always sufficient to ensure that actions align with strategy or that problems are addressed at the right level. Independent evaluation introduces an external checkpoint into this system, raising the standard of accountability across the board (Schindler and Lüthje 2024).

An evaluation conducted by a third-party organization compels project teams to justify their assumptions, explain their methodologies, and defend their progress based on measurable outcomes. It places responsibility where it belongs, on facts rather than interpretations. This in turn encourages more disciplined behavior from internal stakeholders, who understand that their work will be subjected to outside scrutiny. Project documentation becomes more thorough, risk registers more complete, and schedule updates more accurate when teams know they are preparing for an independent review.

The influence of independent evaluation extends to the executive level as well. Senior decision makers are provided with a tool that helps them validate the integrity of internal reporting and separate perception from performance. It gives them the confidence to ask hard questions and demand accountability for results. For boards and oversight committees, such evaluations provide an external signal that governance systems are functioning as intended. They are also useful for demonstrating to shareholders and the public that the organization is acting with integrity and transparency.

Improved Decision Making

Decision making in the context of megaprojects is fraught with complexity. Each choice whether to approve a scope change, adjust the budget, or proceed to execution can have far-reaching implications. These decisions must be made under conditions of uncertainty, with incomplete information and competing priorities. Independent evaluation supports better decision making by providing high-quality, evidence-based analysis at precisely the moments when it is most needed (Rahman and Thibault 2023).

One of the key advantages of independent evaluation is its ability to synthesize a vast amount of project data into actionable insights. Evaluators distill technical reports, schedule and cost performance updates, execution stage time (schedule) and cost estimates, financial models, stakeholder feedback, and risk assessments into coherent findings and recommendations. This enables decision makers to see the full picture, understand interdependencies, and anticipate consequences. It also helps them differentiate between superficial progress and substantive achievement.

Beyond providing clarity, independent evaluation challenges assumptions. It encourages decision makers to reconsider timelines, revisit cost projections, or explore alternative delivery models. By raising issues that may not have been previously discussed or adequately understood, evaluators expand the range of options available to leaders. They also help leaders avoid the trap of escalation bias the tendency to continue investing in failing strategies simply because so much has already been committed. In this way, independent evaluation acts as both a mirror and a compass, reflecting the current state of the project and pointing toward better paths forward.

Project Optimization

Even in well-managed projects, inefficiencies can accumulate over time. These may take the form of redundant processes, misaligned responsibilities, or ineffective communication channels. Left unaddressed, they can erode performance and limit the project's ability to respond to unforeseen challenges. Independent evaluation plays a vital role in identifying these inefficiencies and suggesting improvements.

Evaluators often begin this process by examining the project's scope, organizational structure, governance mechanisms, and operating procedures. They assess whether responsibilities are clearly defined, whether reporting lines are effective, and whether information flows, or will flow, freely between teams. They look for duplication of effort, gaps in accountability, and areas where decision making is delayed or unclear. These findings are then translated into recommendations that target specific areas for improvement.

Optimization also extends to the technical and commercial domains. Evaluators may identify opportunities to streamline engineering workflows, accelerate procurement processes, or improve contractor alignment. They may recommend changes to work packaging, adjustments to resource allocation, or enhancements to quality assurance protocols.

In many cases, these suggestions are drawn from best practices observed on other projects. By bringing external knowledge into the project, evaluators raise the bar on performance and help project teams deliver more value with the right resources.

Another important aspect of optimization is the alignment of execution plans with business objectives. Evaluators assess whether the project is delivering not just technical scope but strategic value. This includes examining interfaces with detail engineering, procurement, contracts, downstream operations, construction, readiness for commissioning, and long-term asset performance. By optimizing for life cycle value rather than just construction efficiency, independent evaluations ensure that the project delivers sustained benefits over time.

Regulatory and Compliance Alignment

In an era of increasing regulatory complexity and public scrutiny, compliance is no longer a peripheral concern. It is a central element of project viability and legitimacy. Independent evaluation helps ensure that megaprojects are in full alignment with applicable laws, regulations, and standards, thereby reducing the risk of legal sanctions, project shutdowns, or reputational harm.

Evaluators review all regulatory permits and approvals required for the project. They assess the status of applications, identify gaps, and verify whether commitments made to regulatory bodies are being met in practice. They also examine the project's approach to environmental stewardship, community engagement, health and safety, and labor practices. This comprehensive review allows decision makers to understand not just where the project stands in terms of compliance but also where it may face future challenges. It is all about ensuring that the project's "license to execute" is in place.

Independent evaluation is particularly valuable in jurisdictions with evolving regulatory frameworks or heightened public interest. In such contexts, the margin for error is small, and noncompliance can have disproportionate consequences. Evaluators bring an external perspective that helps anticipate changes in the regulatory environment and adapt project plans accordingly. Their findings can also serve as evidence of good faith when engaging with regulators or responding to public inquiries.

Compliance alignment is not just about avoiding penalties. It is about demonstrating that the project is being developed responsibly and with respect for the social and environmental context in which it operates. Independent evaluation reinforces this message, providing stakeholders with tangible evidence that the project is aligned with both the letter and the spirit of the law.

Enhanced Project Reputation

Megaprojects often operate in a fishbowl, with their actions and decisions scrutinized by investors, governments, media, and the general public. Reputation, once lost, is difficult to recover, and negative perceptions can undermine stakeholder support even when technical performance is strong. Independent evaluation enhances project reputation by providing a credible, external affirmation of progress, integrity, and responsibility.

A well-conducted evaluation sends a signal that the project is being managed transparently and in accordance with global best practices. It shows that the organization is open to feedback, willing to be challenged, and committed to continuous improvement. This openness builds trust among external stakeholders, making it easier to obtain permits, secure financing, and manage public relations.

The reputational benefits of independent evaluation also extend to the organization as a whole. By embedding evaluation into its governance processes, a company demonstrates its commitment to excellence and ethical conduct. This can improve its standing with regulators, strengthen its brand, and make it more attractive to partners, investors, and top talents. Over time, the consistent use of independent evaluation contributes to a culture of accountability and quality that enhances the organization's long-term competitiveness.

Post completion Review and Future Learning

The final strategic rationale for independent evaluation lies in its contribution to organizational learning. Once a project is completed, the evaluation serves as a valuable repository of insights that can inform future initiatives. These insights go beyond typical project closeout documentation. They capture the root causes of success and failure, the effectiveness of governance structures, and the dynamics of team performance under pressure.

Post completion evaluation allows organizations to compare planned outcomes with actual results. It reveals where assumptions were flawed, where execution deviated from plan, and where mitigation strategies were effective or insufficient. This retrospective analysis creates a foundation for continuous improvement. It enables the organization to refine its development frameworks, update its risk models, and evolve its project management methodologies.

Importantly, these lessons are not limited to the original project team. They can be codified, shared, and institutionalized across the organization. They become part of the corporate memory, helping to derisk future projects and accelerate their path to success. Independent evaluation ensures that these lessons are not lost in the transition from one team or business cycle to the next, but are retained as strategic assets for long-term value creation.

Megaproject Evaluation

Effective megaproject delivery is not a result of luck or technical excellence alone; it is the consequence of a robust, repeatable, and disciplined evaluation process that supports critical decision making at every juncture. Megaproject evaluation serves as a foundational mechanism through which leadership can monitor performance, allocate resources, manage risk, and ensure alignment with long-term objectives. From the early stages of ideation to the final decision to commit capital and initiate execution, each evaluation touchpoint becomes a moment of truth for the project.

The following subsections break down the most essential components of megaproject evaluation, starting with the Stage Gate process, followed by insights on project scoping, the business case for evaluation, and finally, the structure and function of pre-FID evaluation reporting.

Gated Process

Notwithstanding the advent and deployment of the agile project management methodology, the Stage Gate process has become a defining framework for managing complex, high-risk megaprojects across sectors such as energy, construction, mining, and infrastructure. It breaks down the full project life cycle into discrete development stages separated by critical decision points known as "gates." This structure introduces rigor, discipline, and transparency into project development, while simultaneously enabling agile, evidence-based decision making.

Each stage of the process is designed to build upon the outputs of the previous one, progressively refining the technical scope, economic model, risk profile, and execution strategy of the project. Gate reviews, occurring at the end of each stage, serve as formal checkpoints where a project's continuation is either approved, paused, or rejected based on objective performance criteria and alignment with strategic goals.

Stage 1: Idea and Concept Initiation

The initial Stage of any megaproject begins with the identification of a compelling opportunity. At this point, the focus is on defining the project concept, estimating its potential business value, and establishing whether it aligns with the organization's strategic growth agenda. The activities in this Stage typically include market analysis, strategic fit assessments, and high-level feasibility studies. Deliverables may also include early technical evaluations, resource availability studies, high-level fiscal policy, and preliminary risk scans.

The gate criteria at this point are relatively high-level and may include:

- Strategic alignment with business vision and investment goals
- Initial cost–benefit analysis and economic justification
- Clear articulation of the problem or opportunity being addressed

The goal of this Stage is not to deliver detailed engineering but to determine whether a project concept is worthy of further exploration and investment. Some businesses assess the options at this Stage and decide on the Go Forward option such that the next Stage is devoted to the optimization of the one option, while some wait until the next Stage to select the preferred option and also optimize the one option at the back end of the next Stage.

Stage 2: Optimization (Feasibility and Pre-FEED)

If the project concept receives a green light, it progresses to the optimization (feasibility and pre-FEED) Stage. Here, the technical, environmental, social, and financial dimensions of the project are examined in more detail. Key activities during this Stage include the development of preliminary engineering designs, site selection studies, regulatory and permitting investigations, and detailed financial modeling. Stakeholder mapping and engagement planning also begin in earnest.

The gate review at the end of this Stage must confirm:

- Technical feasibility of the project concept
- Financial viability under different scenarios
- Initial environmental and regulatory compliance pathways
- Risk identification across operational, financial, and legal dimensions

A project that exits this gate should demonstrate a coherent plan for moving into FEED and a credible strategy for risk mitigation.

Stage 3: Definition Stage (Front-End Engineering Design)

This is arguably the most critical development stage in the life cycle of a megaproject. It involves finalizing technical specifications, conducting detailed engineering, and producing schedule and cost estimates with a high degree of confidence. The FEED effort refines the scope and forms the technical and commercial baseline for investment evaluation.

During this Stage, the project team must also complete stakeholder alignment, finalize procurement strategies, identify contracting models, and prepare execution readiness plans. At the gate review, the emphasis is on:

- Early precommitment or long lead items' procurement (Optional)
- Completeness and accuracy of engineering design
- Level 3 integrated schedule with contingency analysis

- Class 2 cost estimates with an accuracy of at least -10 percent to $+15$ percent, including cost risk analysis to estimate project contingency
- Procurement and contracting strategies finalized or in negotiation
- Labor and market analysis report
- Stakeholder support and regulatory readiness
- Execution readiness and risk mitigation strategies fully developed, leading to the establishment of the PEP and the Risk Register
- Economic evaluation report
- Independent peer reviews
- DSP

Approval at this gate leads directly to the FID. The stakes are high, and so is the burden of proof on the project team to demonstrate preparedness. Refer to Appendix IV for a sample template for PEP.

Stage 4: Execution (Detail Design, Procurement, and Construction)

Upon receiving investment approval, the project moves into full-scale execution. Activities in this Stage include detailed design implementation, procurement of materials and services, construction activities, with the PEP, quality assurance, project control systems and risk management plans activated and operationalized. Six monthly independent execution Stage reviews are strongly recommended.

The commissioning readiness at the end of the execution Stage requires evidence of:

- Certification of pre-start-up review (PSUR) report
- All permits and approvals to operate the plant obtained
- Mobilization of commissioning contractors and workforce
- Construction management's readiness to commission the plant

Any gaps in these areas may justify delaying execution or scope reconfiguration.

Stage 5: Commissioning and Start-Up

Most of the time, the combined commissioning and start-up is part of the execution Stage in most Stage Gate systems. The transition from construction to operational readiness is managed in this Stage. Commissioning activities verify that facilities and systems function according to design specifications. Start-up procedures are implemented, and performance testing begins. Handover plans are executed in parallel, transferring responsibilities from the project team to the operations group.

Criteria for completing this Stage may include:

- Completion of all system verification and start-up procedures
- Safety and regulatory certifications achieved
- Finalization of operational manuals and staff training
- Performance criteria met for all core systems
- All permits and approvals to operate the plant obtained
- Full financial close and CAPEX/OPEX funding availability to close the warranty period, remaining reporting, review and documentation activities post first production
- Plan for the closure of major contracts and supply agreements established
- Plan for the demobilization of contractors and workforce
- Operations and maintenance team's readiness

End of this gate marks the end of construction and the beginning of sustained operations.

Stage 6: Transition to Operations

Most of the time, the transition to operations (aka handover) is part of the execution Stage in most Stage Gate systems. With the project now technically complete, it transitions into its operational life cycle. The focus shifts to achieving steady-state operations, optimizing performance, and extracting value. The project team begins to wind down, while the operations team assumes full control.

End-of-Stage criteria include:

- All deliverables transferred to operations
- Remaining construction issues resolved
- KPIs established and monitored
- Closure of open items with regulators and stakeholders

This Stage also includes commencement of final document handovers, warranty management, and establishing asset monitoring protocols.

Stage 7: Closeout and Review

Most of the time, the closeout and review (except the formal post investment review) is part of the execution Stage in most Stage Gate systems. This final Stage is where the lessons learned from the project are captured and institutionalized. It involves formal evaluations of project performance against objectives, schedule and cost analysis, stakeholder feedback, and knowledge transfer.

This stage includes:

- Post project evaluation and performance audits
- Financial closeout and contractual settlements
- Debriefings with key stakeholders
- Documentation of best practices and lessons learned
- Establishment of the full project's closeout report

Projects that close well provide a template for future excellence. More importantly, they ensure that knowledge is not lost but fed back into the organizational knowledge base.

Note that Stages 5 to 7 may not be stand-alone Stages in most businesses (as stated above), but one way of delineating each of them is to conduct a readiness review at the beginning of each of those major activities.

It is important to note that the Post Investment reviews are usually conducted within 18 months of first production date, that is, during the Operations Stage. This is meant to confirm that the plant is meeting/exceeding the performance (production) promised the stakeholders at FID.

Also decommissioning (aka Abandonment) scope is executed at the end of the useful life of the asset.

Gate Reviews and Decision Authority

Each Stage and/or Gate function(s) act(s) as governance checkpoint. Project leaders must present evidence to a decision-making body, often comprising senior executives, functional heads, and subject matter experts (external or internal). At each Gate, three decisions are possible:

- **Go**: The project has met all criteria and proceeds to the next Stage.
- **No-go**: The project does not meet expectations and is formally terminated.
- **Hold**: The project is temporarily paused pending further analysis, issues resolution, or rework.

Gate reviews must be supported by detailed documentation, clear risk assessments (Stage and full Project), stakeholder sign-off, and financial readiness. The process not only enforces discipline but also provides assurance that strategic decisions are well-informed.

Benefits of the Stage Gate Process

The Stage Gate process delivers significant value to megaprojects by reducing risks, improving decision quality, and increasing capital efficiency. It introduces structure to what would otherwise be a fluid and chaotic development process. By breaking projects into manageable Stages and embedding decision reviews throughout, organizations can detect problems early, realign efforts promptly, and protect against large-scale failure.

Some of the most tangible benefits include:

- **Systematic risk management** that isolates and addresses high-impact risks early in the life cycle
- **Informed decision making** backed by metrics, benchmarks, and data-driven evaluations

- **Cost control mechanisms** that prevent capital waste by stopping underdeveloped or nonviable projects
- **Stakeholder engagement** through frequent check-ins, reducing surprises and increasing buy-in

Ultimately, the Stage Gate framework instills a culture of accountability, discipline, and transparency—qualities that are indispensable for the successful delivery of large, complex investments.

Focus and Scoping

The success of any megaproject hinges not just on technical sophistication or financial viability but on the clarity and precision of its scope. Evaluation efforts must begin with a comprehensive understanding of the project's scope, boundaries, and objectives. In the absence of such clarity, even the most well-resourced and expertly staffed projects can lose alignment, balloon in cost, or collapse under the weight of complexity.

Scope definition, when properly executed, establishes a common language among all stakeholders. It describes not only what the project is expected to deliver but also what it is not intended to include. This dual clarity prevents misunderstanding, eliminates assumptions, and protects against the dangerous expansion of deliverables, commonly known as "scope creep." In the context of megaproject evaluation, focus and scoping serve as the bedrock upon which risk assessments, schedules, cost estimates, and procurement plans are constructed.

Purpose of Defining Focus During Evaluation

When conducting a megaproject evaluation, the first step must be to define the purpose and focus of the evaluation itself, via a mutually agreed-to ToR. For example, is the review focused on technical readiness, financial viability, stakeholder alignment, or overall investment justification? Evaluations that lack a clear focus often become unfocused audits that generate excessive detail but yield little actionable insight. By contrast, a focused evaluation can target specific performance dimensions, assess readiness in relation to predefined criteria, and direct decision makers to areas of strength and vulnerability. Refer to Appendix III for an Independent Review or Evaluation ToR template.

For example, a project nearing its FID will require a comprehensive evaluation of execution readiness, while an earlier-Stage project may benefit more from a strategic alignment review. In this sense, the focus of the evaluation must match the stage of the project. It must also reflect the needs of the organization, some entities may prioritize schedule assurance; others may focus more heavily on cost competitiveness; while others may focus on supply chain, stakeholder or environmental compliance. Clarifying these objectives before initiating the evaluation helps evaluators design their methodologies, structure their inquiries, and contextualize their findings within the broader business goals.

Scope Definition as a Tool for Control

In megaprojects, scope definition is not a static deliverable; it is a living document that guides planning, design, procurement, and construction. During evaluation, the scope must be reviewed for clarity, completeness, and alignment with stakeholder expectations. This includes verifying whether the project's boundaries are clearly defined in terms of geography, process units, facilities, or service areas. It also involves examining whether interfaces between work packages or contractors have been clearly mapped, and whether responsibilities have been properly allocated.

Scope definition must extend to performance expectations. For instance, it is not sufficient to say that a plant will produce a certain volume of output; evaluators must determine whether the specifications of that output, the tolerance levels, and the quality standards have been fully articulated. Evaluators must also assess whether assumptions related to design standards, regulatory compliance, utility requirements, and maintenance accessibility have been integrated into the scope documentation.

Incomplete or vague scoping documents are among the most common red flags identified in pre-FID evaluations. These gaps often result in cost growth, delay claims, contractor disputes, and design rework during execution. Therefore, scope evaluation must go beyond a review of high-level statements and include detailed analysis of the scope baseline, its alignment with the engineering design, and the mechanisms for change control. An adaptable Scope of Work and Estimate (SOWE) template (with high level time and cost information, and battery limits) is provided in Appendix V.

Managing Scope Interfaces and Dependencies

The complexity of megaprojects is often amplified by the presence of multiple interfaces between technical systems, between organizations, or between project Stages. These interfaces represent points of vulnerability, where misunderstandings, delays, or coordination failures can cause cascading problems. Evaluators must pay special attention to how the scope has been segmented and how integration between components will be managed.

For example, if an upstream processing facility is being built by one contractor and the downstream distribution network by another, the scope evaluation must assess how the interface between those systems will be controlled. Questions arise such as: Are the design assumptions consistent? Are the schedule dependencies acknowledged and mapped? Have roles and responsibilities for integration been formally assigned? and Are interface management plans included in the project execution strategy?

By addressing these questions during the evaluation, the project team can avoid execution-Stage disputes and ensure a seamless transition between work/contract packages and/or work streams. More importantly, well-managed interfaces reduce risk, enhance quality, and improve overall system reliability.

Prioritization and Value-Based Scoping

In many megaprojects, especially those with accelerated schedules or constrained budgets, value-based scoping becomes an essential strategy. This approach involves identifying which elements of the scope contribute the most to project objectives such as revenue generation, regulatory compliance, or stakeholder acceptance and ensuring that these elements are protected during budget reductions or design simplification efforts.

Evaluators must examine whether value engineering has been appropriately conducted and whether critical scope elements are protected against arbitrary removal. It is not uncommon for decision makers to demand scope cuts to meet capital targets without fully understanding the long-term implications. Independent evaluators, therefore, serve as a voice of reason, ensuring that cost reductions are achieved intelligently and do not undermine the strategic value of the project.

Scope prioritization also involves examining the inclusion of "nice-to-have" features, optional components, or speculative extensions. While such features may have merit in isolation, they may complicate execution or dilute project focus. The evaluation must assess whether these elements can be deferred to a future Stage, managed through separate contracts, or eliminated altogether without compromising overall success.

The Business Case

The development of a comprehensive business case is one of the most critical aspects of megaproject evaluation. It provides the financial, strategic, and operational justification for undertaking a project of such scale and complexity. Unlike ordinary capital requests, the business case for a megaproject must synthesize technical feasibility, economic projections, organizational capacity, stakeholder needs, environmental considerations, and long-term sustainability. It becomes the central tool used by decision makers to determine whether to commit resources, approve investment, and initiate execution.

Megaprojects typically span several years, consume significant resources, and carry high risk. Consequently, the business case serves as a filter that prevents ill-conceived or poorly defined initiatives from advancing beyond development. At the same time, it ensures that viable and strategically aligned projects are supported with sufficient evidence and planning rigor to withstand scrutiny from internal and external stakeholders alike.

Strategic Alignment

At the core of the business case lies the requirement that the megaproject must directly support the organization's long-term strategy. This alignment is not a formality; it is a critical factor in evaluating whether the project contributes to sustainable growth, competitiveness, or market leadership. The evaluation must explore how the project supports one or more strategic objectives, such as expanding production capacity, entering new geographic markets, replacing obsolete infrastructure, diversifying revenue streams, or enhancing customer value.

Evaluators must also examine how the project fits into broader industry or national strategies. For example, a new energy facility may align not only with a company's portfolio expansion plan but also with governmental policies related to energy security, climate targets, or local content development. The strength of this alignment increases the project's legitimacy, facilitates stakeholder support, and may open doors to incentives or financing options.

Clear documentation of strategic alignment is vital. It ensures that executive leadership can defend the project's relevance to shareholders, regulators, and boards of directors, particularly in environments where capital allocation is highly competitive and public interest is high.

Risk Management

Megaprojects are exposed to a range of risks that can undermine their performance, delay schedules, inflate budgets, and damage reputations. These include technical failures, labor disputes, regulatory changes, environmental opposition, market shifts, and geopolitical instability. The business case must provide a structured assessment of these risks, supported by quantitative and qualitative analyses.

Evaluation of the business case must examine whether risks have been fully identified and categorized by likelihood and impact. This includes not only construction-stage risks but also risks related to long-term operations, supply chains, product markets, and policy environments. The strength of a business case is partly judged by how well it demonstrates understanding of such risks and the presence of viable mitigation strategies.

Evaluators will also look for contingency planning. This involves determining whether schedule and cost buffers are proportionate to the level of uncertainty, whether contractual structures are designed to allocate risk appropriately, and whether insurance, hedging, or strategic partnerships have been used to reduce exposure.

A business case that lacks a robust risk management section is incomplete. It leaves decision makers vulnerable to underestimating downside scenarios and overcommitting to projects with hidden liabilities.

Cost–Benefit Analysis

One of the most visible components of the business case is the cost–benefit analysis. This financial evaluation must present a clear, defensible comparison between the expected benefits of the project and the costs of delivering those benefits over the project life cycle. The analysis must include both tangible and intangible benefits and must present a comprehensive view of costs, including CAPEX, operating expenses, financing costs, and decommissioning liabilities.

Evaluators must verify that benefit projections are realistic and supported by market analysis, demand forecasts, or proven operational metrics. They also assess whether costs have been benchmarked against similar projects and whether assumptions related to inflation, labor rates, commodity prices, and currency fluctuations are reasonable.

The cost–benefit analysis should also address broader value drivers. For instance, while a project may not deliver an immediate return on investment, it may position the company for future market dominance, enable compliance with new environmental regulations, or enhance resilience against supply disruptions.

Sophisticated financial metrics such as NPV, IRR, Payback Period, and capital efficiency must be presented and stress-tested under multiple scenarios. Evaluators look for sensitivity analyses that demonstrate how changes in key variables affect outcomes. This provides decision makers with insight into project robustness and capital at-risk.

Stakeholder Engagement and Support

No megaproject can proceed without the support of key internal and external stakeholders. The business case must reflect a clear understanding of who these stakeholders are, what their expectations are, and how their needs have been integrated into project planning.

Evaluators assess whether stakeholder mapping has been completed and whether engagement strategies are in place. This includes consultations with local communities, coordination with regulatory bodies, briefings with shareholders or financiers, and alignment with joint venture partners. The presence of letters of support, permits, partnership agreements, or memoranda of understanding can strengthen the case.

In projects with a strong social or environmental footprint, evaluators look for evidence that stakeholder concerns have been meaningfully addressed and that mechanisms exist for ongoing dialogue and issue resolution. A project that faces significant opposition is unlikely to succeed, regardless of its financial promise.

The evaluation also considers internal stakeholder's functional departments such as operations, procurement, and legal. These groups must be aligned with the project's objectives and ready to provide support throughout its life cycle. A business case that lacks cross-functional input is often a red flag, indicating potential future conflicts during execution.

Resource Allocation and Organizational Readiness

A central question in any evaluation is whether the organization has the resources and capabilities required to deliver the project successfully. This includes not just funding but also access to talent, technology, facilities, and systems.

The business case must address how these resources will be acquired, allocated, and managed. Evaluators examine whether staffing plans are realistic, whether key positions have been identified, and whether external resources such as contractors, advisers, or technology providers are integrated into the delivery model.

Readiness also involves internal systems. This includes project management tools, governance structures, control processes, and decision-making frameworks. A business case that proposes a megaproject without demonstrating that the organization is prepared to manage its complexity is likely to be challenged during evaluation.

Organizational capability must be aligned with the scale and novelty of the project. For instance, a company that has never delivered a project of similar magnitude may require new governance layers, executive oversight committees, or external technical assistance. The evaluation must assess whether these enablers are identified and built into the project plan.

Environmental and Social Impact

In today's world, environmental and social sustainability is no longer a secondary consideration, it is a central element of project justification. The business case must present a clear narrative of how the project interacts with its physical and social environment and how it plans to manage its footprint responsibly.

Evaluators review the results of EIAs, stakeholder consultations, community benefit plans, and mitigation strategies. They assess whether the project meets or exceeds local and international standards for emissions, biodiversity, land use, and waste management.

Social considerations are also critical. These include labor standards, indigenous rights, relocation issues, gender equity, and opportunities for local economic development. A business case that ignores these dimensions is likely to face pushback from investors, regulators, and communities.

In addition to managing risk, strong environmental and social strategies can be value-enhancing. They enable access to sustainable financing, improve relationships with governments, and reduce the likelihood of delays or protests. Evaluators look for business cases that integrate these elements not just as compliance obligations but as strategic opportunities.

Return on Investment and Life Cycle Value

The culmination of the business case is a clear articulation of expected return on investment and value over the project life cycle. This includes financial return, strategic benefits, risk-adjusted value, and alignment with future business models.

Evaluators seek clarity in how ROI is calculated, including revenue models, cost structures, maintenance and operating cost forecasts, and projected demand or utilization levels. They also examine how value is distributed over time, whether the project has peak earning periods, and how it behaves under market downturns.

Beyond financial returns, evaluators consider life cycle value whether the asset will remain competitive, compliant, and valuable in a changing world. This includes adaptability to future technologies, compatibility with circular economy principles, and resilience to climate-related or geopolitical disruptions.

A strong business case does not promise the highest return; it promises a balanced, credible, and well-defended value proposition. It shows that the project team understands the business environment, has challenged its assumptions, and is prepared to manage uncertainty while delivering results.

Reporting

No megaproject evaluation is complete without detailed, structured, and decision-oriented reporting. Reports are the vessels through which the results of evaluations are communicated to executives, stakeholders, investors, and regulatory authorities. They provide the evidence base for decisions regarding project continuation, modification, or termination. Evaluation reporting must therefore be accurate, comprehensive, and tailored to the needs of its audience, capturing both the technical depth and the strategic implications of project readiness.

In the context of pre-FID work, two primary types of reports emerge as critical: The **Mega Studies Pre-FID Evaluation Report** and the **FEED Report**. Together, these reports consolidate years of planning, analysis, engineering, risk mitigation, financial modeling, and stakeholder engagement. They mark the culmination of the development Stage and provide the basis upon which the FID is made.

Mega Studies Pre-FID Evaluation Report

The Mega Studies Pre-FID Evaluation Report functions as the executive summary of the entire development effort. It synthesizes the findings from multiple technical, financial, and organizational studies and presents a high-level overview of the project's readiness. This report is often submitted to executive leadership teams, investment committees, boards of directors, and, oftentimes, regulatory authorities as formal justification for proceeding to the execution stage.

a. Executive Summary

This section provides a high-level overview of the project, summarizing key findings, status of the FEED, capital and operating cost projections, identified risks, and the overarching recommendation concerning the FID. It often includes visual dashboards that present the status of engineering, permitting, procurement readiness, stakeholder alignment, and financing in a snapshot format.

b. Project Scope

This section details the project's technical and functional scope, including objectives, key deliverables, high-level design elements, and a timeline broken down into key Stages. It outlines what is included and excluded from the scope and provides rationale for those boundaries. It also summarizes the chosen technology, geographic footprint, facility layout, and major systems and processes.

c. Technical Evaluation

The report then delves into the technical foundation of the project. It includes the current status of engineering deliverables from the FEED, such as process design documents (PFDs, P&IDs), equipment lists, layout drawings, and 3D models. Operational requirements are assessed, and the technology readiness levels of core components are evaluated. This section also discusses safety design considerations, regulatory codes applied, and integration with existing assets, if applicable.

d. Project Schedule

The final section of the evaluation report outlines the integrated master schedule developed during FEED. It includes critical path analysis, interface management plans, and key decision milestones. Construction sequencing, permit lead times, long-lead procurement planning, and commissioning windows are identified and aligned with financial draw-down requirements.

e. Commercial Viability

A review of the commercial landscape helps determine whether the project will be competitive in the market. This includes demand forecasts, price sensitivity studies, competitor benchmarking (schedule, CAPEX, OPEX, CAPEX/production unit, etc.), and contracting strategies. The report also details procurement planning and supplier evaluation, highlighting strategies for local content fulfillment and risk diversification in sourcing.

f. Financial/Economic Evaluation

This section includes detailed CAPEX breakdowns, OPEX projections, and funding models. Sensitivity analyses are provided for key assumptions such as feedstock prices, exchange rates, inflation, and financing costs. Metrics such as NPV, IRR, payback period, capital efficiency, and debt coverage ratios are presented in both base-case and downside-case scenarios. Most executive leaderships and Boards are more interested in the input parameters for the downside case. This is because once they are comfortable with those, they know that the investment outcomes could not get any worse.

g. Risk Management

This section is dedicated to address the risk register, quantify risk exposure, and outline mitigation measures. The evaluation includes risk ranking matrixes, Monte Carlo simulation outputs, escalation triggers, and contingency planning. Key risk categories such as engineering risks, supply chain risks, permitting delays, labor availability, site conditions, and political factors are addressed.

h. *SHSEC Review*

This part of the report summarizes the SHSEC strategy. It includes results from security evaluations, EIAs, hazard identification and operability (HAZID, HAZOP) studies, and reviews against applicable environmental, community and safety standards. This section is critical for regulatory approvals and community engagement.

i. *Stakeholder Engagement*

Stakeholder mapping, engagement and communication plans, community impact analysis, and summaries of consultations with local authorities, regulatory agencies, and the public are documented. The report must demonstrate that the project has developed an inclusive and proactive engagement model and has accounted for local concerns in the design and implementation plan. It should also show how the key stakeholders will be kept engaged during the execution stage.

j. Recommendations

The report concludes with a formal recommendation to proceed, delay, or modify the project. Decision makers rely on this summary to understand the rationale behind the recommendation, the major risks that remain, and the actions proposed to address them. This section must be clear, candid, and based on verifiable evidence.

Front-End Engineering Design Report

The FEED Report is the technical and commercial foundation of the project. It captures the detailed engineering that defines the design basis, timelines, cost estimates, procurement strategies, and construction methodology. The quality of this report is often the most direct determinant of forecast execution success, as it forms the baseline for contractor scopes, timelines, cost control systems, and construction sequencing.

The typical structure of a FEED report includes the following components:

a.   Executive Summary

A concise overview of the FEED outcomes, summarizing scope, schedule, cost, major decisions, and design philosophy.

b.   Project Overview

A description of the project's objectives, KPIs, major design constraints, and project boundaries. It outlines regulatory context, permitting strategies, and alignment with organizational goals.

c.   Engineering Design

This section contains all technical deliverables including:

- Process Flow Diagrams (PFDs)
- Piping and Instrumentation Diagrams (P&IDs)
- Equipment specifications and datasheets
- Civil, mechanical, electrical, and instrumentation designs
- Plot plans and 3D renderings
- Heat and material balances
- Design assumptions and basis of design documentation

d.   SHSEC Assessment

Early SHSEC considerations are documented, including design features that improve security, safety, reduce environmental and community impacts, and ensure operational integrity. Compliance matrixes against applicable standards, risk assessment results, and HAZOP study summaries are included.

e.   Risk Assessment

FEED-stage risk identification and analysis, supported by risk registers, mitigation strategies, and scenario planning. Risk exposure related to design interfaces, procurement timing, site readiness, and permitting is emphasized.

f. Project Schedule

A fully developed integrated project schedule identifying all engineering, procurement, construction, and commissioning activities. Key milestones, float management strategies, and logic relationships are mapped out, along with project phasing strategies.

g. Cost Estimation

It is a detailed breakdown of the project cost estimate, including engineering, procurement, construction, commissioning, owner's cost, and contingency. All cost estimates must include a basis of estimate that outlines all the assumptions, methodology, data source, and execution strategy used to develop the estimate. Cost assumptions include, labor productivity, unit rates, currency basis, escalation models, and cost exclusions.

Typically, benchmarking charts using historical data and comparables are prepared to support the accuracy of the estimate.

h. Procurement Plan

Identification of long-lead equipment, vendor selection processes, prequalification protocols, and bid evaluation criteria. The section also includes a procurement schedule, vendor risk analysis, and logistics plans.

i. Stakeholder Engagement

Summaries of stakeholder consultations, community feedback mechanisms, and social impact mitigation strategies are detailed. This includes the status of permitting processes and alignment with governmental and local authorities.

j. Conclusion and Next Steps

The report concludes with a summary of FEED achievements, alignment with project goals, and recommendations for detailed engineering, EPC contracting, or execution readiness planning.

Role of Reporting in Decision Making

These reports, written by competent subject matter experts, are not simply documentation exercises, they are strategic decision tools. They translate technical detail into executive-level insight, enabling leaders to make billion-dollar decisions with confidence. Reports are often subject to external audits, legal review, and investor scrutiny. Their structure, transparency, and completeness directly impact credibility.

An effective report must therefore be:

- **Accurate**: Data must be validated, and assumptions must be defensible.
- **Accessible**: Content must be structured and written for diverse audiences.
- **Actionable**: Recommendations must clearly guide next steps.
- **Accountable**: Authors and contributors must be identified, and methodologies documented.

Independent evaluators play a key role in both preparing and validating these reports. Their neutrality enhances trust, their experience ensures rigor, and their objectivity reinforces discipline. At the pre-FID stage, when decision makers must balance risk, opportunity, and accountability, well-constructed reports become not just tools for communication but instruments of governance, control, and value protection.

Fundamentals for Megaproject Evaluation Success

The successful evaluation of a megaproject is not simply the product of experience or technical ability; it is rooted in a foundation of structured principles, ethics and disciplined practices that ensure accurate assessment, informed decision making, and the ability to adapt in the face of complexity. To mitigate megaproject's high-risk stakes, project teams and sponsoring organizations must rely on well-defined evaluation fundamentals that guide both the development process and the investment decision.

This section explores the core building blocks that underpin effective megaproject evaluation, each contributing to a broader framework of predictability, transparency, and long-term value.

Clear Definition of Objectives

Every successful evaluation begins with a shared understanding of the project's goals, intended outcomes, and success criteria. Without this clarity, assessments become arbitrary, performance benchmarks become meaningless, and decision making becomes reactive.

A megaproject must articulate its scope, strategic rationale, and desired impact at the earliest stages. This includes defining technical deliverables, market objectives, environmental goals, and operational performance expectations. When these elements are clearly documented, evaluators can measure whether the project is tracking toward its vision or drifting into ambiguity.

Equally important is stakeholder alignment. Successful evaluation requires that the project's objectives are not only internally understood but also externally supported. Investors, regulatory agencies, contractors, and community stakeholders must be engaged early to ensure that expectations are aligned. Misalignment at this level is one of the most common causes of late-stage conflict and execution failure. Therefore, evaluators must verify that the objectives are clearly stated, broadly accepted, and realistically achievable.

Comprehensive Feasibility Study

Evaluation without feasibility is like navigating without a map. Feasibility studies provide the technical, financial, and contextual foundation upon which investment decisions are made. They allow decision makers to understand whether the project can and should proceed and under what conditions.

Three categories of feasibility must be addressed:

- **Technical Feasibility**: Can the project be delivered using existing or planned technologies? Are the required skills, materials, and resources accessible? Are engineering constraints understood and accounted for in the design?
- **Economic Viability**: Will the project deliver a reasonable return on investment? What is the break-even point, and how sensitive is it to key variables such as pricing, inflation, and exchange rates? Is there a path to sustained profitability?
- **Environmental and Social Impact**: Does the project meet environmental regulations and corporate responsibility standards? Will it disrupt local communities, ecosystems, or heritage sites? Are mitigation strategies in place? Does it trigger new security issues for the host community?

Evaluation must verify that feasibility studies are not merely academic exercises but robust, data-driven analyses supported by market research, stakeholder input, and independent validation.

Robust Risk Management

No megaproject is immune to risk. However, projects that evaluate and manage risk systematically are better positioned to respond with agility and resilience. A successful evaluation framework assesses risk management at every stage.

Evaluators should assess whether the project team has a structured method for identifying potential risks. These may include engineering design flaws, scope creep, schedule delays, cost escalations, regulatory delays, geopolitical instability, and stakeholder opposition. Once identified, risks must be quantified in terms of likelihood and impact.

A mature evaluation also examines the robustness of mitigation strategies. Has the team identified ways to eliminate, reduce, transfer, or accept each risk? Are contingency plans defined? Are buffers adequate for schedule or cost disruptions?

Finally, evaluators must ensure that risk monitoring mechanisms are in place. Risks are dynamic and they evolve as the project progresses. A static risk register is unacceptable. Instead, organizations must implement tracking systems, periodic reviews, and risk-based decision triggers that ensure responsiveness throughout the life cycle.

Strong Governance and Leadership

Governance defines how decisions are made, who makes them, and under what conditions. Weak governance structures often lead to project drift, unclear accountability, and decision paralysis. Strong governance, by contrast, enables swift, data-driven decisions aligned with strategic objectives.

Evaluators must determine whether a formal, fit-for-purpose governance framework is in place and functioning. This includes roles and responsibilities, escalation paths, gatekeeping mechanisms, and reporting structures. Each gate review or investment milestone should have clearly defined criteria and decision authorities.

Leadership is equally important. Projects with disengaged leadership often suffer from misalignment between strategy and execution. Evaluation must examine whether executive sponsors are actively involved, whether project managers have authority commensurate with responsibility, and whether governance bodies have the right balance of technical, financial, and strategic expertise.

Ultimately, governance must be more than a checklist; it must serve as the backbone of megaproject discipline.

Effective Stakeholder Management

Stakeholder relationships can make or break a megaproject. Effective evaluation requires not only an understanding of who the stakeholders are but how their influence, expectations, and concerns are being managed.

Evaluators should look for a comprehensive stakeholder analysis that maps key groups by power, interest, and proximity to the project. The engagement strategy must be tailored, not generic. For example, local communities may require participatory forums, while investors may need regular financial updates. Regulatory bodies may demand compliance documentation, while contractors may require collaborative interface planning.

The presence of an active communication plan, grievance redress mechanisms, and feedback integration loops are signs of maturity in stakeholder management. Evaluators must also assess whether the project has established the trust and legitimacy necessary to navigate difficult issues.

Stakeholder engagement is not a one-time event it is a continuous process. Evaluation must reflect whether the project team has committed to long-term relationship-building rather than transactional interactions.

Project Controls Management

Megaprojects are notorious for exceeding budgets and missing deadlines. Effective evaluation helps prevent these outcomes by scrutinizing the integrity of schedule and cost and systems.

Schedule (time/duration estimate) evaluation involves more than checking timelines. It includes analyzing the logic of sequencing, the realism of productivity rates, the adequacy of float, and the treatment of critical path activities. Schedule integration across work packages, contractors, and external interfaces is also essential. These are usually contained in the basis of schedule document.

Cost estimates become the project budget used to control the project cost, hence they must be as accurate as possible, realistic, clearly documented, and based on detailed quantity take-offs, and market rates. Evaluators assess whether estimates include allowances for known unknowns, escalation, and risk-based contingency. They must also examine the quality of the cost basis documents, benchmarking data, and alignment with scope.

Change management is a vital part of scope, schedule, and cost disciplines. Evaluators must ensure that the project has processes in place to evaluate, approve, and monitor scope changes; and that the contingency drawdown protocol is transparent. Projects that lack these controls are at high risk of unplanned delays and cost overruns. Refer to Appendix VI for a sample Project Change Management template.

Integrated Performance Measurement

You cannot manage what you do (or can) not measure. Megaprojects must define, monitor, and report on performance using clear indicators that reflect both progress and outcomes.

Evaluators examine whether KPIs are defined for safety, quality, time, cost, stakeholder satisfaction, and environmental compliance. These KPIs must be measurable, tracked regularly, and reported transparently.

Regular reviews are essential. Monthly dashboards, gate review packages, and executive briefings help maintain alignment and provide early warnings. Evaluation must verify that reviews are grounded in data, not opinions, and that corrective actions are tracked to closure.

Benchmarking is another important tool. Evaluators look for comparisons with industry standards or similar projects to contextualize performance. This enables the identification of best practices and underperformance areas, fostering a culture of continuous improvement.

Sustainability and Long-Term Value

Modern megaprojects must deliver value not only during construction but throughout their operational life. Evaluation must therefore extend beyond technical feasibility and into the realm of long-term sustainability.

Environmental sustainability involves assessing the project's carbon footprint, resource usage, biodiversity impact, and alignment with global climate targets. Evaluators review mitigation plans, life cycle assessments, and environmental certifications.

Social sustainability includes local employment, infrastructure development, and broader contributions to human development. Evaluation should verify that the project is not only avoiding harm but creating lasting benefits for its host region.

Legacy management is another aspect. Evaluators assess whether the project has an operations readiness plan, a long-term maintenance strategy, and the ability to remain functional and profitable over decades. Projects that deliver short-term success but long-term failure are not truly successful.

Technological Integration

As technology reshapes industries, megaprojects must adopt tools that improve accuracy, reduce risk, and enhance collaboration. Evaluation must include an assessment of the project's digital maturity.

This includes the use of BIM for design integration and clash detection, digital twins for performance simulation, and artificial intelligence (AI) for schedule and cost prediction. Evaluators assess whether the technology is appropriate, tested, and integrated with project management systems.

Automation is also a growing trend. Projects that automate data collection, reporting, and compliance tracking gain efficiency and reduce human error. Evaluation must examine the deployment of digital dashboards, remote monitoring, and machine learning in risk management and procurement optimization.

The key question is not whether technology is present, but whether it is delivering measurable value. Evaluators must ensure that digital tools are aligned with project objectives and embedded in workflows.

Continuous Learning and Adaptation

In a megaproject, the learning process never stops. Evaluation is not a single moment in time; it is an evolving journey. Projects that succeed are those that continuously learn, adapt, and improve.

Evaluators should examine whether the project team documents lessons learned throughout each Stage. This includes technical insights, stakeholder feedback, and responses to unexpected events. A centralized knowledge base or digital platform to collect and share lessons across teams, on an ongoing basis (not a one-and-done practice), is a sign of maturity.

Adaptation is equally critical. Evaluation must assess whether the project team is flexible in responding to new data, shifting priorities, or unforeseen challenges. Rigid plans in dynamic environments are a recipe for failure. Agile decision making, scenario planning, and resilience thinking are attributes of projects that finish strong despite obstacles.

A strong evaluation culture values transparency, accepts mistakes as learning opportunities, and fosters innovation. It avoids blame and focuses on solutions. Evaluators must ensure that continuous improvement is not an aspiration, but an operational reality.

Probabilistic Analysis and Contingency Determination

Embracing Uncertainty in Megaprojects

Traditional deterministic approaches to project evaluation often fall short in capturing the inherent uncertainties associated with megaprojects. Factors such as commodity price fluctuations, unforeseen technical challenges, regulatory changes, and weather events can significantly impact project outcomes. To address this, probabilistic analysis offers a more robust and realistic view by considering a range of possible values for key variables rather than single-point estimates.

Monte Carlo Simulation: A Powerful Tool

Monte Carlo simulation is a widely used technique in probabilistic analysis for megaproject evaluation. It involves the following steps:

1. **Identifying Key Uncertain Variables**: Pinpoint project parameters that significantly impact outcomes and are subject to uncertainty, such as reserves size, regulatory changes, fiscal systems, commodity prices, engineering, procurement and construction schedules, capital costs, operating costs, and production rates.
2. **Defining Probability Distributions**: Assign appropriate probability distributions (e.g., normal, triangular, beta, uniform) to each uncertain variable based on historical data, expert judgment, or statistical analysis.
3. **Running Multiple Iterations**: Use simulation software to randomly sample values from each defined distribution and calculate the project outcome (NPV, IRR, payback period, etc.) for each combination. Repeat this process thousands of times to generate a comprehensive range of possible outcomes.

4. **Analyzing the Results**: Examine the distribution of potential project outcomes to understand the likelihood of achieving different results. This includes assessing the probability of a positive NPV, the range of potential returns, and the likelihood of exceeding certain schedule or cost thresholds.

Sample Monte Carlo Simulation Outputs

Note: The following descriptions are accompanied by illustrative charts in the book.

- **Histogram of NPV**: A bar chart displaying the frequency of different NPV outcomes from the simulation, visually representing the range of potential NPVs and the most likely scenarios.
- **Cumulative Probability Distribution of IRR (S-Curve)**: A chart plotting the probability of achieving an IRR less than or equal to specific values, allowing stakeholders to assess the likelihood of meeting hurdle rates or desired returns.
- **Tornado Diagram (Sensitivity Analysis)**: A visual ranking of uncertain variables based on their impact on the project outcome. Wider bars indicate greater sensitivity, helping focus attention on managing the most critical uncertainties.

Contingency Determination

Insights from probabilistic analysis are crucial for determining appropriate contingency levels:

- **Schedule Contingency**: Simulate project schedules under various scenarios to determine the buffer needed to achieve a desired probability of on-time completion.
- **Cost Contingency**: Analyze the distribution of potential project costs to determine the contingency required to achieve a certain confidence level (e.g., 80 percent or 90 percent) in staying within budget.

Key Takeaways for Megaproject Evaluation

- **Embrace Uncertainty**: Recognize that megaprojects are inherently uncertain, and probabilistic analysis provides a more realistic assessment than deterministic methods alone.
- **Focus on Key Drivers**: Identify and model variables that significantly impact project success.
- **Communicate Probabilities**: Present probabilistic analysis results clearly, highlighting the likelihood of different outcomes and associated risks.
- **Inform Contingency Decisions**: Use insights from probabilistic analysis to determine appropriate and defensible contingency levels for both schedule and cost.

Economic Analysis and Data Analytics

The Foundation of Sound Megaproject Evaluation

A robust economic analysis is essential for assessing a project's financial viability, contribution to shareholder value, and broader economic impact. Data analytics enhances this process by extracting meaningful insights from vast datasets to support informed decision making.

Key economic metrics and their derivation are as follows:

- **Net Present Value:**
  - *Concept*: The present value of all expected future cash flows (inflows and outflows) discounted back to the present using a predetermined discount rate (often the weighted average cost of capital—WACC).
  - *Formula:*

$$\text{NPV} = \Sigma \left(\text{CF}_t / (1 + r)^t \right)$$

$$\text{from } t = 0 \text{ to } n$$

  - CF_t = Cash flow in period t
  - r = Discount rate
  - t = Time period
  - n = Total number of periods

- *Interpretation*: A positive NPV indicates that the project is expected to generate value for investors.
- **Internal Rate of Return:**
  - *Concept*: The discount rate at which the NPV of all cash flows equals zero, representing the project's effective rate of return.
  - *Derivation*: Solve for *r* in the NPV equation, where NPV = 0.
  - *Interpretation*: If the IRR exceeds the company's cost of capital or a predetermined hurdle rate, the project is generally considered acceptable.
- **Payback Period:**
  - *Concept*: The time it takes for cumulative cash inflows to equal the initial investment.
  - *Derivation*: Calculate the time required for cumulative cash flows to recover the initial investment.
  - *Interpretation*: A shorter payback period is preferred as it indicates a quicker return of capital.
- **Profitability Index (PI) or Benefit–Cost Ratio (BCR):**
  - *Concept*: The ratio of the present value of future cash inflows to the initial investment.
  - *Formula:*

PI = Present Value of Future Cash Inflows / Initial Investment

  - *Interpretation*: A PI greater than 1 indicates that the project is expected to generate more value than its cost.
- **Break-Even Analysis:**
  - *Concept*: Determines the point at which total revenue equals total costs.
  - *Formula*:

Break-Even Point (Units) = Total Fixed Costs /
(Selling Price per Unit − Variable Cost per Unit)

  - *Interpretation*: Understanding the break-even point is crucial for assessing the project's sensitivity to changes in production volume or sales prices.

- **Capital Efficiency**
  - *Concept:* Capital efficiency describes how effectively an organization converts invested capital into economic value. It reflects the discipline of doing more with less, allocating scarce capital to the opportunities that produce the greatest and most durable returns.
  - *Formula*:

$$\text{Capital Efficiency} = \text{Value Created} \div \text{Capital Invested}$$

(Practically proxied by metrics such as ROIC, IRR, or Value per Dollar Invested.)

  - *Interpretation:* High capital efficiency means each dollar of capital works hard, generating strong returns, faster payback, and resilience through cycles. Low capital efficiency signals trapped value, over-investment, or weak strategic choices, even if absolute growth looks impressive on paper.

The Role of Data Analytics

Data analytics enhances economic analysis in megaprojects through:

- **Historical Data Analysis**: Examining past project performance and economic indicators to inform forecasts.
- **Market Analysis**: Utilizing market research and competitor analysis to estimate future revenues.
- **Econometric Modeling**: Employing statistical techniques to predict the impact of economic factors on project outcomes.
- **Scenario Planning and Sensitivity Analysis**: Developing different economic scenarios and assessing project sensitivity to key variables.
- **Risk Modeling and Simulation**: Integrating economic data into probabilistic models to quantify financial risks and uncertainties.

Applying Economic Analysis and Data Analytics

- **Comprehensive Cash Flow Forecasting**: Develop detailed and realistic cash flow projections over the project's life cycle.
- **Rigorous Discount Rate Selection**: Determine the appropriate discount rate reflecting the project's risk profile and company's cost of capital.
- **Sensitivity Testing**: Analyze how changes in key economic assumptions impact financial viability.
- **Scenario Analysis**: Evaluate project performance under different plausible economic scenarios.
- **Value Driver Identification**: Identify key factors influencing economic returns and focus management efforts on maximizing these drivers.

By employing sound economic analysis techniques and leveraging data analytics, organizations can make well-informed investment decisions, optimize project design, and enhance the likelihood of achieving desired financial outcomes from their megaprojects.

Ethical Evaluation and Decision-Making Impacts

Silent Force Behind Megaproject Success

Megaprojects are not just built on plans and projections. They are built on principles. While technical rigor and financial viability are crucial, it is often ethics that determines whether a project succeeds in the real world or fails behind the scenes.

Ethics is the silent force that shapes every layer of project evaluation. It influences how risks are reported, how stakeholder concerns are addressed, and how uncomfortable truths are confronted. A technically sound evaluation that ignores ethical gaps is not due diligence; it is denial.

In high-stakes environments, ethical lapses do not always appear as blatant violations. They often emerge as unchallenged assumptions, polished optics, and compromised transparency. These quiet, subtle, and easily overlooked moments can ultimately define the trajectory of a project.

To embed ethical integrity into megaproject evaluation, leaders must:

- Insist on data integrity, not only in accuracy but in intent.
- Challenge consensus by actively welcoming independent, dissenting perspectives.
- Translate stakeholder commitments into measurable and auditable terms.
- Include ethical behavior and transparency as formal KPIs.

Ethical evaluation goes beyond asking, "Can we proceed?" and asks, "Should we proceed, and are we doing it right?"

It slows down bad decisions and accelerates credibility. It protects legacy as much as it protects capital.

Because when the numbers have faded and the infrastructure is complete, what remains is the story of how the project was built and the values it embodied.

Summary

The fundamentals of successful megaproject evaluation are not abstract ideals, they are practical disciplines grounded in experience, evidence, and intent. They reflect a commitment to clarity, discipline, transparency, and value creation across the life cycle. From clearly defined objectives and rigorous feasibility studies to effective stakeholder engagement, financial integrity, digital innovation, and long-term sustainability, these fundamentals guide project teams and decision makers alike.

In addition to the core disciplines of megaproject evaluation, this chapter also recognizes the critical importance of Mega M&A Evaluation, a specialized domain where strategic intent, technical due diligence, risk mapping, financial realism, cultural alignment, stakeholder engagement, and execution readiness converge. Evaluating M&As in the megaproject space demands a future-back, multidisciplinary perspective that integrates engineering complexity with financial and organizational realities. Successful mega M&A deals don't just acquire assets; they transform organizations, requiring alignment between strategy and execution to unlock value beyond the balance sheet. This expanded focus reflects the evolving landscape of capital projects, where growth through acquisition is as vital as project delivery itself.

When practiced consistently, they transform evaluation from a compliance requirement into a competitive advantage. They provide the assurance that the project can meet its goals, avoid unnecessary risks, and deliver enduring value to its sponsors, stakeholders, and the broader community.

We've explored the strategic rationale for independent evaluation, delved into the gated process, and highlighted the critical elements of focus, scoping, the business case, and effective reporting. We then underscored the fundamentals for megaproject evaluation success, emphasizing practical subjects like clarity, discipline, transparency, and value creation. Building upon this, we examined the importance of Probabilistic Analysis and Contingency Determination, showcasing how techniques like Monte Carlo simulation help quantify uncertainty and inform robust contingency planning. We also detailed Economic Analysis and Data Analytics, outlining key financial metrics and the crucial role of data in providing a comprehensive understanding of the project's economic viability and potential. We also introduced the importance of **ethical evaluation and decision making**, emphasizing that megaproject success is not determined by technical and financial diligence alone. Ethics plays a pivotal role in shaping responsible decisions, building trust, and ensuring transparency. By embedding integrity into data, challenging assumptions, and holding stakeholders accountable, evaluators ensure that projects are not only feasible but also justifiable, and that the legacy left behind is one of truth, courage, and principled execution. But evaluation alone does not deliver results. It must evolve into execution. The insights, recommendations, and decisions formed during evaluation must now be translated into a coherent, actionable, and measurable execution plan. In the next chapter, we explore how to bridge that critical gap from insight to implementation by building effective execution strategies that carry the vision forward with precision and discipline. Finally, we wrapped it up by veering into the world of **ethics**—the most underrated driver of megaproject success. This is because ethical decision making doesn't slow down success—it sustains it. It doesn't limit innovation; it legitimizes it. And it doesn't weaken outcomes; it defines them. Because in the end, when the concrete has dried, the pipe is buried, and the ribbon is cut ... all that remains are your name ... your choices ... and your legacy. Let that legacy be one of courage, truth, and ethical excellence. In the next chapter, we veer into the exciting collaborative world of execution planning—the what, the why, the how, and the when.

Reflection Questions

1. Why is it important to distinguish between evaluating mega transactions and evaluating mega construction projects?
2. What are some of the limitations of conventional evaluation approaches (e.g., basic NPV/IRR), and how do they impact project decisions?
3. How does an enhanced evaluation readiness improve the quality of FIDs in megaprojects?

CHAPTER 4

Execution Planning

Learning Outcomes

After reading this chapter, you will be able to:

1. Define EPC readiness in the context of megaprojects.
2. Identify key factors that influence readiness for execution, including engineering maturity, contracting strategy, and procurement planning.
3. Understand how gaps between development and execution phases contribute to delays and cost overruns.
4. Analyze how organizational structure, contracting approaches, and contractor engagement affect project execution capability.
5. Apply readiness models and lessons learned to improve the transition from the FID to full-scale execution.

Overview

Execution planning stands at the critical junction between ideation and realization in the megaproject life cycle. While the conceptual and development Stages formulate the business case, refine the scope, and develop preliminary assessments, it is the execution planning that transforms these building blocks into a comprehensive, implementable roadmap. This chapter focuses on providing a detailed, practical understanding of execution planning in the context of megaprojects in the energy, metals, and mining sectors—the sectors characterized by capital intensity, operational complexity, and significant reputational risk.

A **PEP** is the cornerstone of project delivery. It is the single most important document that captures the "how" of the project, the strategy, methodologies, processes, and resources that will be employed to deliver the project objectives within defined constraints (Sullivan 2023). It offers clarity of purpose, fosters alignment, promotes accountability, and enhances the predictability of outcomes. In high-stakes environments where margin for error is thin and the cost of failure is high, the PEP becomes a nonnegotiable tool for governance, execution control, and stakeholder assurance. The PEP defines how the full scope of the project will be executed to achieve the business and project objectives in compliance with the strategic plan. It is one of the most important deliverables during the definition Stage because it will have a significant effect on the ultimate project schedule, cost, and other KPIs.

The execution planning process begins during the definition stage, and, though it is a living document, the first complete PEP must be fully defined prior to FID. It is both iterative and integrative. It is iterative in the sense that it evolves with new information, updated assumptions, risk reviews, stakeholder feedback, and lessons learned. It is integrative in that it consolidates inputs from multiple disciplines and work streams, such as stakeholder requirements; scope definition; contractual strategies; procurement plans; scheduling; cost estimation; risk management; SHSEC; quality assurance and quality control; detailed EPC; commissioning; and transition to operation frameworks.

Each megaproject is unique. While templates and organizational standards provide a baseline, no two execution plans are identical. The context of the project geography, regulatory environment, sociopolitical landscape, technological maturity, stakeholder ecosystem, and delivery strategy shapes the content and structure of the PEP. A well-defined execution plan is one that is developed by the core team that will execute the project (or, at least, reviewed and approved by them). It must be a compilation of all the various plans in a single document, project-specific, realistic, defensible, transparent, and usable.

Let us consider the overarching **purpose** of a PEP:

- It defines how the project will be delivered from detail engineering through procurement to commissioning.
- It clarifies the organizational structure, reporting lines, roles, and responsibilities.

- It documents key project objectives and outlines how performance will be measured.
- It consolidates the strategies for schedule, cost, quality, safety, environmental stewardship, stakeholder engagement, and risk management, among others.
- It identifies interfaces between disciplines, workstreams, teams, systems, and contractors.
- It provides decision-making frameworks, escalation protocols, and governance checkpoints.
- It establishes communication flows both internal and external.

In essence, the PEP is not merely a document; it is a **living, breathing management tool**. It communicates the project philosophy and guides daily actions, tactical decisions, and long-term strategic moves. It is used by the project team to track progress, by stakeholders to evaluate risk posture, by governance bodies to ensure alignment with enterprise goals, and by external reviewers to assess project readiness, and health during the execution Stage.

A Systemic View of Execution Planning

A robust execution plan connects the **strategic intent** of the project with the **operational execution**. It translates boardroom decisions into site-level actions. To achieve this, execution planning must address both the **macro** and **micro** dimensions of the project.

At the **macro level**, the PEP should address:

- Strategic delivery approach (e.g., EPC, EPCM, alliance, public–private partnerships [PPPs])
- Governance and assurance framework
- Contracting and procurement strategy
- Risk allocation and mitigation strategy
- Interface and integration planning across assets, Stages, and/or contract packages
- Regulatory and permitting strategy
- Mobilization and execution readiness criteria
- Scenario planning for major disruptions or black swan events (project business continuity planning)

At the **micro level**, the PEP dives into:

- WBS and work package sequencing
- Project controls implementation plan
- Construction execution plans (e.g., modularization, offsite fabrication)
- Logistics and supply chain management
- Field supervision and craft labor strategy
- Site HSE (Health, Safety, Environment) management
- Commissioning and start-up plan
- Document control and knowledge management
- Change control and issue resolution process

Without this systemic lens, execution plans often become too tactical, fragmented, or overly idealistic leading to disconnection between plan and reality (Martins and da Silva 2024). This disconnect is a recurring cause of megaproject distress, ranging from missed deadlines and cost overruns to eroded stakeholder confidence.

Iterative and Collaborative Development

One of the most common mistakes in execution planning is treating the PEP as a one-time deliverable developed in isolation. In reality, it is a **collaborative and evolving** document. Its quality depends on the maturity of inputs from other project functions/disciplines, including:

- **Stakeholder Requirements Specification (SRS)**—Defines what success looks like from the perspective of internal and external stakeholders
- **Risk and Opportunity Register**—Identifies critical threats and upside levers that must be managed during execution
- **Schedule and Cost Estimate**—Provides the timeline, phasing, and budget baselines against which execution performance will be measured and controlled

- **Contract Strategy and Procurement Plan**—Details who will do what, under which commercial terms, and how delivery will be assured
- **Scope of Work and Deliverables Register**—Sets the boundaries of responsibility, deliverables, and acceptance criteria for the project scope

The integration of these elements into the PEP is not passive; it requires deliberate coordination, structured workshops, assumption validation, and buy-in from key players. Execution planning is, therefore, both a **technical** and a **social** exercise. It tests not just the engineering or commercial logic of the plan but the team's ability to align around a shared vision (Nguyen and Le-Hoai 2024).

Governance and Sign-Off

A completed PEP is **not valid** until it is endorsed by key project stakeholders, especially those who will be expected to execute the project. Sign-off serves several purposes:

- It confirms alignment on strategic priorities.
- It authorizes the allocation of resources.
- It defines the control gates and review points for the execution Stage.
- It holds stakeholders accountable for their roles in project success.

Typical signatories for a megaproject's PEP include:

- Project sponsor or business unit leader
- Governance team chair or assurance lead
- Operations representative or facility owner
- Program management office (PMO) director or steering committee chair
- Project execution leadership team

By endorsing the PEP, these individuals take collective ownership of the execution strategy and signal organizational readiness to move forward. This is particularly crucial in **joint ventures, cross-border projects, or multientity investments**, where clarity of execution strategy mitigates future disputes or delivery failures.

Execution Planning as a Risk Mitigation Tool

Perhaps the most underappreciated value of execution planning is its role in **risk mitigation**. While risk registers identify threats and quantify exposure, the PEP puts in place the systems, buffers, and levers to **absorb shocks and maintain resilience** during delivery. Execution planning enables project teams to:

- Anticipate resource bottlenecks
- Simulate schedule slippage impacts
- Identify interface misalignments
- Detect procurement vulnerabilities
- Integrate constructability and operability insights early
- Plan for execution Stage decision delays and their consequences

In this way, the PEP becomes a **bridge between risk analysis and project operational agility**. It turns theoretical risk into practical action plans, enabling the project to pivot quickly in the face of uncertainty.

Tailoring the Plan to Project Characteristics

One size never fits all in megaproject execution planning. Every project has its **own DNA**, a blend of technical, economic, social, and environmental variables. For example:

- A LNG plant in a politically unstable region requires a different execution strategy than a mining expansion in a remote but stable jurisdiction.

- A brownfield refinery upgrade with multiple shutdowns and tie-ins has vastly different execution constraints than a greenfield solar farm built on flat land.
- A project funded by public–private partnership has higher transparency requirements and longer decision cycles than one funded solely by private equity.

Therefore, the PEP should be **custom-built**, not copy-pasted. A useful technique is to develop a **Project Execution Strategy Matrix** that considers factors such as:

- Capital size and funding structure
- Delivery location and local content requirements
- Environmental and social impact
- Labor market dynamics
- Technology maturity and integration
- Logistics and infrastructure support
- Stakeholder complexity and media scrutiny

This matrix becomes the lens through which the team prioritizes execution planning elements and determines the appropriate level of detail, control, and contingency.

Why Plan the Execution Stage Work?

In the life cycle of a megaproject, planning the execution stage is the linchpin that transforms strategy into action. It is the discipline through which intent becomes impact, where scope turns into schedule, design morphs into construction, and commitments mature into results (Alotaibi and Ghosh 2023). If the development and evaluation Stages of a project are about imagining, assessing, and deciding, then execution planning is about **delivering**. But delivering what, exactly?

It is not just about the physical asset, nor is it limited to meeting a Gantt chart deadline or a financial milestone. Planning the execution stage is about delivering **total project success**, encompassing the technical product, project governance, stakeholder satisfaction, regulatory alignment, and sustainable value. It involves designing an operating environment where risks are known and mitigated, expectations are calibrated, teams are aligned, and the sequence of execution is so well understood that surprises are reduced to an acceptable minimum.

The execution stage of a megaproject is a period of intense activity, financial exposure, reputational risk, and operational vulnerability. In such a context, a strong, current, and well-communicated execution plan is not optional; it is indispensable.

Key points to take into account in preparing the PEP are as follows:

- It must be project specific; do not use a boilerplate document.
- It must be a compilation of all the various plans in a single document (at summary level).
- Avoid high-level generalities; provide real information and instructions.
- Obtain input from the whole team and undertake comprehensive reviews.
- Refer to Appendix IV as a guide to the minimum requirements of the PEP.
- The quality of FEL for a PEP must be at least as good as that of other study activities.

Note that higher quality of PEP definition implies to:

- Shorter start-up duration
- Enhanced early operational performance
- Limits the amount of contingency required
- Reduces the number of design changes in execution

Defining Success Holistically

A good execution plan articulates the **full definition of success**. It goes beyond technical completion or schedule and cost control. It includes:

- How every scope element will be implemented?
- The discipline-specific deliverables and the sequencing of activities

- Performance targets across schedule, cost, quality, and risk
- Human resource plans, safety culture protocols, and leadership structures
- Environmental and community considerations
- Technology deployment and integration strategy
- Compliance with laws, licenses, permits, and stakeholder obligations

In other words, the plan becomes the **single point of reference** for understanding how all components such as technical, managerial, commercial, and human converge to deliver the intended outcomes.

Megaprojects often fail not because the teams are technically incompetent, but because of **incomplete definitions of success**. Some focus exclusively on the product like a refinery, a mine, a gas pipeline without paying attention to the project governance systems. Others focus too narrowly on the project management triangle of time, cost, and quality, while ignoring stakeholder and environmental factors. A good execution plan resists this fragmentation. It unifies all dimensions of delivery and anchors every work stream around a coherent success narrative. A complete PEP must enhance the achievement of project success as the summation of project management success (to specifications, on time, and on budget) and product success (the predefined value to the business).

Enabling Strategic Execution Discipline

Execution planning introduces **discipline into execution**, the ability to deliver according to plan, even when the environment is volatile. Strategic discipline means decisions are made based on preagreed frameworks, assumptions are validated before actions are taken, and the team is not constantly reacting to surprises.

The execution plan provides the necessary structure to resist pressure from ad-hoc decisions or political interventions that can derail the project (Kwak et al. 2023). It becomes a control mechanism that enforces transparency, traceability, and accountability.

This discipline is even more important in projects with multiple stakeholders, such as joint ventures, public–private partnerships, or cross-border developments. In such cases, each party brings its own priorities, standards, and assumptions. Without a shared execution plan, the risk of misalignment is high. With one, conflicts are minimized, decisions are streamlined, and performance is monitored objectively.

Managing Multidisciplinary Deliverables

Megaprojects involve **hundreds, sometimes thousands, of individual deliverables**, across disciplines like engineering, procurement, construction, commissioning, safety, legal, communications, and stakeholder engagement. Each of these has a different rhythm, format, risk profile, and set of dependencies.

An execution plan becomes the tool that **organizes and orchestrates** these deliverables. It defines:

- Which team owns each deliverable
- What dependencies exist between them
- When each deliverable is due and what triggers it
- How progress will be tracked and deviations addressed

The execution plan enables clarity and coordination across these silos. It allows project managers to detect when engineering delays will affect procurement, or how regulatory approvals are gating construction. It transforms what could be chaos into a structured, interdependent system.

Without this integrative logic, megaprojects often experience breakdowns in communication, scope gaps, or duplicated efforts. These breakdowns manifest as cost overruns, time slippage, or stakeholder dissatisfaction.

Governing the Investment Wisely

In megaprojects, the stakes are high. Capital is deployed over long time horizons, and small errors in planning can have exponential impacts. Execution planning is a form of **investment governance**; it protects shareholder value by ensuring that resources are deployed in the right sequence, under the right conditions, with the right oversight.

Execution planning enables leaders to:

- Validate investment assumptions before spending begins.
- Prioritize high-risk activities for early mitigation.
- Establish controls that prevent financial leakage.
- Set approval thresholds for deviations.
- Align project pacing with funding availability.

For example, without execution planning, a megaproject might mobilize field crews before permits are in place or long-lead equipment is secured, resulting in idle labor costs and reputational damage. A robust execution plan, on the other hand, sequences mobilization with risk clearance and procurement cycles.

Investors and executive sponsors also use the execution plan as a **dashboard for governance**. It allows them to monitor whether funds are being spent in accordance with the business case, whether the risk posture has changed, and whether the project remains aligned with strategic priorities.

Aligning with Regulatory and Contractual Requirements

Megaprojects operate within complex **regulatory ecosystems**. From environmental permits and zoning laws to safety codes and community development agreements, there are dozens of compliance layers. Any breach can result in delays, penalties, legal battles, or even license revocation.

Execution planning ensures that **compliance is embedded into delivery**, not treated as an afterthought. The plan outlines:

- Applicable regulations and their enforcement timelines
- Required submissions, audits, and inspections
- Role of legal and regulatory advisers
- Training and awareness protocols for the workforce
- Interface between project schedule and regulatory deliverables

Similarly, megaprojects involve a dense **contractual landscape**, with multiple vendors, service providers, and partners. The execution plan must align with these contracts, ensuring that deliverables, payment terms, KPIs, and change protocols are honored. Contract strategy and execution planning must be tightly interwoven, with clear communication flows, decision matrixes, and conflict resolution mechanisms.

Failure to align execution with regulatory and contractual realities exposes the project to claims, penalties, or disputes, and can cause cascading effects across schedule and budget.

Managing Risk and Opportunity Proactively

Execution planning is also a form of **risk management**. It turns risk registers into proactive control plans. By identifying high-impact risks during the planning Stage, the team can embed mitigations into the execution sequence, resource allocations, and contingency buffers.

A good execution plan addresses:

- Safety risks: Through safety-in-design, worker protection protocols, and emergency response plans
- Technical risks: Through peer reviews, redundancy, and Staged testing
- Commercial risks: Through contract buffers, escalation clauses, and price hedging
- Supply chain risks: Through logistics planning, dual sourcing, and warehousing strategies
- Reputational risks: Through community engagement and media handling frameworks

Importantly, the execution plan also highlights **opportunities**, areas where productivity can be increased, value can be unlocked, or innovations can be tested. By structuring in flexibility, the team can pivot to pursue these opportunities without derailing the baseline plan.

Execution planning brings risk and opportunity into the **operating rhythm** of the project. It ensures that these are not side conversations, but central to how the work is sequenced and delivered.

One of the most compelling reasons to plan the execution stage is that it allows the project team to operate with foresight instead of constantly reacting to events. This difference in mindset, proactive versus reactive, often distinguishes successful megaprojects from those that spiral into crisis. In the absence of a cohesive plan, even minor issues can escalate rapidly. A delayed shipment, an unanticipated weather disruption, or a misunderstanding with a subcontractor can trigger cascading failures across multiple work streams. But with a well-developed execution plan in place, the team already knows the alternatives, escalation paths, and trade-offs. The disruption is absorbed, not amplified.

Another critical value of execution planning is that it lays the groundwork for **clear communication**. In a megaproject environment, where teams are often spread across regions, time zones, and companies, communication challenges are inevitable. Different disciplines speak different technical languages. Engineers focus on specifications and tolerances. Procurement professionals prioritize timelines, budgets, and vendor relationships. Contractors look at labor availability, material delivery, and field logistics. Meanwhile, project sponsors and governance teams want to see metrics, trends, and assurance.

A detailed execution plan acts as a translation mechanism. It aligns language and expectations across disciplines and levels. When the electrical team knows when civil works will be complete and the commissioning team is confident that vendors will meet start-up timelines, friction is reduced. Misalignment drops. Performance improves.

The execution plan is also a platform for **accountability**. It defines who is responsible for what, when, and how. This may seem basic, but in many megaprojects, lines of accountability blur under the pressure of delivery. Decisions are delayed because nobody is sure who has authority. Issues remain unresolved because no one owns them. A well-structured plan resolves this by detailing decision rights, response protocols, and ownership matrixes, whether formally via a responsibility assignment matrix or informally through clarity of roles and escalation channels.

Beyond internal dynamics, execution planning helps manage the project's **external identity**. Megaprojects attract public attention, regulatory oversight, investor scrutiny, and media coverage. Without a strong execution strategy, the project risks appearing disorganized or opaque. With a clear plan, however, the project leadership can confidently share milestones, manage expectations, and demonstrate readiness. Regulators are more likely to trust a well-prepared team. Investors feel more secure about the return on capital. Community members see progress rather than disruption.

Moreover, execution planning is where the **human factor** comes into focus. Teams are not machines. Execution brings long hours, shifting deadlines, difficult terrain, and sometimes hazardous environments. Morale, safety, and mental resilience matter just as much as logistics or design. A thoughtful execution plan considers how to motivate, support, and protect its people. It includes workforce rotation strategies, health and wellness policies, safety culture integration, and mechanisms for recognizing effort. Projects that care for their teams tend to deliver better outcomes, not because of sentiment, but because a motivated team is a productive one.

Planning the execution stage also provides the opportunity to incorporate **lessons learned** from previous projects. It becomes a mechanism for organizational learning. Rather than repeating past mistakes, teams can embed tested practices into their current workflow. Whether it's a specific procurement sequence that mitigated material delays, a contract structure that balanced risk more effectively, or a logistics route that reduced shipping time, all of these elements can be brought into the execution plan early. This ensures that knowledge is retained and applied, not lost to turnover or forgotten files.

Another dimension where execution planning plays a strategic role is in **interface management**. Megaprojects are inherently interdependent systems. The output of one contractor becomes the input for another. Delays in fabrication affect shipping schedules. Late procurement impacts installation. Regulatory approvals affect commissioning. These interfaces are invisible unless actively managed, and execution planning brings them to the surface. Through proper sequencing, communication loops, and interface control documentation, the plan ensures that no handoff is left to chance.

As the project enters the execution Stage, the environment becomes increasingly dynamic. Conditions on the ground change rapidly; weather, political developments, supply chain pressures, or labor disputes can all impact progress. A strong execution plan does not guarantee these events won't occur. Rather, it ensures that when they do, the team is not blindsided. It has the frameworks, contingencies, and decision logic to respond effectively. This ability to stay resilient under pressure is often what distinguishes well-planned projects from reactive ones.

Execution planning is also an opportunity to optimize **resource utilization**. In a typical megaproject, thousands of workers, dozens of subcontractors, and millions in material assets are mobilized. Without a coordinated plan, resources get underutilized, overbooked, or misallocated. Workers may wait on site for equipment that hasn't arrived. Multiple teams may crowd the same workface, causing safety hazards and productivity drops. With a proper plan, teams are sequenced, materials are delivered just-in-time, and site access is optimized. This reduces cost and improves efficiency.

Furthermore, the plan provides structure for **schedule and cost control**. It is the baseline against which performance is measured. Without a baseline, project managers cannot tell whether they are ahead, behind, or on track. Worse, they cannot understand why variances are occurring. A well-documented execution plan, with defined milestones and deliverables, allows for real-time tracking, trend analysis, and predictive reporting. It empowers project controls teams to intervene early and course-correct before deviations become disasters.

Finally, the execution plan supports **governance and assurance**. It is the document that is reviewed by internal and external audit teams, by executive sponsors, and by financiers. It is the foundation for the project's quarterly reviews, steering committee meetings, and investor updates. In essence, the execution plan is the formal declaration that the project is ready to proceed responsibly, intelligently, and effectively.

To summarize, execution planning is not simply a task on a checklist. It is a deeply strategic activity that touches every part of the megaproject. It provides clarity in complexity, structure in chaos, foresight in uncertainty, and alignment across functions. It is the mechanism through which intent becomes impact, and strategy becomes measurable, sustainable success.

In the megaproject world, where the stakes are enormous and the variables countless, planning the execution stage is what separates vision from value. It ensures that every hour spent, every dollar invested, and every risk managed leads to the creation of something that not only works but works well, on time, on budget, and with purpose.

Megaproject Execution Planning Steps

Execution planning is the heart of converting a megaproject's aspirations into reality. Unlike smaller projects, megaprojects require layered planning systems that cover both strategic intent and operational execution. The complexity of such projects often spanning continents, cultures, regulatory frameworks, and disciplines demands a sequence of steps that are both structured and dynamic. These steps, when properly implemented, provide a roadmap that aligns every team member, process, and resource with the overarching project goals.

The following subsections break down the key planning steps that contribute to the formulation of a robust PEP, each described as a vital gear in the machinery of megaproject implementation.

Setting the Foundation: People and Ownership

The most important element of megaproject execution planning is people. A well-articulated plan without the right people behind it is merely a document, not a deliverable. Planning begins by determining who will do what. Leadership is central, but successful execution requires distributed responsibility. The project director should not act as the sole architect of the plan. Instead, a Coordinating Team should be empowered to lead the development of the PEP. This fosters shared responsibility, faster decisions, and higher team morale.

Engaging the broader project team in authoring parts of the plan, particularly the "how" aspects, brings a sense of ownership that cannot be manufactured by top-down delegation. When individuals are encouraged to articulate their vision, concerns, and methodologies, the result is not only a better plan but a more invested team. Many successful megaprojects include narrative inputs from each team leader written memos that outline personal goals, areas of concern, and proposed execution strategies. This collaborative method integrates a range of experiences, identifies blind spots early, and sets the tone for participatory project governance.

Establishing the Table of Contents: The What, Why, and How

Before diving into specifics, the execution team must define the structure of the plan. Developing the Table of Contents (ToC) is more than an administrative step; it is a conceptual exercise. It allows the team to define what needs to be planned, why it matters, and who should lead each section. The ToC must reflect the complexity of the project, drawing from previous lessons learned, regulatory demands, stakeholder expectations, and anticipated challenges. However, it is equally important to keep the document adaptable. The ToC may evolve as more is known about risks, design changes, or site conditions. This foundational framework sets the stage for developing meaningful content in the execution plan.

Defining Objectives and Scope

Every megaproject must begin with clarity of purpose. Execution planning starts by refining the project's objectives and scope. These elements define not only what the project aims to deliver but also its justification and intended benefits. Whether the project seeks to improve infrastructure, expand production, or enter a new market, the scope must align with these business drivers.

Clear definition of scope allows for boundary management. It helps in separating what the project will deliver from what it will not, thus avoiding scope creep, one of the most dangerous risks in megaprojects. Alongside scope, KPIs must be developed. These indicators translate abstract goals into measurable targets and guide subsequent scheduling, budgeting, and quality planning. KPIs must be created early and embedded into team dashboards, reporting structures, and incentive systems to ensure alignment throughout execution.

Developing a Project Charter

Once objectives and scope are finalized, the project needs a formal charter. The charter outlines the project's high-level goals, governance structure, authority levels, and key stakeholders. In megaprojects, the charter serves as a constitution; it defines what the project stands for, how decisions will be made, and who holds ultimate accountability. It is typically signed off by executive sponsors, lending institutions, and steering committees.

This document sets the tone for all downstream planning and ensures that team alignment begins before resources are mobilized. A well-crafted charter bridges corporate strategy with on-the-ground execution, linking the project to enterprise-level risks, business models, and growth trajectories.

Conducting Feasibility and Readiness Assessments

Although feasibility studies are often conducted earlier in the project development cycle, the execution plan must revisit them with a more granular focus. These assessments examine the technical, economic, environmental, and social viability of the proposed project. The execution planning Stage benefits from updated studies that incorporate any new regulations, design changes, site conditions, and stakeholder feedback.

In this stage, readiness assessments are equally important. These include reviews of logistics, permitting status, procurement maturity, and contracting preparedness. Execution teams use these studies to inform sequencing, budget contingencies, and resource mobilization strategies. Ignoring this step can lead to mobilizing teams and materials before the site or supply chain is prepared, resulting in costly inefficiencies.

Establishing the Detailed Execution Plan

The core of execution planning lies in creating a detailed project plan that outlines exactly how the work will proceed. This includes time-based schedules, resource allocations, interdependency mapping, equipment needs, and sequencing of activities. The plan must account for geographic, logistical, regulatory, and technical constraints.

A robust execution plan also includes detailed WBSs, integrated schedules, and milestone charts (Cheng and Kumaraswamy 2024). It clearly shows critical paths, float times, and high-risk activities. Teams rely on this plan to make daily decisions, evaluate contractor performance, and escalate bottlenecks. Importantly, the plan must include alignment mechanisms such as joint planning sessions, integrated schedule reviews, and rolling wave planning techniques to keep it relevant throughout the project.

Crafting the Risk Management Framework

Megaprojects inherently involve uncertainty. Execution planning must therefore develop a strong risk management framework that not only identifies potential hazards but actively integrates risk mitigation strategies into the project workflow.

This process begins by mapping risks across all project dimensions such as technical, commercial, environmental, social, and operational. Each risk must be assessed for likelihood, impact, and controllability. Beyond documentation, the plan must include action items for mitigation, early warning signs, and trigger conditions for activating contingency plans. In high-risk projects, scenario analysis and simulation techniques help the team understand potential outcomes and plan accordingly. Execution planning ensures that these risk strategies are embedded, tracked, and adjusted as project conditions evolve.

Assembling the Right Project Team

Execution is as much about people as it is about plans. Once the execution strategy is defined, the project team must be built around it. The planning Stage should identify not just required positions but the specific skill sets, experience levels, and behavioral competencies needed.

Effective teams blend subject matter expertise with communication skills, cultural intelligence, and adaptability. Leadership roles must be clearly defined, including chain of command, escalation paths, and decision-making authority. Interface management roles should be prioritized, as many failures in execution result from poorly managed transitions between teams or Stages.

Recruiting, onboarding, and integrating team members must be treated as strategic planning activities, not HR functions. The execution plan should include workforce ramp-up and ramp-down schedules, succession plans, and mechanisms for conflict resolution and performance monitoring.

Creating a Cohesive Communication Strategy

Information flow is the lifeblood of execution. In megaprojects, where stakeholders span geographies, languages, and disciplines, communication breakdowns can derail progress quickly. The execution plan must include a comprehensive communication strategy that governs internal coordination and external stakeholder engagement.

This strategy should define reporting cadences, communication tools, meeting protocols, and decision documentation processes. It should also provide guidelines for media relations, regulatory updates, and crisis communication. A successful communication strategy minimizes noise, avoids duplication of efforts, and promotes transparency.

Establishing Robust Project Controls

Project controls are systems used to monitor, evaluate, and adjust the project's progress against its baseline plan. In the execution Stage, these controls are vital for making informed decisions, identifying trends, and adjusting strategies before issues become irreversible.

The planning steps should define the control metrics, data collection methods, reporting cycles, and review boards. Controls must cover schedule, cost, quality, scope, and safety dimensions. Modern megaprojects often leverage digital dashboards, integrated software platforms, and predictive analytics to enhance control capabilities. These tools provide real-time feedback and help project leaders stay ahead of emerging risks. Usually coordinated by Project Controls, additional templates that will enhance overall project definition, planning and execution are contained in Appendices VII to XVI.

Designing the Procurement and Contracting Plan

Given the capital intensity of megaprojects, procurement strategy is central to successful execution. Planning must outline how goods and services will be acquired, including the selection of vendors, negotiation of terms, risk sharing, and delivery timelines.

This step should address contracting models such as EPC, EPCM, or hybrid structures and allocate responsibilities clearly. It must also consider supplier diversity, local content regulations, and logistics planning. The execution plan should integrate procurement milestones with construction sequencing, thus ensuring that long-lead items are ordered, tracked, and delivered as needed.

Integrating Health, Safety, and Environmental Planning

The health and safety of workers and the protection of the surrounding environment are nonnegotiable in any megaproject. The execution planning Stage must include detailed health, safety, and environmental (HSE) strategies, protocols, training modules, and compliance audits.

Safety planning should be embedded into the daily operations, from site access controls to emergency response systems. Environmental management must account for waste handling, emissions control, and biodiversity impacts. Community health and safety also need to be considered, particularly in areas with nearby populations. The HSE plan must be more than a document; it must be a living practice enforced at every level.

Preparing for Completion and Closeout

While it may seem counterintuitive, execution planning must also prepare for the project's closure. This includes final inspections, systems handover, knowledge transfer, postimplementation reviews, and demobilization. Planning ahead ensures a structured transition from project mode to operational mode and avoids the common problem of open-ended closeouts that drain resources and erode trust.

Documentation of lessons learned, stakeholder debriefs, and final performance audits should also be included in this Stage. A well-prepared closeout increases the likelihood of successful commissioning and sets the stage for repeatable success in future projects.

The Case for Robust Execution Planning

The case for robust execution planning in megaprojects is not simply theoretical. It is a real and urgent necessity driven by the nature, scale, and expectations of modern capital-intensive initiatives. Megaprojects are defined not only by their size and complexity but also by their visibility, political entanglements, and long-term economic implications. Unlike traditional projects where setbacks may be contained or corrected without severe ramifications, megaprojects operate at a level where even minor errors can escalate rapidly into major disruptions. For this reason, the case for robust execution planning is not just compelling but also foundational to project success.

Effective execution planning acts as a counterweight to the inherent risks and uncertainties that accompany large-scale developments. It is the single most powerful tool for organizing complexity, aligning diverse stakeholders, managing risk, and driving project delivery toward measurable and sustainable outcomes. Whether the project involves building a transnational gas pipeline, developing a deep-sea oil extraction facility, or constructing a multibillion-dollar mining plant, the principles remain the same: success depends on the strength, depth, and adaptability of the execution plan.

High Financial Investment and Exposure

One of the most obvious and urgent reasons for robust execution planning is the sheer volume of financial investment involved in megaprojects. These projects often exceed one billion dollars in CAPEX. In some cases, especially in the oil and gas, mining, or infrastructure sectors, the budgets can stretch well beyond that into tens of billions. With capital investment of this magnitude, the risks are just as large. Poor planning, faulty sequencing, scope creep, contractor misalignment, or logistical delays can easily lead to hundreds of millions of dollars in cost overruns.

A detailed and methodically developed execution plan provides the framework to contain these financial risks. It sets realistic budget baselines and defines the cost control systems necessary to monitor performance throughout the life cycle. Without a strong plan in place, financial losses can multiply. A few days of idle labor on a megaproject site or a delay in material delivery due to customs clearance issues can cascade into costly schedule disruptions. Cost overruns are not merely spreadsheet issues, they trigger erosion of investor confidence, difficulty securing additional financing, and pressure on executive leadership.

Moreover, cost blowouts often lead to political ramifications in publicly visible projects. Governments and private sector sponsors become risk-averse in future investments, making it harder for other essential developments to get off the ground. Robust planning is therefore not just about saving money. It is about preserving reputation, investor relations, and future funding potential.

Managing Complexity and Interdependencies

Megaprojects are inherently complex systems composed of multiple subprojects, stakeholders, disciplines, and supply chain networks. They often span across continents and involve cross-functional teams from various cultures and legal jurisdictions. Each of these variables introduces its own set of challenges and risks. Even a minor misalignment between two interdependent systems such as engineering and procurement or logistics and construction can result in schedule misfires and budgetary complications.

Robust execution planning provides the integration point for these moving parts. It maps out interdependencies and clarifies sequences. For example, the plan should show that underground piping must be completed before concrete foundations can be poured or that the electrical switchgear must be ordered before structural steel erection begins in a certain plant zone. Without this level of integrated detail, one team may end up working on assumptions that another team has already invalidated, leading to costly rework or conflict.

Furthermore, robust planning ensures that the right questions are asked at the right time. Are the engineering drawings complete and constructible? Are vendor packages synchronized with site readiness? Has the customs clearance timeline been included in the material delivery forecast? These questions cannot be answered reactively. They must be embedded within the planning framework from the beginning.

Schedule Management and Time Sensitivity

Time is money in megaprojects. Every day of delay is not just a scheduling issue; it is a value erosion event. Whether the delay is due to equipment availability, weather disruptions, workforce shortages, or political unrest, its impact on the financial performance of the project is significant. Many contracts contain clauses that penalize late delivery. For projects tied to public infrastructure or private utilities, delays can lead to service interruptions, regulatory fines, and strained community relations.

Robust execution planning enables accurate scheduling, complete with float management, critical path identification, and risk-adjusted timelines. It also incorporates scenario planning to simulate what might happen if key milestones slip. This allows teams to develop contingency strategies before they are needed.

By investing time in robust schedule planning, project teams can visualize the execution horizon in detail. They can simulate crew loading curves, construction sequencing, logistical bottlenecks, and turnaround strategies. More importantly, they can communicate these plans transparently with stakeholders, managing expectations and building trust.

Without robust scheduling, even the most well-intentioned project teams become reactive. They spend their days firefighting rather than executing. They are constantly in recovery mode rather than control mode. Robust planning reverses this dynamic, empowering the team to lead rather than chase.

Risk Identification and Proactive Mitigation

Risk is not a possibility in megaprojects; it is a certainty. From political instability and price volatility to design errors and labor strikes, the risk landscape is wide and constantly shifting. A megaproject can be brought to a halt by the smallest of disruptions if risks are not managed proactively.

Robust execution planning enables comprehensive risk identification, not as a one-time event but as an ongoing discipline. It allows project teams to assess not only what can go wrong but also what must go right for the project to succeed. Planning provides a forum for risk workshops, peer reviews, design simulations, and field readiness reviews that expose hidden threats.

Once risks are known, robust planning embeds mitigations directly into the plan. For example, if equipment delivery is considered high risk due to port congestion, the execution plan might include early ordering or dual sourcing. If local community opposition is anticipated, the plan would outline engagement strategies, grievance protocols, and escalation frameworks.

The best execution plans go further by incorporating leading indicators metrics that warn the team before a risk manifests. A rise in absenteeism might indicate workforce morale issues. Delays in drawing approvals could suggest bottlenecks in engineering. These early signals allow the team to intervene before the problem matures into a crisis.

Achieving Stakeholder Alignment and Governance Clarity

One of the most difficult aspects of managing a megaproject is ensuring that stakeholders remain aligned. Stakeholders may include government agencies, investors, community leaders, regulatory bodies, contractors, joint venture partners, and internal executives. Each of these parties has different priorities, expectations, and risk tolerances.

A robust execution plan acts as a unifying tool. It outlines not only what will be delivered but how, when, and under whose authority. It defines governance structures, communication protocols, reporting requirements, and decision gates. This clarity reduces the number of misinterpretations, escalations, and political conflicts.

Execution planning also builds trust. When stakeholders see that their concerns have been considered, that transparency is embedded into delivery, and that milestones are well defined, they are more likely to remain supportive, even when problems occur. Trust becomes a performance multiplier. It encourages collaboration, accelerates approvals, and reduces friction.

To further illustrate the level of detail required for robust execution planning, Table 4.1 presents a structured summary adapted from the widely recognized IPA FEL Index. This index outlines critical elements across engineering definition, site factors, team structure, stakeholder engagement, and operational planning, each of which directly contributes to megaproject readiness and successful delivery.

The relationship between front-end planning effort and execution outcomes is further illustrated in Figure 4.1. This industry-recognized visual emphasizes that robust FEL not only maximizes value but also

Table 4.1 IPA Front-End Loading (FEL) Index—Execution readiness components

Category	Elements/considerations
Site Factors	Local labor (cost, productivity), materials availability, site data, and soils data
Contracting Strategy	Who is contracting? How will contracts be managed?
Engineering Definition	Equipment layout, environmental and safety requirements, engineering tasks including scope, feedstock/product properties, heat and mass balance, PFDs, P&IDs, GAs, major equipment specs, and cost estimate
Team Structure	Team participants and defined roles
Stakeholder Buy-In	Commitment from operations, maintenance, and business units
Integration Scheduling	Identification of critical path items, tie-in shutdowns, and overtime requirements
Execution Planning	Plans for commissioning, start-up, operations, manpower, and quality assurance

enables smoother, more predictable execution Stages. In contrast, inadequate FEL results in diminished performance despite similar capital investments.

A well-developed FEL process is a critical success factor for megaprojects. As shown in Figure 4.1, it establishes a strong foundation that improves execution certainty, cost efficiency, and overall value delivery.

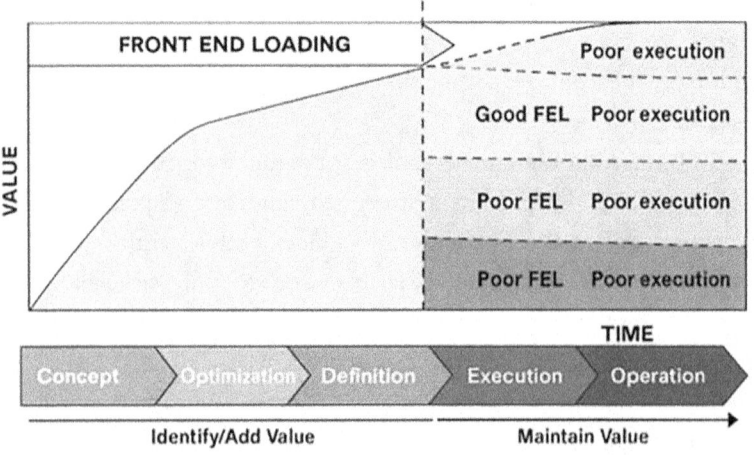

Figure 4.1 The value of front-end loading

Promoting Efficiency and Optimizing Resource Utilization

Megaprojects consume enormous quantities of materials, equipment, labor hours, and energy. Any inefficiency in planning leads to exponential waste. Idle workers waiting for instructions, trucks delayed by unclear routes, or duplicative efforts due to poor coordination, all of these are signs of weak planning.

Robust execution planning provides the operational logic to deploy resources efficiently. It maps out the sequence of work, allocates the right resources at the right time, and avoids congestion or duplication. It allows procurement teams to time deliveries precisely, construction crews to mobilize when truly ready, and support functions like safety and quality to align their interventions with the actual work plan.

Efficient resource utilization is not just about cost savings. It also has environmental and social implications. Projects that use fewer materials and less fuel generate smaller carbon footprints. Projects that avoid night shifts or double handling are less taxing on communities and workers. Efficiency, therefore, becomes a marker of responsibility, not just performance.

Ensuring Regulatory Compliance and Environmental Stewardship

Compliance with legal and environmental regulations is not optional. It is a prerequisite for operational continuity. In many countries, megaprojects are monitored closely by regulators, environmental activists, media outlets, and the public. Any failure to comply can result in work stoppages, litigation, or even license cancellations.

Robust execution planning ensures that compliance is not a separate work stream but an integrated part of project delivery. It includes permitting schedules, compliance audits, training programs, and reporting protocols. It tracks milestones such as environmental assessments, safety drills, emissions controls, and local hiring quotas.

Furthermore, robust planning enables environmental sustainability. It identifies opportunities to reduce waste, reuse materials, lower emissions, and enhance biodiversity. It anticipates the project's life cycle impact and provides mechanisms to mitigate long-term harm. In doing so, it aligns the project with broader societal goals, enhances corporate reputation, and builds credibility with regulators.

Facilitating Innovation and Technology Integration

Modern megaprojects are increasingly dependent on advanced technologies. These include digital twin platforms, AI for schedule optimization, automated construction equipment, and real-time data dashboards. Integrating these tools into the execution environment requires planning.

Robust execution planning provides the roadmap for technology adoption. It defines timelines for implementation, training schedules, data flows, system compatibility, and backup procedures. It ensures that technology supports project objectives rather than becoming a distraction or source of delay.

Innovation is not just about new tools. It is also about mindset. Robust planning creates space for innovative thinking, whether in contract models, delivery methods, or stakeholder engagement. It encourages teams to test new ideas in controlled environments and scale what works.

Execution-Stage KPIs

To ensure robust execution does not merely exist on paper but translates into measurable results, the project team must define and monitor clear KPIs. These KPIs serve as the benchmarks of success during the implementation Stage, allowing teams to assess progress, identify deviations, and respond swiftly. The minimum KPIs for the execution Stage typically include:

- **Safety performance**: Measured through indicators such as total recordable injury frequency rate (TRIFR) or lost time injury frequency rate (LTIFR), ensuring that all activities are conducted in a safe working environment.
- **Milestone achievement**: Tracking the timely completion of critical construction and commissioning milestones to ensure alignment with project schedules.

- **Cost control**: Monitoring actual spend versus budget across all project dimensions, highlighting cost efficiencies or overruns.
- **Operational readiness and ramp-up**: Measuring the speed and efficiency of transitioning into operations, including the ability to reach intended production rates within specified timelines.

Final Thoughts on the Case for Robust Execution Planning

The case for robust execution planning is not built on abstract theory. It is grounded in practical experience, painful lessons, and hard-earned wisdom from decades of megaproject delivery. The projects that succeed on time, on budget, and to quality, are not lucky. They are planned, managed, and executed with rigor.

In an era of rising capital costs, climate change pressures, community activism, and digital transformation, megaproject execution is more demanding than ever. It is no longer enough to be reactive or technically competent. Project teams must be proactive, collaborative, and strategically disciplined.

Robust execution planning is the engine that drives this transformation. It turns good intentions into great outcomes. It connects vision with value. It aligns ambition with action. And most importantly, it prepares the team not only to deliver a project but to deliver it well.

This chapter explores the critical importance of execution planning in megaprojects, presenting it as the foundation upon which project success is built. It emphasizes that a robust execution plan is not just a procedural document but a living framework that aligns people, processes, and objectives before any physical work begins. The chapter walks through the planning steps in detail, from defining project scope and team roles to integrating risk management, procurement strategies, scheduling, and stakeholder alignment. It makes a compelling case that without a well-thought-out execution strategy, even the most well-funded and technically sound projects are vulnerable to delays, cost overruns, and stakeholder conflicts. Drawing from real-world insights, the chapter reinforces that strong execution planning is a proactive discipline that mitigates complexity and drives value delivery.

Execution planning in megaprojects is more than developing a list of tasks and timelines. It is a strategic exercise of aligning people, processes, and performance with the project's purpose. It defines how intent is translated into impact, how complexity is harnessed into control, and how vision is made executable. However, even the most robust plans must ultimately support sound decisions, on resource allocation, risk trade-offs, timing, and governance. In the next chapter, we examine the principles and frameworks that guide effective decision making in megaprojects, and how planning insights shape the choices that define project success.

Reflection Questions

1. What are the critical indicators of EPC readiness, and how do they help predict execution success?
2. How do misalignments between development and execution phases typically manifest in megaprojects?
3. In what ways can organizations improve their pre-FID planning to ensure smoother EPC transitions, and execution success?

CHAPTER 5

Decision Making

Learning Outcomes

After reading this chapter, you will be able to:

1. Understand the distinction between decision support and actual decision making in capital-intensive projects.
2. Recognize common biases and organizational dynamics that influence megaproject investment decisions.
3. Analyze how risk perception, groupthink, and decision timing affect the quality of project approvals.
4. Apply principles of good governance and decision quality to improve strategic investment outcomes.
5. Evaluate the effectiveness of decision-making frameworks used in major project environments.

The Context for Strategic Decision Making

Strategic decision making lies at the heart of megaproject development, shaping both the trajectory and eventual outcomes of initiatives that are often colossal in scale, investment, and societal impact. These projects, in infrastructure, energy, oil and gas, mining, transportation, and other capital-intensive sectors, operate within a unique and multifaceted decision-making context. Unlike smaller-scale projects where decisions can be made based on a narrow set of technical or financial factors, megaprojects necessitate a broader, integrated, and long-term perspective (Flyvbjerg 2023).

The context for strategic decision making in megaprojects is defined by several intersecting dimensions each contributing to the complexity, uncertainty, and scope of the decisions that must be made. These include project scale and complexity, stakeholder diversity, risk and uncertainty, capital intensity, regulatory frameworks, technological innovation, and broader socioeconomic trends. This section explores each of these contextual factors in detail, highlighting how they shape strategic choices and demand a sophisticated, often adaptive approach to governance and leadership.

Scale and Complexity

Megaprojects are characterized by their extraordinary scale, both in terms of physical size and investment. This scale inherently brings complexity, as decisions must span numerous domains and layers of activity. Technical intricacies must be balanced with financial structuring, legal compliance, environmental impact, and community engagement. Moreover, the interconnectedness of project components such as engineering, procurement, construction, and operations requires decisions to be made with a systems-thinking mindset.

For example, a decision about the design of a tunnel in a metropolitan transit megaproject may impact not only construction logistics but also urban planning, environmental permitting, and future maintenance strategies. As such, decision makers must adopt a holistic perspective, relying on cross-disciplinary teams and IPD approaches. The conventional siloed decision-making models are insufficient for megaprojects; instead, a coordinated approach is required that aligns decisions across technical, commercial, regulatory, and social spheres (Priemus and van Wee 2022).

The scale of these projects also means that decisions are often irreversible or costly to reverse. Once significant capital is committed or a particular design path is chosen, changing direction can lead to massive delays and financial losses. Therefore, early-stage decision making assumes heightened importance and must be informed by rigorous scenario planning, feasibility studies, and stakeholder consultation.

Stakeholder Management

Megaprojects are inherently public, even when privately funded. Their impact stretches beyond shareholders and clients to include entire communities, governments, environmental bodies, and future generations. As a result, the stakeholder landscape is unusually broad and often includes parties with divergent or even conflicting interests.

Strategic decision making in such an environment must be politically and socially astute. Government agencies may prioritize public value, environmental sustainability, or job creation. Private investors may be focused on return on investment and risk mitigation. Local communities may be concerned about land use, cultural preservation, and employment opportunities. International organizations might insist on compliance with global environmental standards or human rights principles.

Decisions, therefore, cannot be made in isolation. Stakeholder mapping, early engagement, continuous communication, and collaborative governance structures are essential. Ignoring stakeholder dynamics has led to the failure of otherwise technically sound projects. Protests, legal challenges, or a loss of social license can bring a megaproject to a standstill. Conversely, effective stakeholder engagement can unlock synergies, mitigate opposition, and align diverse interests toward a shared vision (Davis 2023).

It is also crucial to recognize that stakeholders are not static. Political shifts, economic cycles, and social movements can rapidly change the stakeholder landscape. Decision makers must be agile and responsive, adapting strategies and engagement plans as new actors emerge or priorities shift.

Risk and Uncertainty

Risk is an ever-present reality in megaprojects. Given their long timelines, complex supply chains, and significant capital outlay, these projects are exposed to a wide array of risks such as financial, operational, environmental, and geopolitical. Strategic decision making, therefore, is as much about managing uncertainty as it is about setting direction.

Financial risks may include inflation, currency fluctuations, cost overruns, and market volatility. Operational risks encompass construction delays, supply chain disruptions, labor shortages, and equipment failures. Environmental risks arise from regulatory changes, climate-related events, and unforeseen site conditions. In many cases, these risks are interdependent, compounding their impact and complicating mitigation efforts.

Effective strategic decision making requires the institutionalization of robust risk management frameworks. These frameworks should include early risk identification, scenario analysis, sensitivity testing, and dynamic response mechanisms (Ward and Chapman 2024). Moreover, risk-sharing arrangements such as public–private partnerships, performance-based contracts, and insurance mechanisms can be employed to distribute risk across stakeholders more equitably.

Crucially, risk must be understood not just in probabilistic terms but in terms of its impact on strategic objectives. A risk that threatens schedule adherence may be tolerable, whereas a risk that jeopardizes regulatory approval or social acceptance may be existential. Strategic decisions must prioritize resilience and adaptability, incorporating contingency planning and fallback options wherever feasible.

Long-Term Impacts

Megaprojects are long-term undertakings with enduring effects. They shape urban landscapes, influence national economies, and alter ecological systems. As such, strategic decisions must extend beyond immediate project goals to consider future generations and systemic implications.

For instance, the development of a hydroelectric dam may achieve energy generation targets but could also displace communities, disrupt ecosystems, and impact downstream water usage. A new international airport may catalyze economic growth but also contribute to urban sprawl and carbon emissions.

Long-term thinking must therefore inform every strategic choice from site selection and design specifications to procurement strategies and operational models. Decision makers should employ tools such as life cycle costing, sustainability assessments, and post project evaluations to understand the full ramifications of their choices.

Moreover, legacy considerations are increasingly central to megaproject discourse. Stakeholders demand that projects not only meet performance benchmarks but also leave behind a positive social, economic, and environmental legacy. This requires strategic decisions to integrate sustainability, equity, and future-readiness as core criteria, not afterthoughts (van Marrewijk and Smits 2023).

Capital Intensity and Financing

Megaprojects are among the most capital-intensive ventures undertaken by human societies. The scale of investment required often in the billions of dollars' demands sophisticated financial planning and innovative funding structures. Strategic decision making must therefore include careful deliberation around financing models, capital allocation, and cash flow management.

Financing for megaprojects may come from diverse sources: public budgets, private equity, multilateral development banks, sovereign wealth funds, and blended finance mechanisms. Each source brings its own expectations, risk appetite, and governance requirements. Strategic decisions must reconcile these inputs, aligning financial flows with project timelines and risk profiles.

A common challenge is the mismatch between CAPEX and revenue generation. Many megaprojects require heavy upfront investment but only deliver returns over long periods. This creates liquidity challenges that must be addressed through bridging finance, Staged implementation, or performance-based payment structures.

Strategic decisions also involve choosing between various financial instruments like debt, equity, bonds, guarantees and structuring contracts to incentivize performance and share risks appropriately (Yescombe 2022). Transparency, accountability, and compliance with financial regulations are nonnegotiable, particularly when public funds are involved or when international financiers demand adherence to anti-corruption and governance standards.

Regulatory and Legal Constraints

The regulatory environment is a critical context for megaproject decision making. These projects typically intersect with a dense matrix of national laws, regional agreements, and international norms. Legal compliance is not optional; it is foundational.

Environmental regulations may dictate the scope of permissible development, requiring detailed impact assessments and mitigation plans. Labor laws shape workforce composition, safety standards, and wage policies. Land acquisition regulations can delay or derail project implementation if not navigated properly. Taxation, procurement rules, and dispute resolution mechanisms further complicate the legal landscape.

Strategic decisions must be informed by legal due diligence and supported by a strong legal advisory team. Regulatory risks should be identified early, and compliance pathways should be integrated into project planning. Where projects cross borders or jurisdictions, harmonizing regulatory approaches becomes essential.

Moreover, legal constraints are not static. Changes in political leadership, public policy, or international treaties can introduce new requirements or shift the legal landscape. Strategic decision making must therefore include legal monitoring and adaptive governance structures capable of responding to evolving regulatory contexts (Lehtonen and de Jong 2024).

Technology and Innovation

The twenty-first century has ushered in a wave of technological transformation that is reshaping how megaprojects are conceived, designed, and delivered. From AI and machine learning to digital twins, drones, and modular construction, the opportunities for innovation are vast.

Strategic decision making must grapple with the pace of technological change and the associated uncertainties. Adopting new technologies can enhance safety, improve efficiency, and reduce costs but it also introduces risks related to obsolescence, interoperability, and workforce readiness. Decisions around technology must balance innovation with pragmatism.

A further challenge is integrating legacy systems with new digital platforms, particularly in infrastructure rehabilitation projects. Strategic choices must also consider intellectual property rights, cybersecurity, and data governance, areas that are increasingly critical in the digital age.

Organizations leading megaprojects must foster a culture of innovation, invest in upskilling their workforce, and establish partnerships with technology providers and academic institutions. Decision-making structures should include technology steering committees or innovation task forces to guide adoption and ensure alignment with broader project goals (Papadonikolaki and Liu 2023).

Global and Local Economic Conditions

The economic environment both at the global and local level profoundly influences strategic decision making in megaprojects. Fluctuations in interest rates, commodity prices, inflation, and exchange rates can significantly affect the financial viability of a project. Likewise, local economic indicators such as unemployment rates, labor costs, and gross domestic product (GDP) growth shape the socioeconomic feasibility and implementation strategy.

For example, an oil and gas megaproject may be highly attractive when crude prices are rising but could become economically nonviable during a downturn. Similarly, a major infrastructure development in a rapidly growing economy may attract strong investor interest, while the same project in a stagnating economy may struggle to secure funding or community support.

Strategic decision makers must therefore conduct rigorous economic scenario planning, incorporating macroeconomic forecasts and localized economic impact analyses. Currency hedging, inflation-indexed contracts, and Staged investment strategies are commonly used financial instruments to navigate economic uncertainties.

Moreover, megaprojects are increasingly evaluated not only on their IRR but also on their broader economic impact such as job creation, stimulation of adjacent industries, regional development, and contribution to GDP. These socioeconomic multipliers must be considered in strategic choices, especially when public or multilateral funding is involved.

In volatile economic conditions, decision makers must also assess the resilience of the supply chain, availability of local resources, and elasticity of labor markets. Understanding the nuances of both global and local economic trends enables more grounded, responsive, and effective strategic planning (Odeck and Welde 2023).

Sustainability and Social Responsibility

The imperative for environmental sustainability and social responsibility has moved from the margins to the mainstream of megaproject decision making. Increasingly, stakeholders, including regulators, investors, and the public demand that projects align with principles of environmental stewardship, social equity, and long-term ecological balance.

Sustainability considerations now influence every stage of project planning and execution. Strategic decisions must address issues such as carbon emissions, biodiversity loss, water usage, waste management, and resilience to climate change. EIAs, once a regulatory formality, are now critical tools for identifying potential risks and designing mitigation strategies.

On the social side, projects are expected to demonstrate respect for human rights, support local economic empowerment, preserve cultural heritage, and engage communities transparently and ethically. Projects that fail to meet these expectations risk public opposition, reputational damage, legal challenges, and even project cancellation.

Strategic decisions around project design, procurement, technology, and operations must be guided by ESG principles. For example, choosing a modular construction method may reduce on-site waste and energy consumption. Selecting local contractors and suppliers supports community livelihoods and builds local capacity.

Beyond compliance, sustainability can be a source of competitive advantage. Projects that adopt innovative green technologies, circular economy principles, and inclusive engagement models often attract impact investors and gain faster regulatory approvals. Sustainability should not be treated as a constraint but as a strategic pillar integrated into core objectives and performance indicators (Jefferies and Rowlinson 2024).

Governance Structures

The governance of megaprojects plays a pivotal role in shaping strategic decision making. Given the high stakes and complexity involved, decisions are rarely made unilaterally. Instead, they emerge from interactions among multiple entities, including project owners, government agencies, private contractors, financiers, and regulatory bodies.

Governance structures typically include a combination of project steering committees, PMOs, boards of directors, and advisory panels. The effectiveness of these bodies depends on their composition, mandate, accountability mechanisms, and ability to coordinate across organizational boundaries.

Strategic decisions often require consensus among diverse stakeholders with varying interests and levels of authority. This can lead to delays, diluted objectives, or compromised outcomes if not managed effectively. Therefore, governance structures must be designed to facilitate transparent, timely, and informed decision making. Clear roles and responsibilities, decision rights, escalation protocols, and performance monitoring systems are essential.

Moreover, decision makers must be equipped with the right information at the right time. This demands robust project information systems, risk dashboards, and real-time reporting tools. Governance also involves ensuring that ethical standards are upheld, conflicts of interest are managed, and regulatory obligations are met.

In an increasingly globalized and digital world, governance structures must also adapt to manage distributed teams, cross-border regulations, and remote collaboration technologies. Agile governance where decisions can be adjusted based on new information or changing conditions is becoming a hallmark of successful megaprojects (Müller and Turner 2023).

Integrated Decision Making in Practice

The complexity of the megaproject context requires integrated decision-making frameworks that transcend functional silos. Financial decisions must account for technical constraints. Regulatory strategies must align with stakeholder engagement plans. Risk mitigation must be embedded into design and procurement choices.

Integrated decision making involves cross-functional collaboration, iterative feedback loops, and systems thinking. It recognizes that megaprojects are not static but dynamic ecosystems where every decision triggers a cascade of effects. Project managers and executives must be skilled not only in their core disciplines but also in facilitating interdisciplinary dialogue and trade-off analysis.

Tools such as decision trees, value engineering, Monte Carlo simulations, and multicriteria decision analysis (MCDA) can support the evaluation of complex options under uncertainty. However, tools are only as effective as the quality of data and the judgment of decision makers.

Building organizational capability in strategic analysis, scenario planning, and systems integration is therefore a key enabler of effective megaproject delivery.

Case studies consistently show that successful megaprojects are not those with the best technical designs or largest budgets, but those where strategic decisions were timely, transparent, inclusive, and aligned with a long-term vision.

Strategic decision making in megaprojects does not occur in a vacuum. It is profoundly shaped by a unique and often volatile context defined by scale, complexity, stakeholder diversity, risk, capital intensity, legal frameworks, technological disruption, economic variability, sustainability imperatives, and governance structures.

Each of these contextual elements introduces specific challenges and considerations that must be understood and addressed holistically. Success in megaprojects hinges not just on what decisions are made but on how, when, and by whom they are made.

Understanding the full context of strategic decision making equips project leaders to make choices that are not only technically sound and financially viable but also socially responsible, environmentally sustainable, and politically resilient. It is this integrated and forward-thinking approach that distinguishes successful megaproject governance from short-term, reactive management.

Opportunity Management

The complexity of the megaproject context requires that emphasis also be placed on identifying and managing opportunities. In megaprojects, the traditional focus on risk mitigation must be balanced with a proactive approach to opportunity management. Opportunities, defined as uncertain events that, if realized, would have a positive impact should be identified, tracked, and deliberately pursued. These can range from technological innovations and cost savings to policy shifts or stakeholder partnerships that can accelerate timelines or improve outcomes.

Effective opportunity management involves embedding this thinking into early-stage planning, maintaining a dynamic opportunity register, and assigning clear ownership for exploration and implementation.

Figure 5.1 is an example of decision-making layers that consider different stakeholder groups and/or subject matter expertise:

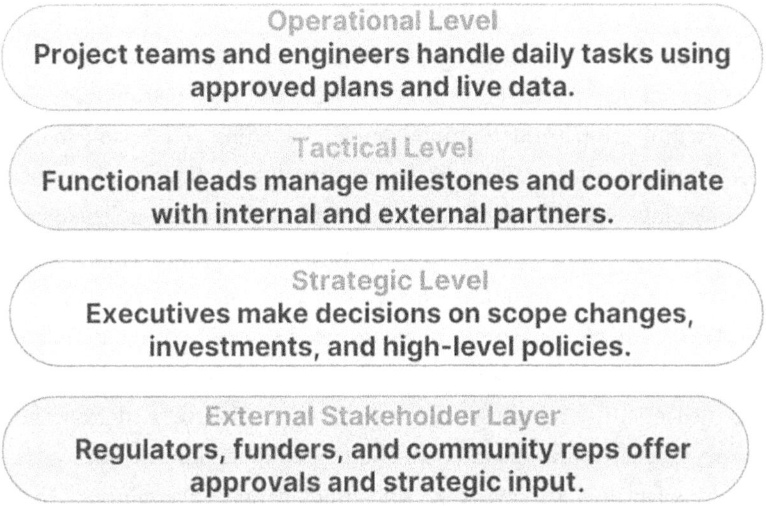

Operational Level
Project teams and engineers handle daily tasks using approved plans and live data.

Tactical Level
Functional leads manage milestones and coordinate with internal and external partners.

Strategic Level
Executives make decisions on scope changes, investments, and high-level policies.

External Stakeholder Layer
Regulators, funders, and community reps offer approvals and strategic input.

Figure 5.1 Decision-making layers in megaprojects

Figure 5.1 illustrates the layered structure of decision making in megaprojects, from operational execution to external stakeholder influence. Each level plays a crucial role in ensuring alignment, coordination, and effective governance across the project's life cycle.

As we move to the next section, we will explore the **frameworks, processes, and tools** that support effective decision making in this demanding environment, beginning with the foundations of strategic planning and the alignment of decisions with organizational and project-level objectives.

Uncertainty Management

Uncertainty management in megaprojects is not merely a supplementary function of risk mitigation; it is a central component of strategic project governance. Given the enormous scale, extended timelines, and dynamic environments in which megaprojects operate, uncertainty permeates all Stages from conceptualization and planning to execution and operation.

A proactive and structured approach to managing uncertainty can significantly enhance the resilience, adaptability, and eventual success of these large-scale endeavors.

Understanding the Nature of Uncertainty

Megaprojects, often exceeding $1 billion in investment and extending over several years, operate within a high-uncertainty environment. This uncertainty arises from multiple sources including fluctuating market conditions, evolving regulatory frameworks, unpredictable geopolitical shifts, technological innovation, and environmental changes. These variables introduce ambiguity not only in project scope and timeline but also in cost structures, stakeholder expectations, and long-term benefits.

Unlike conventional projects, where uncertainties can often be isolated and addressed through standard protocols, megaprojects face layered and interdependent uncertainties that require a systems-level understanding. Strategic decision makers must differentiate between known risks, which can be quantified and managed, and fundamental uncertainties, which demand flexibility, scenario analysis, and adaptive strategies.

Planning and the Need for Flexibility

Traditional planning tools such as NPV analysis or fixed scheduling techniques often assume a relatively stable and predictable future. These methods may fail to account for significant shifts in the underlying assumptions of a megaproject. This shortfall underscores the need for planning approaches that can accommodate variability and allow for mid-course corrections.

Real options logic has emerged as a powerful framework in this context. It views investment decisions not as fixed commitments, but as staged options that provide the flexibility to adapt or abandon based on how uncertainties unfold. This adaptive planning approach enhances the strategic agility of the project and allows decision makers to better align resource allocation with evolving conditions.

Additionally, FEL practices emphasizing comprehensive early-stage analysis can help identify critical uncertainties before full-scale investment is committed. Techniques such as scenario planning, Monte Carlo simulation, and Delphi methods are also being integrated into early project planning to forecast uncertainty ranges and inform robust contingency strategies.

Proactive Risk Identification and Mitigation

Effective uncertainty management begins with a robust process for identifying and assessing risks early in the project life cycle. This involves scanning both internal and external project environments to uncover potential disruptors. These could range from supply chain vulnerabilities and resource shortages to policy shifts or shifts in public sentiment.

Key to this approach is the development of a comprehensive risk register that is dynamically updated as new information becomes available. Risks must be prioritized based on both likelihood and impact, with mitigation strategies tailored accordingly. This could include technical design buffers, financial hedging mechanisms, or the development of alternative suppliers and logistics routes.

Moreover, megaprojects must incorporate "robustness" into their design ensuring that the system can continue to function under a wide range of conditions. This involves stress-testing key components, embedding redundancies where necessary, and applying modular designs that can be adjusted as project realities evolve.

Building Adaptive Capacity

Uncertainty management is not solely about predicting potential problems; it is equally about building the capacity to respond when those problems materialize. Adaptive capacity refers to an organization's ability to recognize, interpret, and respond to changing circumstances without losing strategic direction.

This requires a project culture that values agility, continuous learning, and empowered decision making. Leaders must be attuned to early warning signals and prepared to pivot when assumptions prove invalid. Governance frameworks should include defined decision points or "gates" where project direction can be reevaluated and adjusted.

Moreover, adaptive capacity can be institutionalized through mechanisms such as change control systems, real-time project monitoring dashboards, and decentralized decision-making structures. These systems enable rapid assessment of deviations and coordinated responses that minimize disruption.

Leveraging Collaborative Networks

Given the range of stakeholders involved in megaprojects including governments, financial institutions, private contractors, civil society, and local communities, uncertainty management must be a shared responsibility. Collaboration across these entities enhances knowledge sharing, aligns expectations, and strengthens collective problem-solving capacity.

Joint risk assessment workshops, integrated project teams, and shared information platforms are practical mechanisms to promote transparency and foster cooperative decision making. Furthermore, formalizing stakeholder engagement through structured dialogue processes can reduce conflict, build trust, and uncover latent sources of uncertainty.

Public–private partnerships (PPPs), in particular, demand a high degree of alignment on risk-sharing arrangements. Effective uncertainty management in PPPs involves contractual clarity, dynamic performance monitoring, and continuous recalibration of roles and responsibilities based on real-time developments.

Emerging Tools and Methodologies

To address the challenge of uncertainty in megaprojects, researchers and practitioners are developing new tools and decision-support systems. These include simulation models that visualize the impact of different risk scenarios, digital twins that replicate project behavior in virtual environments, and AI-based analytics that detect early anomalies in performance metrics.

These tools not only enhance the ability to foresee potential disruptions but also support dynamic scenario testing, allowing project leaders to evaluate the implications of different decisions before implementation. Decision makers are now equipped with real-time data feeds, machine learning algorithms, and cloud-based collaboration platforms that enable more timely, data-driven, and coordinated responses to uncertainty.

Importantly, the adoption of these tools must be accompanied by adequate training, change management, and integration with existing project governance processes. Tools alone cannot manage uncertainty; their value lies in how effectively they are embedded into organizational workflows and decision-making cultures.

Managing uncertainty in megaprojects is not about eliminating unpredictability but about preparing for it with foresight, flexibility, and resilience. By understanding the sources and nature of uncertainty, adopting flexible planning models, proactively identifying risks, building adaptive capacity, fostering collaboration, and leveraging advanced tools, megaprojects can significantly enhance their ability to navigate complexity and change.

A strategic, integrated, and forward-looking approach to uncertainty management is therefore not optional but essential. It transforms uncertainty from a threat into an opportunity for innovation, learning, and value creation, positioning megaprojects not only to survive but to thrive in an ever-changing world.

Benchmarking Megaprojects

Benchmarking megaprojects is an essential strategic practice aimed at evaluating and enhancing performance by systematically comparing project processes and outcomes against established standards, industry norms, or best-in-class projects. *It is a major step in the decision-making process.* This exercise transcends mere comparison; it is an active process of learning, adaptation, and strategic alignment that underpins continuous improvement in complex, capital-intensive initiatives. In megaproject development and execution, where billions of dollars are at stake and failure can have far-reaching implications, benchmarking provides a data-driven foundation for informed decision making, risk mitigation, and stakeholder confidence.

Understanding the Role of Benchmarking in Megaprojects

Megaprojects operate in dynamic, uncertain, and multifaceted environments. The inherent complexity of such undertakings marked by multiple stakeholders, long timelines, and broad economic and social impacts requires a structured framework for performance assessment. Benchmarking delivers that framework by aligning current project metrics with recognized standards from comparable projects globally. This alignment allows for the identification of performance gaps, underutilized capabilities, inefficiencies, and opportunities for excellence.

Strategically, benchmarking serves five primary roles in the megaproject context: evaluation, risk mitigation, learning, performance improvement, and communication. Each of these roles supports the overarching goal of delivering megaprojects on time, within budget, and in accordance with expected quality, safety, environmental, and social standards.

Benchmarking as a Tool for Strategic Evaluation

At its core, benchmarking enables objective performance evaluation. Traditional project assessments often rely on internal reviews or project-specific metrics, which may not fully capture performance relative to external standards. Benchmarking bridges this gap by placing project data within a comparative framework, offering visibility into how a project is performing across key dimensions such as quality assurance, safety standards, schedule adherence, cost efficiency, and labor productivity.

For instance, a transportation megaproject in Southeast Asia might benchmark its performance against similar infrastructure projects in South America or Europe. This provides a wider perspective and generates insights that may not emerge from internal analysis alone. This external view challenges assumptions, validates practices, and prompts strategic shifts when needed.

Enhancing Predictability Through Benchmarking

Predictability is a fundamental yet elusive goal in megaproject delivery. By leveraging benchmarking, project leaders can better forecast outcomes, anticipate potential pitfalls, and create realistic expectations. Predictability is enhanced through early comparison of planning assumptions, budget allocations, resource plans, and timeline estimates against aggregated data from completed projects. This allows for the identification of discrepancies or overoptimistic projections early in the planning cycle.

Moreover, benchmarking fosters the discipline of realism in planning. Projects that benchmark assumptions before finalizing funding or initiating execution are less likely to suffer from chronic underestimation of durations and costs, a phenomenon widely referred to as the planning fallacy in project management parlance.

Benchmarking for Risk Recognition and Proactive Management

A critical advantage of benchmarking lies in its capacity to unearth and categorize risks that may not yet be visible in the current project context. Benchmarking databases often contain insights into common failure modes or challenges encountered in similar megaprojects. By studying patterns of budget overruns, schedule slippages, regulatory hurdles, or procurement issues in peer projects, project leaders can anticipate and prepare for analogous issues in their own initiatives.

Benchmarking thus becomes an early-warning system. It draws attention to outlier performances, whether positive or negative and provides the rationale for adopting specific risk mitigation measures. This insight is particularly valuable during the front-end planning stages, where strategic decisions carry long-term implications.

Supporting Organizational Learning and Knowledge Transfer

Beyond individual projects, benchmarking serves as a conduit for organizational learning. Project organizations especially those managing portfolios of megaprojects across multiple geographies can use benchmarking data to develop internal performance baselines. This supports a culture of learning where lessons are not only documented but actively applied across future projects.

Instituting a benchmarking framework also encourages disciplined data collection and codification of project outcomes. When data from past and ongoing projects are systematically captured and analyzed, it creates an internal knowledge repository. This body of knowledge fosters faster onboarding of project personnel, reduces learning curves, and enables more consistent delivery across projects.

Leveraging Benchmarking for Stakeholder Engagement and Transparency

Megaprojects often operate under intense public scrutiny and must navigate a dense web of stakeholder relationships. Benchmarking provides an objective and credible communication tool in this environment. Project proponents can use benchmark data to justify decisions, defend budget estimates, explain schedule variances, and demonstrate accountability.

Benchmarking can also enhance trust and transparency. When stakeholders including government agencies, investors, and community representatives are presented with comparative data showing how the project aligns with or outperforms similar initiatives, it strengthens confidence and supports constructive dialogue. This is particularly relevant in public–private partnerships (PPPs) or internationally financed projects where transparency is a nonnegotiable requirement.

Developing a Benchmarking Strategy for Megaprojects

Implementing an effective benchmarking strategy in megaprojects involves a structured, systematic approach that includes the following steps:

Establishing Benchmarking Objectives

The first step is to define the objectives of benchmarking. These could include enhancing schedule reliability, improving cost accuracy, evaluating productivity, or learning from past project outcomes. The objectives should be aligned with project priorities and stakeholder expectations.

Identifying Benchmarking Sources and Partners

Successful benchmarking relies on access to reliable data. External sources such as the Independent Project Analysis (IPA), the Construction Industry Institute (CII), and sector-specific benchmarking consortia offer databases built on thousands of projects. Internal benchmarks can be derived from previous projects within the organization or joint ventures. Partnerships with universities or industry groups can also facilitate access to high-quality data.

Selecting Relevant Benchmarking Metrics

While there are many possible indicators, effective benchmarking focuses on those that matter most. These often include but are not limited to:

- **Quality metrics**: defect ratios, rework hours, acceptance rates
- **Safety metrics**: injury frequency rates, safety near-miss reporting trends
- **Schedule indicators**: engineering and construction durations, productivity rates, on-time delivery ratios
- **Cost indicators**: cost per unit of output, indirect/direct cost ratios, overhead percentages
- **Operational metrics**: equipment utilization rates, downtime statistics, commissioning times, production rate(s)
- **Sustainability metrics**: carbon emissions, water usage, environmental compliance rates

Normalizing Benchmark Data for Applicability

Benchmarking across projects necessitates adjustments for contextual factors. These include geographical conditions, project scope, regulatory environments, climate considerations, labor availability, and political factors. Normalization ensures that comparisons are meaningful and not distorted by contextual differences.

Interpreting Benchmarking Results and Identifying Gaps

After data normalization and comparison, project teams must analyze the outcomes to pinpoint gaps between current performance and industry best practices. This analysis should be both quantitative (e.g., 15 percent cost overrun compared to peer projects) and qualitative (e.g., differences in procurement strategy or design approach).

Developing Actionable Improvement Plans

Like knowledge, benchmarking is only effective if it leads to action. The insights derived must be translated into improvement initiatives, such as process redesigns, resource reallocation, skill development, or technology adoption. These actions should be tracked for progress and evaluated for impact.

Updating Benchmarks Throughout the Life Cycle

Megaprojects span several years, during which conditions and performance dynamics evolve. As such, benchmarking must be a continuous process. Regular updates ensure that the data remains relevant, and the project stays aligned with changing benchmarks. This also allows real-time course corrections.

Beyond Performance: Strategic Benchmarking for Innovation and Transformation

While operational performance remains the main focus of benchmarking, there is growing interest in using benchmarking to drive innovation and transformation in megaprojects. This includes benchmarking digital maturity, organizational agility, stakeholder integration, and sustainability practices.

For instance, a project team may benchmark their use of digital twin technologies or BIM against leading practices in the industry. Similarly, diversity in project governance or stakeholder feedback mechanisms can be benchmarked to assess inclusivity and responsiveness. These dimensions offer new lenses through which megaprojects can create value and deliver broader societal benefits.

The Future of Benchmarking in Megaproject Management

As the megaproject landscape evolves, so too will the role of benchmarking. The increasing availability of big data, advances in analytics, and emergence of AI will allow for more predictive and prescriptive forms of benchmarking. Rather than merely comparing past outcomes, future systems may simulate project scenarios, forecast potential deviations, and recommend corrective measures.

Additionally, the integration of sustainability, equity, and innovation into mainstream benchmarking will reshape what is measured and why. Projects will not only be judged by schedule and cost adherence but also by their contributions to climate resilience, community empowerment, and ethical governance.

Benchmarking is more than a performance review tool; it is a strategic enabler of excellence in megaproject development and delivery. Through comparative analyses, continuous improvement, and informed decision making, benchmarking supports the realization of megaprojects that are not only efficient and cost-effective but also resilient, inclusive, and transformative. For leaders operating in this space, embedding benchmarking into the DNA of project planning and execution is no longer optional— it is imperative.

Megaproject Key Performance Indicators

Introduction

KPIs are central to the strategic decision making and subsequent execution of megaprojects. Given the immense scale, investment, and stakeholder engagement associated with megaprojects, KPIs provide a structured and quantifiable means to evaluate project health, performance, and alignment with objectives. In this section, we explore the core types of KPIs relevant to megaprojects, how they are applied, and their strategic importance.

Defining Megaproject KPIs

Megaproject KPIs are quantifiable metrics used to assess the performance of large-scale capital projects. Typically valued at over $1 billion, these projects often span years or even decades. Their success depends not only on schedule and cost adherence but also on stakeholder satisfaction quality, safety, production, and long-term sustainability. Therefore, KPIs must reflect a comprehensive performance profile beyond traditional scope–time–cost parameters.

Classification of Key Performance Indicators

Quality Performance

Quality KPIs assess the standard of output delivered:

- **Defect Density:** The number of defects per unit of completed work
- **Rework Percentage:** Amount of work redone due to quality issues
- **Compliance with Standards:** Conformance to regulatory, environmental, and contractual quality specifications

Safety Performance

Safety is a nonnegotiable aspect of megaprojects, particularly in sectors like oil and gas or construction:

- **Total Recordable Incident Rate (TRIR):** Measures the frequency of recordable incidents per 200,000 work hours
- **LTIFR:** Tracks the number of lost time injuries relative to hours worked
- **Near Miss Reporting Frequency:** Indicates the safety culture's maturity

Risk Management

Megaprojects face multifaceted risks. Risk KPIs help monitor preparedness:

- **Risk Exposure Index:** Aggregated risk severity score weighted by probability and impact

- **Mitigation Action Closure Rate:** Percentage of implemented mitigation strategies within the planned timeframe
- **Contingency Drawdown Rate:** Tracks usage of contingency reserves, indicating financial flexibility

Schedule Performance

Schedule-related KPIs help track time efficiency and adherence to planned timelines. Key metrics include:

- **Schedule Performance Index (SPI):** SPI = Earned Value (EV) ÷ Planned Value (PV). An SPI value below 1 signals a delay.
- **Milestone Achievement Rate:** The proportion of milestones completed on time compared to the project schedule baseline. This measure provides insight into project momentum.

Cost Performance

Effective cost control is fundamental in megaprojects due to their budget sensitivity:

- **Cost Performance Index (CPI):** CPI = EV ÷ Actual Cost (AC). A CPI less than 1 indicates overspending.
- **Cost Variance (CV):** CV = EV − AC. It reflects whether the project is under or over budget at any given time.
- **Budget at Completion (BAC) Versus Estimate at Completion (EAC):** This comparison indicates the forecasted cost overruns or underruns.
- **Critical Ratio:** CR = SPI × CPI. This is also referred to as the Cost-Schedule Index (CSI), and it is a statistical indicator of the overall project health (Meredith and Mantel 2000; Lewis 2001). A CR of 1 indicates that the overall project performance is on target. More than 1 indicates good overall project performance. Less than 1 indicates poor overall project performance. Performance trends are visually presented via a graph of the CR over time and, oftentimes, the impact of interventions as a result of perceived performance issues.

Embedding Earned Value Management for Performance Control

EVM Concept Overview

Earned value management (EVM) is a project control methodology that integrates scope, schedule, and cost to assess project performance. It is most effective when applied to well-defined projects, whether a contract, budget, or work package with a specific scope of work, a time-staged baseline schedule, and an authorized budget.

Without these foundational elements, EVM loses its relevance and cannot generate meaningful insights, particularly when unapproved changes dilute its structure.

EVM relies on **three core dimensions** of performance measurement:

- **Planned Value**
  1. What work has been authorized?
  2. What is the budget for the work authorized?
- **Earned Value (EV)**
  1. What work has been accomplished?
  2. What was the budget for the work accomplished?
- **Actual Costs (AC)**
  1. What are the ACs of the work accomplished?

These form the basis of key EVM indicators such as:

- **Schedule Performance Index (SPI)** = EV ÷ PV
- **Cost Performance Index (CPI)** = EV ÷ AC
- **Critical Ratio (CR)** = SPI × CPI

"You may practice good project management without EVMS, but you cannot practice EVMS effectively and efficiently without good project management."

—Akin Oni

Performance Chart Example

Figure 5.2 illustrates the trend of schedule and cost performance over a defined project duration, enabling early detection of deviations (Table 5.1).

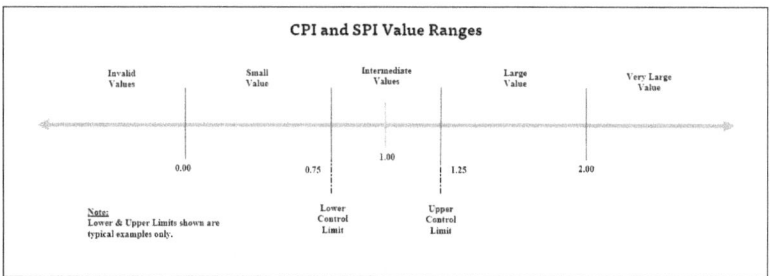

Figure 5.2 CPI and SPI tracking over time

Table 5.1 Value ranges for EVM metrics

Metric	Value range	Interpretation
CPI > 1.0	Over 1.0	Cost-efficient (under budget)
CPI = 1.0	Exactly 1.0	On budget
CPI < 1.0	Below 1.0	Over budget
SPI > 1.0	Over 1.0	Ahead of schedule
SPI = 1.0	Exactly 1.0	On schedule
SPI < 1.0	Below 1.0	Behind schedule
CR = SPI × CPI	Around 1.0	Overall project health (values below 1.0 warrant attention)

Interpreting EVM Metrics

Stakeholder Satisfaction

Managing expectations and perceptions is critical:

- **Stakeholder Survey Scores:** Quantitative analysis from structured stakeholder feedback forms
- **Grievance Redress Time:** Average time taken to resolve community or stakeholder concerns
- **Media and Public Sentiment Index:** Analysis of media tone and public feedback

Resource Utilization

Monitoring labor, equipment, and material use ensures operational efficiency:

- **Labor Productivity Rate:** Output per labor hour
- **Equipment Utilization Rate:** Percentage of time equipment is in productive use
- **Material Waste Index:** Quantifies unused or wasted materials per output unit

Environmental and Sustainability Metrics

Modern megaprojects must comply with environmental standards:

- **Carbon Emissions per Output Unit:** Measures project-related emissions normalized by project output
- **Recycled Material Utilization:** Proportion of reused/recycled materials
- **Environmental Compliance Score:** Percentage of completed environmental audits without noncompliance issues

Strategic Importance of KPIs in Megaprojects

Monitoring Performance in Real Time

By providing current and historical performance data, KPIs allow project managers to assess if objectives are being met and pinpoint areas needing corrective action. For example, real-time SPI or CPI dashboards can alert teams to performance dips that may warrant immediate response.

Data-Driven Decision Making

In a megaproject context, every major decision carries financial and operational consequences. KPIs provide a factual foundation for these decisions. For instance, an underperforming CPI may prompt cost reallocation or renegotiation with contractors.

Enabling Predictive Analytics

Beyond monitoring, KPIs also help in forecasting future project outcomes. Integration of KPIs with project simulation tools allows teams to anticipate issues such as likely schedule slippage or cost overruns, facilitating proactive planning.

Enhancing Accountability

Defined KPIs establish clear expectations for team performance. When linked to contracts or performance incentives, KPIs encourage accountability from all stakeholders, including contractors, consultants, and internal teams.

Stakeholder Engagement and Transparency

KPIs offer a concise and structured language for communicating with stakeholders. Transparent KPI reporting can build trust, demonstrate competence, and support community or investor relations.

Supporting Post project Learning

Once a megaproject concludes, retrospective analysis of KPI performance helps identify best practices and areas for improvement. This knowledge can be fed back into future project planning and execution.

Challenges in KPI Implementation

Despite their value, KPIs are not always easy to implement effectively. Key challenges include:

- **Data Availability:** In many cases, collecting real-time, reliable data for KPI analysis remains difficult due to fragmented systems.
- **Standardization:** Lack of universal definitions or formats for KPIs can make interproject comparisons challenging.

- **Overreliance on Quantitative Metrics:** While numerical KPIs provide precision, they may miss nuances such as team morale, political dynamics, or long-term reputational impact.
- **KPI Fatigue:** Monitoring too many KPIs may overwhelm teams and dilute focus. It is critical to select a manageable set of high-impact indicators.

KPI Best Practices for Megaprojects

Effective KPIs are the lifeblood of megaproject governance—translating complex ambitions into measurable, actionable insights. The following best practices provide a structured approach to designing, managing, and sustaining KPIs that drive alignment, accountability, and performance excellence throughout the project life cycle.

1. **Align KPIs with Strategic Objectives:** Every KPI should map directly to a critical project goal, whether financial, operational, social, or environmental.
2. **Ensure Measurability and Simplicity:** KPIs should be easy to understand, measurable, and interpretable by all stakeholders.
3. **Utilize Integrated Project Dashboards:** Employ digital dashboards that pull data from multiple sources and display KPI trends graphically in real time.
4. **Maintain KPI Flexibility:** Megaprojects evolve. Review and refine KPIs periodically to ensure continued relevance.
5. **Engage Stakeholders in KPI Design:** Including stakeholders in KPI development enhances relevance, buy-in, and shared accountability.
6. **Conduct Periodic KPI Audits:** Regular reviews of KPI definitions, data sources, and reporting frequency help maintain quality and consistency.

In the volatile, complex landscape of megaprojects, KPIs serve as the navigational tools guiding teams toward successful delivery. They ensure transparency, foster accountability, drive performance, and build the foundation for strategic agility. With effective KPI frameworks, project managers and executives can transform raw data into actionable intelligence, maximizing the chances of megaproject success in a high-stakes environment.

Early Warning Signs and the Strategic Decision-Making Construct

Megaprojects, by nature, are high-stakes ventures marked by extensive complexity, prolonged timelines, and massive investments. As such, the ability to detect early warning signs (EWS), especially prior to FID, and respond with timely, strategic decision making is crucial. Early detection of potential pitfalls allows for proactive intervention, ultimately safeguarding project performance, timelines, costs, and stakeholder trust.

This section explores the typical early warning signs encountered in megaprojects and presents strategic decision-making constructs to mitigate associated risks effectively. More broadly, early bad news (especially through warning signs) is much better than late bad surprises.

Early Warning Signs in Megaprojects

Early warning signs are critical indicators that suggest potential or emerging problems, before or after FID. Left unaddressed, these issues can escalate into severe disruptions. Identifying these signs early facilitates corrective action before the project veers off course. They are by no means an exhaustive list.

Scope Creep

Scope creep is one of the most persistent threats to megaproject success—often subtle at first but ultimately capable of derailing budgets, schedules, and stakeholder trust. Recognizing its early warning signs and applying disciplined control measures is essential to preserving project integrity and strategic focus.

- **Warning Signs:**
  - Uncontrolled or undocumented scope additions
  - Lack of formal change control procedures

- **Strategic Response:**
  - Strengthen scope definition and documentation.
  - Implement a robust change control process.
  - Enforce approvals for any scope changes.

Quality Issues

Quality issues, if left unchecked, can silently erode a megaproject's value, leading to costly rework, schedule slippage, and reputational damage. Proactive monitoring, rigorous assurance processes, and continuous workforce training are vital to maintaining construction integrity and long-term asset performance.

- **Warning Signs:**
  - High volume of nonconformance reports (NCRs)
  - Delays in inspections
  - Increased rework
- **Strategic Response:**
  - Enhance QA/QC procedures.
  - Provide training to improve workmanship.
  - Increase inspection frequency and rigor.

Security, Health, Safety, Environmental,
and Community Concerns

SHSEC performance is a defining measure of megaproject excellence and corporate responsibility. Breakdowns in security, health, safety, environmental stewardship, or community relations can halt progress and erode stakeholder trust. Sustained success demands vigilance, accountability, and a culture that places people and the environment at the heart of project execution.

- **Warning Signs:**
  - Frequent security, health, safety, environmental, and community (SHSEC) incidents
  - Environmental violations
  - Declining worker morale, for a variety of reasons or factors

- **Strategic Response:**
  - Strengthen SHSEC protocols and enforcement.
  - Conduct audits, security, and safety drills, or behavior assessments.
  - Foster a culture of security, health, safety, environmental, and community responsibility.

Schedule Slippage

Schedule slippage is one of the most visible indicators of a megaproject in distress, often signaling deeper issues in planning, coordination, or execution discipline. Preventing and recovering from delays requires a credible baseline, continuous performance tracking, and decisive intervention along the project's critical path.

- **Warning Signs:**
  - Defective baseline schedule
  - Missed intermediate milestones
  - Delays in procurement or contractor mobilization
  - Lagging critical-path activities
- **Strategic Response:**
  - Validate the baseline schedule prior to establishing it for execution.
  - Reevaluate the project schedule on an ongoing basis, if warranted.
  - Prioritize critical path items.
  - Apply schedule acceleration techniques such as crashing or fast-tracking.

Cost Overruns

Cost overruns remain one of the most common and consequential challenges in megaproject delivery, often reflecting weaknesses in scope control, forecasting accuracy, or execution discipline. Sustaining financial integrity requires rigorous cost monitoring, early variance detection, and timely corrective action to preserve project viability and investor confidence.

- **Warning Signs:**
  - Budget consistently exceeded
  - Rising labor and material costs
  - Frequent or uncontrolled change orders
- **Strategic Response:**
  - Conduct cost variance analysis.
  - Perform root cause analysis.
  - Adjust project scope or financing strategy.
  - Tighten cost control mechanisms.

Resource Bottlenecks

Resource bottlenecks can quickly disrupt progress and productivity on a megaproject, often cascading into schedule delays and cost escalation. Proactive resource planning, flexible sourcing, and contingency readiness are essential to sustaining momentum and ensuring execution resilience.

- **Warning Signs:**
  - Shortage of critical labor or equipment
  - Poor subcontractor performance
  - Delays in material delivery
- **Strategic Response:**
  - Realign resource allocation.
  - Negotiate alternative sourcing strategies.
  - Maintain buffer stocks and develop contingency plans.

Stakeholder Misalignment

Stakeholder misalignment is a silent disruptor that can undermine even the most technically sound megaprojects. Sustained success depends on transparent communication, shared vision, and deliberate alignment of interests across all parties throughout the project life cycle.

- **Warning Signs:**
  - Conflicting stakeholder objectives
  - Communication breakdowns
  - Low stakeholder engagement

- **Strategic Response:**
  - ○ Increase engagement frequency.
  - ○ Clarify expectations and responsibilities.
  - ○ Facilitate alignment workshops and review sessions.

Strategic Decision-Making Constructs for Risk Mitigation

Detecting warning signs is only half the equation. Strategic decision making enables project leaders to act on insights efficiently, limiting the adverse effects on project outcomes. The following constructs form the backbone of effective decision making in the face of early warning signs.

Risk-Based Decision Making

  - ○ Prioritizes actions based on the severity and probability of identified risks
  - ○ Involves conducting risk assessments and updating the risk register regularly
  - ○ Guides allocation of resources to the highest-impact issues

Scenario Planning

  - ○ Envisions various outcomes (e.g., best case, worst case, base case)
  - ○ Facilitates preparedness for diverse developments
  - ○ Supports better evaluation of alternative strategies

Real-Time Data Analytics

  - ○ Uses dashboards and integrated software platforms to provide real-time insights
  - ○ Detects deviations from schedule, budget, and quality baselines
  - ○ Enables fast, data-driven decisions

Agile Project Management Elements

  - ○ Incorporate flexibility and short planning cycles
  - ○ Encourage iterative adjustments and frequent reviews
  - ○ Help quickly pivot in response to emerging issues

Collaborative Decision Making

- ○ Integrates perspectives from multiple stakeholders
- ○ Promotes shared ownership of project risks and actions
- ○ Enhances buy-in and alignment on remedial strategies

Governance Structures and Escalation Protocols

- ○ Clearly define thresholds and authority levels for decision making
- ○ Ensure early signs are escalated to the right governance tier
- ○ Facilitate rapid mobilization of response teams

Integrated Project Controls

- ○ Merges risk, schedule, cost, and performance data into a centralized system
- ○ Allows cross-functional teams to detect interrelated problems
- ○ Supports unified strategic responses

Benefits of Early Warning Integration with Strategy

Incorporating EWS into strategic decision making leads to the following benefits:

1. **Proactive Issue Management:** Problems are addressed before they become crises.
2. **Improved Project Outcomes:** Enhanced ability to meet scope, quality, time, and cost goals.
3. **Increased Stakeholder Confidence:** Transparent management inspires trust.
4. **Organizational Learning:** Feedback from EWS fosters a culture of continuous improvement.
5. **Adaptive Capability:** The project team becomes more agile and responsive to change.

As discussed in this chapter, identifying early warning signs and linking them to structured, responsive decision making is vital to steering megaprojects away from failure. However, these efforts are only effective when embedded in a larger system of governance and oversight.

In the next chapter (Chapter 6: Capturing Learning), we will explore the mechanics of capturing, organizing, and sharing knowledge, and institutionalizing it to sustain high performance throughout the megaproject life cycle, and beyond.

Reflection Questions

1. Why is it important to distinguish between the technical analysis of a project and the actual decision-making process?
2. How do organizational politics and biases influence FIDs in megaprojects?
3. What steps can organizations take to improve decision quality and governance in high-stakes capital projects?

CHAPTER 6

Capturing Learning

Learning Outcomes

By the end of this chapter, readers will be able to:

1. Understand the strategic importance of capturing lessons learned in megaprojects to avoid repeated mistakes and improve project outcomes.
2. Identify and apply various methods for capturing, organizing, and sharing knowledge, including After-Action Reviews (AARs), knowledge repositories, and structured workshops.
3. Recognize the behavioral and cultural enablers necessary for a learning-centric project environment, such as psychological safety, leadership modeling, and stakeholder alignment.
4. Distinguish between explicit and tacit knowledge, and learn practical approaches for preserving both forms within a megaproject ecosystem.
5. Explore tools and systems that support knowledge capture, from traditional databases and mentorship programs to AI-powered assistants and gamified learning platforms.
6. Analyze how knowledge management drives behavioral change, fostering continuous learning, collaboration, and resilience among individuals and teams.
7. Evaluate the governance mechanisms and leadership mandates required to embed learning into decision-making processes and project execution.
8. Appreciate the importance of feedback loops, reflective practices, and knowledge application, transforming lessons learned into performance improvement and risk reduction.

Overview

The success or failure of megaprojects is often determined long before the first shovel hits the ground. Among the most powerful determinants is an organization's ability to learn consistently, deeply, and in a timely manner. This chapter explores the often underappreciated yet transformative role of capturing and applying knowledge. It introduces a structured approach to institutional learning by outlining the value, methods, behavioral implications, and tools that together create a learning-driven project environment.

Capturing lessons learned from megaprojects is crucial for improving future project outcomes and avoiding past mistakes. Megaprojects, by nature, are characterized by large capital outlays, extensive timelines, multidisciplinary involvement, and substantial strategic importance. The value of capturing learnings lies in systematically transforming past experiences into actionable intelligence that informs current and future projects (Davenport and Prusak 1998).

Importance of Capturing Megaprojects Learning

1. Preventing Repeated Mistakes: Megaprojects often involve significant investments and complex coordination. Learning from past projects helps avoid repeating costly errors. The case of the Denver International Airport's (DIA) failed baggage handling system is a notable example. The project's overreliance on untested technology and lack of stakeholder alignment led to operational chaos and reputation damage. If similar large-scale infrastructure initiatives capture such lessons in a structured manner, similar pitfalls can be avoided.

2. Improving Efficiency: By understanding what worked well and what didn't, future projects can be planned and executed more efficiently. For instance, the Panama Canal expansion demonstrated how the learnings from previous failed attempts were incorporated into the planning and design of the successful lock-based canal, rather than persisting with a sea-level concept that had failed previously. This led to more streamlined construction efforts and lower overall risk (Levitt 2012).

3. Enhancing Decision Making: Captured knowledge serves as a vital resource for decision makers, offering context, clarity, and continuity. When project leaders and executives have access to detailed case histories, evaluation reports, and postmortem analyses, they are better equipped to assess risks, identify opportunities, and justify strategic moves. Structured practices like AARs support this process by enabling teams to reflect critically on project events and translate those reflections into actionable improvements and informed choices.

4. Adapting to Complexity: Megaprojects are inherently complex due to their size, scope, and strategic importance. Learning from past projects helps teams better manage this complexity. Continuous improvement strategies, such as those highlighted in the Lessons Learned Workshop for Project Foxtrot, provide a blueprint for managing organizational knowledge in a way that adapts to changing project environments and stakeholder expectations.

Methods for Capturing Learning

1. *Post project Reviews:* These are structured evaluations that occur at the end of a project or major Stage. They involve team debriefings, analysis of key metrics, and open discussions on what went well and what could be improved. This format, also known as "After-Action Reviews," is valuable for understanding project dynamics and pinpointing failure and success factors.

2. *Knowledge Repositories:* Organizations can create centralized, searchable databases where lessons learned are stored. These repositories must be easy to access and structured to allow filtering by project type, Stage, or discipline. The IPMA (International Project Management Association) lessons-learned system for construction PM (project management) recommends a structured repository as a critical component in long-term knowledge retention and accessibility.

3. *Regular Workshops and Forums:* Holding periodic lessons-learned workshops fosters a culture of shared learning. Workshops like the one for Project Foxtrot use structured agendas, participant roles (facilitator, scribe, etc.), and safe-space rules to encourage honest

discussions. This method not only gathers insights but reinforces collaboration and transparency within the project team.

4. *Modular and Iterative Approaches:* Project teams can capture and apply learning in real time through modular development processes. This means embedding short review loops within the life cycle where minor but significant learnings are documented, reviewed, and applied continuously. Such a system improves agility and the ability to adapt rapidly without waiting for end-stage reviews.

5. *Brainstorming Templates:* Structured brainstorming templates offer a practical and ready-to-use format for capturing detailed feedback across specific project activities or challenges. These tools typically include columns or fields for items discussed, comments, impact assessments, severity levels, and recommended corrective actions. They also encourage the classification of lessons into themes such as procedural, organizational, or technical making it easier to analyze patterns and prioritize future improvements. When deployed during workshops or review sessions, such templates guide discussions, ensure consistency in documentation, and support data-driven decision making across the project life cycle. Appendix XV contains a sample template for effectively capturing learnings during (or at the end of) the project, for the project, by the project team.

Key Elements for Success

1. *Clear Strategic Vision:* Megaprojects benefit from a strong overarching vision. Lessons learned must be linked to the strategic intent of the project. For example, failures stemming from misaligned goals often trace back to a disconnect between day-to-day decisions and strategic outcomes. Captured learnings that reinforce this linkage are vital.

2. *Total Alignment:* Stakeholder alignment is a foundational requirement for effective knowledge capture. Lessons from the DIA project underline the chaos that ensues from poorly aligned stakeholder expectations. To ensure lessons learned are valid and actionable, all relevant stakeholders, owners, contractors, users, and sponsors must be engaged in the process.

3. *Behavioral and Cultural Enablement:* A culture that supports honest feedback and knowledge sharing is essential. The Foxtrot Workshop emphasized a "no rank in the room" principle, allowing all voices to be heard equally. This egalitarian structure encourages more nuanced insights and ensures that critical information isn't lost due to hierarchical barriers.

4. *Documentation Integrity and Clarity:* Learnings must be captured clearly, unambiguously, and immediately after the event. The business case slides reinforce the need for clean documentation that's not diluted by politics or post event rationalization. Statements should reflect the exact sentiment and experience of the contributors.

5. *Timing of Capture:* Lessons must be gathered not just at the end of a project but during key project milestones when events, decisions, and insights are most immediate and relevant. Capturing knowledge in real time during the project, for the project, ensures that it reflects current challenges and evolving conditions. This approach enhances the likelihood of timely corrective action and supports adaptive project management practices by informing adjustments while they can still influence outcomes.

6. *Categorization of Knowledge Types:* Not all lessons are the same. Tactical learnings (e.g., procurement process improvements) differ from strategic learnings (e.g., risk posture changes). Project teams must identify and classify these types appropriately. The brainstorming template suggests categories such as safety, schedule, cost, and end product performance.

7. *Leadership Mandate*: A strong commitment from senior leadership to enforce lessons learned practices can determine whether such efforts succeed or fail. Informed executives often require evidence of applied learnings from similar past projects before greenlighting new ones. This institutional expectation creates a culture of accountability and reflective practice.

8. *Usability and Access:* Lessons captured must be easy to retrieve, browse, and apply. Repositories should offer filtered access by project type, discipline, or problem type. The business case makes it

clear that knowledge must be embedded in decision support tools, planning checklists, and risk management frameworks for it to be useful.

9. *Tools and Systems Integration:* Integrating lessons learned processes into everyday project tools such as scheduling systems, risk registers, and performance dashboards ensures that knowledge is continuously referenced. This operationalizes learning rather than isolating it to stand-alone documentation.

10. *Celebrating Wins and Recognizing Contributors:* Acknowledging both successful practices and the individuals who contributed to knowledge capture fosters continued engagement. The Panama Canal case demonstrated how celebrating milestones sustained morale and reinforced desired project behaviors.

By systematically capturing and applying lessons learned, organizations can enhance the success rates of their megaprojects, leading to better resource utilization and more predictable outcomes. Effective learning systems minimize the likelihood of project derailment, reduce waste, and build a repository of institutional knowledge that becomes a competitive advantage.

The following sections delve into the mechanics of lessons learned capture, the role of behavioral change in embedding learnings, and tools that can support a high-impact knowledge management system.

The Mechanics of Megaproject Knowledge Management

To effectively harness the lessons of past projects and ensure knowledge is embedded into future practices, organizations must understand the internal mechanics of knowledge management. This section explores the essential elements of how knowledge is captured, stored, shared, and applied within large, complex project environments. These mechanics form the operational backbone of any high-performing learning ecosystem.

Managing knowledge in megaprojects involves a structured, multi-faceted approach that ensures critical insights are not just captured but actively stored, accessed, and leveraged. The mechanics of megaproject knowledge management (KM) encompass processes, tools, people, and policies that work together to enable continuous improvement, informed decision making, and sustainable performance across geographically and culturally diverse environments.

Knowledge in megaprojects spans both explicit and tacit dimensions. Explicit knowledge is codified and easily documented such as manuals, procedures, reports, and lessons learned databases. Tacit knowledge, on the other hand, resides in individuals' experiences, intuitions, and cultural awareness, making it difficult to articulate or formalize. Capturing explicit knowledge requires robust documentation processes and accessible storage systems, while preserving tacit knowledge often depends on human-centric strategies such as mentoring, communities of practice, succession planning, and key employee retention programs (KERP; Nonaka and Takeuchi 1995). The real challenge lies not only in recording knowledge but in embedding it deeply into the operational rhythms and decision-making life cycles of megaprojects. Every megaproject team should pay particular attention to the following with respect to knowledge management:

1. Knowledge Capture

Knowledge capture is the foundational step in KM. It requires intentional efforts to gather explicit knowledge (such as design documents, work processes, risk assessments) and tacit knowledge (like experiential insights and soft signals from stakeholder interactions). One of the most effective approaches is the use of structured brainstorming templates and real-time documentation practices. These tools enable project teams to collect and record insights based on impact severity, associated comments, and responsible actions.

Experiential learning has proven to be as valuable as technical documentation. Mentoring, leadership dialogue, and facilitated workshops help ensure the transfer of contextual insights that are often lost in formal documents. Structured lessons learned sessions and visual facilitation methods like live scribing are particularly effective in preserving nuanced inputs.

Tools:

- Knowledge capture checklists embedded into project closeout forms
- Interactive interviews and mentoring circles
- Templates for categorizing procedural, organizational, and technical knowledge

2.   Knowledge Storage and Organization

Capturing knowledge without a reliable structure for storage renders it inaccessible. Effective megaproject KM requires developing intuitive, centralized repositories digital libraries that serve as the single source of truth.

IPMA's lessons-learned system for construction PM suggests that organizing knowledge by stage, domain, or stakeholder function significantly enhances its retrievability. Furthermore, version control systems ensure that the most recent data is consistently used across teams, preventing confusion and inefficiencies.

The Panama Canal effort demonstrated the effectiveness of documentation continuity, where each engineering shift updated centralized logs to prevent decision lag. Similarly, digital repositories like SharePoint or ERP-integrated document control systems enable global accessibility.

Tools:

- SharePoint with custom taxonomy for megaprojects
- Metadata tagging tools for filtering by life cycle Stage
- Enterprisewide KM dashboards

3.   Knowledge Sharing

Without dissemination, captured knowledge becomes inert. Sharing knowledge involves active practices, such as setting up forums and creating digital collaboration spaces (Wenger et al. 2002). Communities of Practice (CoPs), as referenced in the business case presentation, help transcend organizational silos by linking experts across domains to share applied insights.

The DIA baggage system failure underlines the dangers of poor knowledge sharing. Teams working in isolation without the benefit of past failure insights repeated critical mistakes in integration and risk evaluation. Lessons Learned Workshops, as in Project Foxtrot, utilize S-P-A-C-E-R frameworks to foster safe environments for open feedback.

Tools:

- Digital CoP spaces with discussion boards
- Synchronous collaboration tools (e.g., Teams, Slack)
- Storytelling and case study databases

4. Knowledge Application

Effective KM culminates in the application of knowledge. Knowledge must inform not just historical records but decision points, course corrections, and continuous improvements. A core weakness of many lessons learned programs is that they stop at documentation rather than feeding into execution tools. This explains why the common saying that "knowledge or information is power" isn't entirely true; instead, knowledge or information with action is power. If knowledge is power, there won't be so many cases of megaproject teams making the same set of mistakes from project to project.

The business case slide deck outlines the four stages of KM application: identify, store, apply, and verify. Project dashboards should integrate these learnings to provide real-time decision support. For instance, a risk identified in a prior project should automatically flag a risk category or mitigation checklist in a new project dashboard.

Panama Canal's adoption of lock-based infrastructure, after failures of the sea-level design, illustrates the strategic advantage of applying historical learnings to current projects. Lessons must evolve into standardized practices, referenced in team charters, and reflected in performance metrics.

Tools:

- Decision support engines integrated with KM logs
- Training updates linked to learning outcomes
- AI-powered suggestion engines for risk management

5.   Knowledge Governance

Strong governance ensures accountability for KM practices. Defined roles such as knowledge champions, content curators, and data stewards help drive organizational discipline around knowledge practices. The business case underscores the importance of executive mandates, where leadership insists on the inclusion of learnings in investment requests.

Governance also includes standards for documentation quality, frequency of updates, and compliance with jurisdictional data privacy laws. In multinational megaprojects, knowledge governance must accommodate diverse legal and operational landscapes.

The Foxtrot Workshop's code of conduct ("no rank in the room") reinforces a culture of transparent knowledge dialogue critical for equitable governance.

Tools:

- KM accountability frameworks
- SOPs for capture and reporting
- GDPR-compliant data vaults and audit trails

6.   Challenges in Megaproject KM

Cultural and Geographical Barriers: Multinational teams may face difficulties in alignment. For example, time zones, language, and communication etiquette may hinder knowledge exchange unless platforms and norms are standardized.

Technology Integration: Megaprojects often involve multiple contractors, each with their own systems. KM frameworks must allow interoperability and standard data protocols to avoid fragmented learning.

Resistance to Sharing: Project team members may fear that disclosing problems could reflect poorly on their performance. Establishing trust, recognition, and nonpunitive environments (like Foxtrot's lessons learned session) helps mitigate this.

Knowledge Loss: High staff turnover in megaprojects leads to massive loss of tacit knowledge. Structured exit interviews, mentoring programs, and recorded debriefs are critical.

Panama Canal's archival records and staff logs preserved institutional knowledge that otherwise would have been lost during contractor handovers and political transitions.

Megaproject knowledge management is not an administrative task it is a strategic capability. Effective KM enhances risk resilience, accelerates decision making, and enables replicable success. By integrating lessons learned into the DNA of project systems and practices, organizations can institutionalize continuous learning.

We will explore how this embedded learning drives behavioral change and what practical tools can be deployed to reinforce this transformation at every level of megaproject delivery.

Learning as a Vehicle for Behavioral Change

While systems and tools are critical, they are only as effective as the people who use them. True learning in megaprojects must lead to behavioral change, shaping how individuals think, collaborate, and lead. This section delves into how learning drives transformation at individual, team, and organizational levels, highlighting the conditions that foster a culture of curiosity, adaptability, and continuous improvement.

Learning is more than the passive acquisition of information; it is the catalyst for behavioral transformation in complex environments. In megaprojects, where scale, uncertainty, and multidisciplinary coordination are the norm, behavioral change is often the determining factor between project success and failure. This section explores how intentional learning frameworks, organizational practices, leadership behaviors, and cultural shifts converge to foster meaningful behavioral change that directly impacts megaproject performance.

The impact of a positive learning culture extends beyond individual development; it influences team agility, departmental responsiveness, and overall business growth. Organizations that cultivate such a culture are significantly more likely to outperform their peers across multiple dimensions. The illustration below highlights the tangible business value of a positive learning environment (Figure 6.1).

Note: Promoters are employees who view their company's learning culture positively, while Detractors see it negatively.

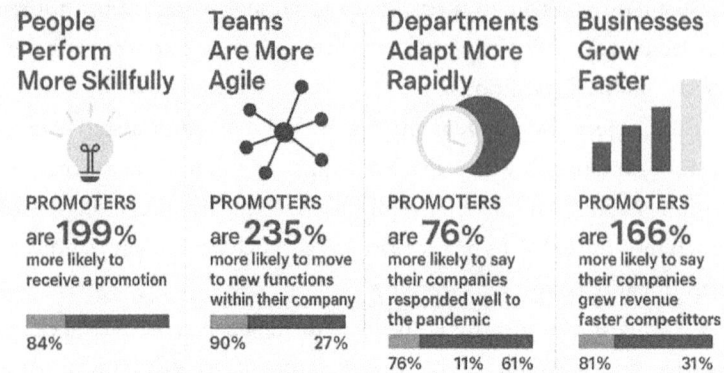

Figure 6.1 Illustrative summary of research findings on the business value of a positive learning culture

Source: Adapted from industrywide data on organizational learning behavior.

For learning to become a vehicle for behavioral change, please pay attention to the following:

1.   Continuous Learning and Adaptation

Megaprojects are not static ventures. They unfold over several years, are influenced by economic, technological, and regulatory changes, and often evolve in scope and complexity. Continuous learning equips project stakeholders with the ability to adapt proactively. This learning is not simply about keeping up with external developments but also about internalizing ongoing feedback and refining execution strategies in real time (Senge 2006).

A culture of continuous learning fosters innovation and risk resilience. It encourages experimentation while creating space for thoughtful iteration. Teams that prioritize learning in every Stage such as initiation, planning, execution, and closure position themselves to navigate change effectively and outperform reactive counterparts.

Learning cycles embedded in the project structure enhance agility. Periodic review mechanisms enable course corrections and foster awareness of evolving risk patterns. These feedback mechanisms, when institutionalized, reduce inertia and eliminate the common pitfall of sticking rigidly to outdated plans.

The mindset of adaptation also allows teams to respond with humility to failure. Instead of viewing setbacks as a threat, they are embraced as data points. This subtle but powerful shift enables psychological safety and cultivates resilience among project personnel.

2. Knowledge Sharing and Collaboration

Knowledge is the currency of transformation. Its value multiplies when it is shared. In the context of megaprojects, knowledge sharing takes on critical importance due to the multidisciplinary and multicultural nature of project teams.

Collaboration enables distributed intelligence. When teams function as integrated systems rather than disconnected units, they harness the collective power of their expertise. Silo-breaking initiatives such as inter-departmental learning exchanges and interface management workshops are essential in cultivating a learning ecosystem.

Open dialogue fosters emergent leadership and ownership. When individuals are trusted to contribute insights and are acknowledged for doing so, engagement deepens. This co-ownership of outcomes improves accountability and accelerates the diffusion of innovation.

Successful megaprojects often institutionalize collaborative routines such as cross-functional design reviews, interface alignment meetings, and integrated risk assessments. These structured opportunities provide fertile ground for knowledge convergence and the normalization of adaptive behaviors.

Moreover, effective collaboration requires a shared language. Creating standard terminologies, definitions, and project taxonomies enhances clarity. It ensures that insights, once shared, are understood consistently and acted upon reliably.

3. Training and Development Programs

Targeted training builds behavioral muscle. Programs tailored to address specific project challenges whether technical, relational, or strategic enable teams to transition from knowing to doing. Training should be dynamic and iterative, evolving with project needs and participant feedback.

The integration of experiential learning techniques such as simulations, scenario planning, and war-room exercises adds realism to training and improves retention. When individuals practice under near-authentic conditions, their confidence and competence increase exponentially (Argote and Miron-Spektor 2011).

Behavioral modeling during training is a subtle yet powerful driver of change. Facilitators who model transparency, curiosity, and active listening influence participants more effectively than static presentations. Peer-based learning structures, such as mentorship circles and rotating facilitation roles, promote inclusivity and engagement.

Development is not limited to structured sessions. Informal learning opportunities like daily stand-ups, shadowing senior leads, or participating in decision-making forums are equally potent. These interactions build contextual intelligence and reinforce desired behaviors through social reinforcement.

Organizational investment in training sends a clear message about priorities. Budgeting for continuous education, allocating time for reflection, and including learning milestones in project charters establish learning as a strategic pillar rather than a peripheral task.

4. Behavioral Change Through Learning

Learning drives behavior when it leads to belief revision. Teams abandon outdated approaches only when they internalize new paradigms. This internalization is achieved not through coercion but through relevance, repetition, and reinforcement.

Successful behavioral shifts are observable at multiple levels. At the individual level, they manifest in improved judgment, openness to feedback, and willingness to assume responsibility. At the team level, changes appear as psychological safety, distributed decision making, and collective accountability. At the organizational level, they result in streamlined governance, enhanced risk culture, and proactive stakeholder engagement.

Behavior change is often driven by small wins. When teams see tangible improvements from altered behavior such as fewer change orders or smoother vendor negotiations, they are more likely to sustain the shift. Capturing and celebrating these wins reinforces new norms and boosts morale.

The link between learning and values is critical. When learning is framed as a means to uphold the organization's values like integrity, innovation, and excellence, it becomes intrinsically motivating. People are more likely to embrace behavior change when it aligns with their sense of purpose.

5. Feedback Loops and Reflective Practices

Reflection is the bridge between experience and insight. Structured feedback loops institutionalize reflection by embedding it into regular workflows. Whether through AARs, lessons learned debriefs, or weekly retrospectives, these mechanisms transform events into education.

Feedback must be multidirectional. Teams benefit most when feedback flows across hierarchies and functions. Encouraging upward and peer feedback increases inclusivity and ensures that blind spots are surfaced early.

Reflection practices should balance factual accuracy with emotional resonance. By examining both what happened and how it felt, teams can uncover deeper truths about motivation, decision-making patterns, and relational dynamics.

Reflection also includes pre action contemplation. Before initiating major Stages, teams should anticipate potential challenges and identify strategies in advance. This proactive learning approach builds foresight and reduces reactivity.

Creating psychological safety is a prerequisite for reflective honesty. Teams must know they can speak openly without fear of punishment. Leaders who listen actively and respond constructively cultivate such environments.

6. Leadership and Learning Culture

Leadership behavior sets the tone for the entire organization. Leaders who model learning, who ask questions, admit mistakes, and remain curious signal that learning is not a weakness but a strength. They normalize vulnerability and create room for authentic engagement.

Culturally, learning becomes embedded when it is celebrated. Recognizing contributors to learning, spotlighting improved outcomes, and sharing stories of transformation create a positive narrative around change. Culture becomes self-reinforcing when learning is seen not just as a response to failure but as a pathway to excellence.

Leadership must also align incentives with learning. Performance management systems should reward not just outcomes but learning behaviors. Promotion pathways should consider growth mindset, knowledge contribution, and collaboration. Policies should remove barriers to experimentation and encourage intelligent risk-taking.

The use of learning champions within project teams adds further depth. These individuals advocate for reflective practices, curate relevant insights, and help translate knowledge into action. Their presence reinforces the value placed on learning at the grassroots level.

Organizations that lead in megaprojects invest in institutional memory. They create systems to retain, retrieve, and reapply learning over time. Whether through digital knowledge bases, curated case libraries, or story-driven repositories, these systems preserve behavioral gains and make them accessible across generations of teams.

Learning is not an optional feature of megaproject management; it is the engine of behavioral transformation. By enabling continuous adaptation, promoting knowledge sharing, equipping individuals with relevant training, reinforcing feedback loops, and modeling change through leadership, organizations transform not just projects but people.

In the context of global megaprojects, where costs are counted in billions and implications stretch for decades, behavioral change through learning is not a soft skill. It is a strategic imperative.

Successful megaprojects embed learning into their operating models. Every structure, tool, and conversation must ultimately serve the goal of shaping adaptive, empowered, and resilient behaviors.

The next section explores the tools for capturing learning, ensuring that behaviors influenced by knowledge are recorded, tracked, and shared with consistency and clarity.

Tools for Capturing Learning

The ability to systematically capture, retain, and reuse knowledge depends heavily on the tools employed by the organization. From structured databases to AI-driven assistants, these tools provide the infrastructure that supports an evolving learning ecosystem. This section provides a deep dive into a comprehensive set of tools designed to turn raw experience into strategic advantage across the life cycle of megaprojects (Alavi and Leidner 2001).

Lessons-Learned Databases

Lessons-learned databases are structured repositories where organizations store documented experiences from past projects. These include details about what worked well, what went wrong, and why specific decisions were made. For megaprojects, where scale and complexity magnify both successes and failures, lessons learned databases provide a reference point that can prevent the repetition of mistakes and promote the replication of successful strategies.

Each entry typically consists of a title, description, project Stage, root cause analysis, resolution strategy, and recommendations for future action. The value of these databases lies in their ability to deliver actionable insights to project planners and teams in the early planning or risk assessment stages.

An effective lessons learned database must have a consistent structure, support advanced search functionality, and include categorization by life cycle stage, and by discipline (engineering, procurement, safety, quality, risk, schedule, cost, construction, commissioning, etc.), and a position-based learning approval workflow. Integration with decision-support tools, workflows and training content enhances its utility.

Some megaproject teams and businesses capture learning through their robust benchmarking database. Some also have Project Closeout Report and Post Investment Review data collection tool(s).

Knowledge Management Systems

Knowledge management systems (KMS) are centralized platforms that combine technologies, processes, and people to manage organizational knowledge. These systems help capture, organize, share, and retrieve both explicit knowledge (documents, processes, plans) and tacit knowledge (insights, best practices).

In megaprojects, a good KMS enables cross-functional and cross-border teams to remain aligned. Systems like SharePoint, Confluence, and custom portals allow teams to share updates, access archives, and contribute learning materials. They serve as a dynamic learning repository where lessons are not only stored but actively used in project decision making.

Effective use of KMS relies on organizational policies around contribution, review, and validation of content. Dedicated knowledge stewards or curators ensure the content remains relevant and high quality.

After-Action Reviews

AARs are structured sessions conducted at the conclusion of a project Stage, major milestone, or specific task. They involve key stakeholders reflecting on four central questions: What was supposed to happen? What actually happened? Why did it happen that way? What can we learn from this?

AARs foster a culture of openness, continuous improvement, and accountability. Unlike traditional reviews that focus on reporting, AARs emphasize dialogue and shared understanding. Documented outcomes from AARs should feed directly into KMS and lessons learned databases.

They are particularly effective when facilitated by an impartial moderator and supported by real-time documentation tools such as collaborative digital boards.

Project Management Information Systems

Project management information systems (PMIS) refers to the tools used to plan, monitor, and control megaproject execution. Platforms such as Microsoft Project, Primavera P6, and Asana include functionality for schedule management, issue tracking, and risk assessment.

When used intentionally for knowledge capture, PMIS can include fields for rationale behind major decisions, mitigation responses, change requests, and unresolved issues. These digital footprints become invaluable when planning future projects, conducting root cause analysis, or handling audits.

Customization of PMIS with lessons capture modules or plug-ins can transform these systems into live repositories of experiential knowledge.

Workshops and Training Sessions

Knowledge is best transferred in environments where teams can discuss, reflect, and practice together. Lessons learned workshops are commonly held at the end of project stages or after key activities. They are designed to solicit insights from team members while events are still fresh.

These sessions generate deep reflections, especially when structured with predefined prompts or categories. Training sessions can incorporate lessons into simulation exercises, case-based learning, or real-world walkthroughs.

When paired with a documentation strategy (digital scribing, templates, etc.), workshops and training become active tools in embedding learning into the organization.

Mentorship Programs

Mentorship is a powerful tool for transferring tacit knowledge and unwritten experience-based insights that formal documents cannot easily capture. Pairing seasoned professionals with younger or newly assigned project staff promotes mutual learning.

Effective mentorship structures include:

- Onboarding tracks for new team members
- Rotation assignments
- Buddy systems
- Knowledge diaries shared between mentors and mentees

These relationships build continuity across megaproject Stages, especially when transitions are frequent and teams are dynamic.

Document Repositories

A central repository of project-related documents including design plans, change orders, technical reviews, contracts, and stakeholder communications serves as an invaluable archive. These repositories ensure knowledge remains accessible and not lost with individual departures or team turnover.

Best practices include:

- Version control and audit trails
- Metadata tagging and folder structuring aligned with project stages
- Integration with KMS and PMIS for seamless access

A well-organized repository ensures that documentation does not merely exist, but is retrieved and reused effectively.

Surveys and Feedback Mechanisms

Structured surveys gather stakeholder insights at various project stages. These instruments are useful for capturing both individual perceptions and systemic feedback. Surveys can be internal (team-focused) or external (client, vendor, community).

Feedback may cover areas like leadership effectiveness, communication, quality assurance, or innovation. Tools such as Google Forms, SurveyMonkey, or enterprise platforms automate collection and analysis.

Results should be synthesized and shared in lessons learned workshops, informing SOPs, performance reviews, and future strategies.

Case Studies

Documenting project outcomes in the form of case studies turns experience into curriculum. These narratives outline the context, objectives, challenges, decision paths, outcomes, and key lessons.

Effective case studies:

- Include visual elements (charts, diagrams).
- Highlight critical decisions and turning points.
- Compare expected versus actual performance.

Case studies can be used for onboarding, training, strategic reviews, and stakeholder engagement. They provide vivid, real-world reference points and humanize learning.

Collaboration Tools

Platforms such as Slack, Microsoft Teams, Trello, and Basecamp enable real-time communication, knowledge sharing, and informal documentation. These tools are increasingly becoming the frontline interface where team knowledge is exchanged.

Collaboration tools can support:

- Group chats that document live decisions
- Channel-based knowledge archives
- Shared task boards linked to file repositories

When linked with KMS or configured to archive searchable conversations, these tools transform from basic communication channels into living knowledge systems.

Digital Whiteboards and Visualization Platforms

Visual thinking tools allow teams to collaborate in spatial, nonlinear ways that promote creativity and clarity. Digital whiteboards like Miro, MURAL, and Lucidspark enable geographically dispersed stakeholders to ideate, map out processes, and cocreate timelines or frameworks.

These tools are especially useful during planning, retrospective, and problem-solving workshops. Captured boards can be exported, versioned, and embedded in project repositories or reports. Over time, they form a visual history of team evolution, reasoning, and brainstorming.

To maximize value:

- Establish standard templates for common discussions (e.g., risk workshops, stage-gate reviews).

- Encourage annotation, tagging, and visual metaphor use to anchor complex ideas.
- Create galleries of boards for new team members to study and learn from.

Interactive Dashboards and Data Analytics Engines

Data-driven learning is accelerated when information is visualized in meaningful, accessible ways. Dashboards pull together KPIs, real-time performance metrics, project health indicators, and even qualitative data (e.g., feedback scores).

Tools like Power BI, Tableau, and Google Data Studio allow teams to track trends, anomalies, and performance patterns. These dashboards can embed links to supporting documents, analysis narratives, and actions taken, turning them into learning tools rather than static reports.

When designing dashboards for learning:

- Incorporate historical benchmarks and comparative metrics.
- Visualize correlations between decisions, risks, and results.
- Enable interactivity to let users explore underlying causes or outcomes.

Standard Operating Procedure Libraries

Standard operating procedures (SOPs) are structured documents that translate learned practices into actionable, repeatable steps. Megaprojects require SOPs across functions such as procurement, quality control, design approvals, and safety inspections.

A robust SOP library integrates:

- Indexed SOPs aligned to project life cycle stages
- Change history and rationale behind procedural updates
- Cross-referencing with tools, templates, and policies

SOPs should be treated as living documents, updated post project to reflect actual lessons learned. Governance for reviews and updates must be formalized.

Playbooks and Implementation Guides

Playbooks go beyond SOPs by offering flexible, scenario-based guidance. They combine frameworks, checklists, tips, and decision aids tailored to specific functions or project types.

Effective playbooks:

- Reflect patterns derived from past projects.
- Offer what-if scenarios and branching logic.
- Use storytelling and real examples to show application.

Project managers use playbooks for onboarding, contingency planning, and real-time troubleshooting. Including embedded hyperlinks to repositories, dashboards, and contacts makes them user-friendly and powerful.

Innovation Logs and Experiment Trackers

Megaprojects are also sites for experimentation. Whether testing modular construction, new contracting models, or sustainability approaches, these trials must be documented.

Innovation logs record:

- Hypotheses tested
- Methods, data, and observations
- Lessons, scalability, and next steps

They ensure institutional memory captures not only what worked but how it was proven. Logs can also inspire new experiments and signal an open culture of inquiry.

Gamification Platforms for Learning Reinforcement

To sustain learning engagement, gamification elements can be embedded in tools or learning journeys. Platforms might reward knowledge sharing, offer points for participating in reviews, or build leaderboards for learning milestones.

Applications include:

- Quizzes based on recent project cases
- Scenario simulations scored for decision quality
- Recognition systems tied to knowledge contributions

Gamification, when aligned with professional development goals, builds a fun, motivating learning ecosystem.

AI-Powered Knowledge Assistants

AI agents can analyze language patterns, summarize reports, suggest related content, and even tag learnings automatically. As these tools mature, they help manage the scale and complexity of megaproject documentation.

Some capabilities include:

- Recommending similar past projects based on risk profiles
- Flagging contradictory learnings across documents
- Predicting likely points of failure from planning inputs

When deployed ethically and with oversight, AI enhances both speed and depth of learning capture.

Organizational Wikis and Open Contribution Platforms

Crowdsourced learning platforms allow any team member to contribute updates, insights, or critiques. These democratic models increase coverage and inclusion.

Moderated wikis allow:

- Real-time updates with historical versioning
- Multiauthor annotation of policies, methods, or glossaries
- Social features like upvoting or discussion threads

Establishing editorial standards, curator roles, and recognition systems ensures quality without stifling contribution.

Retrospective Portals and Story Archives

Beyond factual logs, capturing narratives of transformation stories of turning points, leadership challenges, or adaptive wins builds cultural memory. These can be presented as:

- Audio journazl or mini-documentaries
- Annotated timelines with inflection points
- Internal podcasts with rotating project voices

These human-centered accounts make learnings relatable and memorable. They foster empathy, legacy thinking, and cross-generational transfer.

Integrated Learning Ecosystems

The most mature organizations create interconnected learning environments. All tools from dashboards to repositories, playbooks to AI agents are linked through shared platforms and taxonomies.

In these systems:

- Learning flows across Project Stages or Gates.
- Outcomes automatically feed into risk models, templates, or approvals.
- Each new project begins with insights baked into workflows.

This systemic approach makes learning continuous, contextual, and dynamic.

The breadth of tools available for capturing learning in megaprojects is immense. But tools alone are not enough. Their impact depends on leadership commitment, cultural norms, and integration into everyday workflows.

Organizations that prioritize learning architecture not as an afterthought but as a project pillar, benefit from resilience, agility, and competitive advantage. By enabling a living system of knowledge, megaproject teams can ensure that every lesson hard-won or serendipitous becomes a stepping stone to enduring success.

Summary

This chapter delves deeply into the critical role that learning plays in the success of megaprojects, and in any project environment. It begins by framing learning not as a support function, but as a central driver of performance, risk mitigation, and long-term value. Through structured knowledge practices, organizations can reduce uncertainty, avoid the repetition of past mistakes, and build confidence in both planning and execution.

The chapter first explores the internal mechanisms required for effective knowledge management. These include the capture of **explicit and tacit** knowledge, centralized storage and retrieval systems, mechanisms for real-time sharing, and strategies for applying learning to current and future projects. It emphasizes that for learning to be meaningful, it must be seamlessly integrated into project workflows and supported by governance, timing, and accessibility frameworks.

Beyond systems and processes, the chapter highlights the human side of learning. It shows how learning drives behavioral change by influencing how individuals communicate, collaborate, make decisions, and lead. Continuous learning allows teams to adapt to change, while shared learning fosters a collaborative culture. Structured training programs, feedback loops, reflective practices, and leadership modeling are all shown to be essential in embedding a mindset of continuous improvement.

A substantial portion of the chapter is dedicated to exploring the tools that support learning in megaprojects. Twenty categories of tools are examined in detail, from well-established systems like lessons learned databases, document repositories, and mentorship programs to more advanced solutions such as interactive dashboards, AI-powered knowledge assistants, gamified platforms, and integrated ecosystems. These tools serve not only to capture learning but to connect people, structure insights, and drive action across the entire life cycle of a megaproject.

The chapter closes by reinforcing the idea that tools and systems alone are not enough. The effectiveness of any knowledge strategy depends on leadership support, cultural readiness, and operational integration. When learning is treated as a strategic asset and embedded into the DNA of megaproject delivery, it becomes a source of resilience, innovation, and sustainable success.

With a comprehensive foundation now laid for how knowledge is built and preserved, the next logical step is to explore how that knowledge is used. Chapter 7 shifts the focus from learning to conclusive notes on megaproject development, evaluation, and investment decision making, defining execution readiness, the transformative role of AI in megaproject planning and execution, and how leaders take the lessons from evaluation, development, and planning and turn them into confident, forward-looking investment decisions. Where learning connects us to the past, decision making is what defines the future of every megaproject.

Reflection Questions

1. What behavioral and cultural shifts are necessary to make learning a routine practice in megaproject environments?
2. How can organizations ensure that lessons captured are not just documented but actively applied in future projects?
3. What tools or methods—such as AARs or knowledge repositories—have been most effective in your experience, and why?
4. How can project teams balance capturing both explicit and tacit knowledge, especially during key transitions like project closeout or staff turnover?
5. In what ways can leadership reinforce and reward knowledge-sharing behaviors to create a sustainable learning culture across projects?

CHAPTER 7

Conclusion

Learning Outcomes

By the end of Chapter 7, the reader should be able to:

1. Understand the critical factors that define execution readiness in a megaproject, including governance, resource planning, stakeholder engagement, and project controls.
2. Evaluate the transformative role of Artificial Intelligence in megaproject planning and execution, including applications such as predictive analytics, risk assessment, and AI-driven stakeholder engagement.
3. Identify the evolving dynamics of the future of work in the megaproject landscape, such as remote collaboration, automation, demographic shifts, and ESG imperatives.
4. Distinguish between common pitfalls and best practices in megaproject execution and learn how to design flexible systems that support agility and resilience.
5. Synthesize strategic recommendations for project professionals and leaders that encompass planning, decision making, innovation, sustainability, and capacity building.

Practical Matters of the Execution Stage: Considerations, Readiness, and Success Factors

The FID represents a pivotal turning point in the life cycle of a megaproject. It is at this juncture that the project formally transitions from conceptualization, evaluation, and planning into the realm of physical execution. This Stage, while highly visible and resource-intensive, is often where the compounded consequences of earlier missteps become apparent. Therefore, execution readiness must be viewed not as a singular milestone, but as the culmination of disciplined planning, stakeholder alignment, risk navigation, and leadership maturity established in the preceding Stages.

Transitioning from FID to Execution

The shift from development to execution marks the transition of responsibility from strategists, engineers and, planners to those tasked with actual delivery. This transition must be seamless. It demands detailed documentation, clarity of roles, governance structures, and a complete understanding of the work ahead. The most successful megaprojects ensure that their Execution Planning documents are not static blueprints, but living tools that inform and guide day-to-day activity (Miller and Hobbs 2024).

The initial days post-FID are critical. Teams should reconvene to validate assumptions, confirm the alignment of resources, revisit risk profiles, establish schedule baselines and turn approved estimates into control budget. Misalignment or ambiguity at this point can cascade into schedule slippage, cost overruns, or even project failure.

Key Execution Stage Considerations

Execution is a battlefield of competing interests, evolving conditions, and high stakeholder visibility. As such, a project's success hinges on recognizing and addressing several key considerations:

1. **Detailed Planning and FEED:** A megaproject must not proceed into execution without a rigorous and complete FEED. This ensures that technical, operational, and commercial assumptions are tested and validated. Furthermore, realistic scheduling, proper sequencing, and risk mitigation strategies must be fully baked into the plan. The absence of these contributes significantly to project derailments.

2. **Stakeholder Alignment and Engagement:** Internal and external stakeholders must remain aligned not just at the FID gate but

throughout the execution Stage. Local communities, regulators, financiers, contractors, and end-users all play critical roles. Stakeholder management is not an administrative task; it is strategic. Engagement strategies should emphasize clear, consistent communication, managing expectations, and proactive conflict resolution.

3. **Contracting Strategy and Accountability:** Robust EPC contracts with clear scopes, incentives, and penalty mechanisms form the spine of execution accountability. Before execution begins, contractors should undergo readiness reviews to assess their ability to deliver, both in technical capacity and resource availability. Contracts should support a culture of collaboration, not just legal enforcement.

4. **Supply Chain and Logistics Preparedness:** The execution Stage depends heavily on timely availability of materials, equipment, and services. Global megaprojects must navigate customs, regulatory bottlenecks, weather disruptions, and capacity constraints. Delays in procurement or shipping can cause ripple effects. Thus, a resilient supply chain strategy with identified critical path items and alternative sourcing plans is essential.

5. **Project Controls and Monitoring:** Execution is where schedule and cost pressures manifest. Integrated project control systems are required to manage these variables dynamically. Tools such as EVM, real-time dashboards, and predictive analytics empower project teams to detect and correct deviations before they become unmanageable. Minimize (or avoid, if practical), the scenario of incomplete offsite or yard fabrication scope being carried to installation site. It could delay project completion with the attendant safety issues, and cost overruns, if not well-managed (through a robust assessment of the human resources, scope, risks, and estimates requirement).

6. **Resource Allocation and Workforce Mobilization:** The execution Stage typically mobilizes hundreds, if not thousands, of workers, oftentimes including expatriate resources (where needed). Effective workforce planning ensures the right mix of skills at the right time.

This may include visas for expatriate resources. Thus, robust planning for resources' mobilization, across the board, is vital to success. Additionally, training programs should continue through execution to address evolving challenges. Projects that fail to scale their labor resources responsibly often suffer from quality issues and labor unrest.

7. **Technological Readiness:** Execution efficiency is increasingly driven by digital tools ranging from BIM and Digital Twins to AI-powered scheduling assistants. These tools must be fully operational and integrated into the workflows before construction begins. Tech readiness isn't about having the latest software; it's about using the right tools at the right stage with the right people trained to use them. Thus, for no reason should any critical decision be left in "the hands" of an AI tool.

8. **Leadership and Governance:** Strong project leadership is the glue that holds execution together. Leaders must not only be experienced but empowered with decision-making authority. Governance structures should enable rapid decisions and escalations without being bureaucratic. Leadership must also embody the project's values particularly around safety, ethics, and sustainability.

9. **Security, Health, Safety, Environmental, and Community Readiness:** Megaprojects often span hazardous environments. A security, health and safety-first culture embedded at every level is nonnegotiable. Environmental plans must go beyond compliance, integrating sustainability metrics and minimizing the project's ecological footprint. A single safety lapse or environmental infraction can halt work, erode public trust, and inflate costs. At FID, it is expected that the community engagement is complete, expectations mutually understood and ongoing communication plan fully developed and approved by authorized persons.

10. **Flexibility and Adaptability:** No plan survives first contact with reality. Projects must maintain the flexibility to adapt to design changes, regulatory shifts, market disruptions, or community concerns. A successful project is one that adjusts without compromising its core objectives.

Indicators of Readiness for Execution

Execution readiness can be assessed across several dimensions. These include the following:

- Completion of FEED and all required permits
- Confirmed funding and insurance coverage
- Fully resourced teams across disciplines, with a qualified single point of accountability
- Core project processes and systems in place
- Validated procurement and logistics plans
- Established baseline schedules and budgets
- Approved safety, environmental compliance, and community engagement plans
- Completed readiness reviews and independent peer assessments
- Finalized contracts with critical suppliers and partners; some fully executed with exit strategy, and some ready for mutual execution
- Key operations and maintenance resources are engaged/defined, to be mobilized more fully later in the project

These indicators provide the green light for moving forward. Without them, the project team should pause and rectify the gaps.

Common Pitfalls and How to Avoid Them

Even the most meticulously planned megaprojects can stumble. Common execution pitfalls include the following:

- **Scope Creep**: This arises when new elements are added mid-execution without adequate impact assessment. To mitigate this, enforce a disciplined change control process.
- **Unrealistic Timelines**: Overly ambitious schedules often ignore realities on the ground. Ground-truth your plans with local intelligence.
- **Poor Risk Contingency Planning**: Many projects assume risks are past once execution starts. On the contrary, new operational and geopolitical risks emerge. Constant risk reassessment is essential.

- **Lack of Communication**: Silos form quickly in large teams. Use integrated communication platforms and regular briefings to maintain transparency.
- **Inflexible Contracts**: Contracts that are too rigid discourage innovation or adaptation. Structure contracts with optionality built in.

Sustaining Strategic Alignment During Execution

The execution Stage is where the strategic goals of a megaproject are tested. Delays, budget overruns, or reputational issues can derail broader business objectives. Hence, alignment must be actively maintained.

This can be achieved through the following:

- **Periodic Strategic Reviews**: Revisit business case assumptions and confirm alignment with current realities.
- **Leadership Visibility**: Executives must stay engaged, visiting sites and reinforcing the importance of project objectives.
- **Continuous Learning**: Embed feedback loops that incorporate lessons learned from execution into ongoing project activities.
- **Cultural Reinforcement**: Use team charters, shared KPIs, and recognition programs to promote alignment.

Execution is the moment of truth in a megaproject's life cycle. It is where promises made during development must become tangible results. When approached with discipline, adaptability, and aligned leadership, execution becomes not just a Stage, but a validation of all that preceded it.

In the next section, we examine how emerging technologies, particularly AI, are beginning to reshape the contours of megaproject execution and decision making.

Artificial Intelligence and Megaprojects

As discussed in Chapters 3 and 5, the future of project evaluation and strategic decisions will increasingly depend on data-driven tools and adaptive governance models. The intersection of AI and megaproject management represents one of the most transformative frontiers in the modern infra-structure, energy, metals, and mining sectors. As megaprojects continue to grow in scale, complexity, and global interconnectedness, the integration of AI into their development and execution has the potential to radically reshape how projects are conceived, evaluated, managed, and delivered.

AI, encompassing machine learning, natural language processing, pre-dictive analytics, robotics, and automation, provides a new arsenal of tools that megaproject teams can use to address persistent challenges such as de-lays, cost overruns, data silos, risk underestimation, and decision-making bottlenecks. AI not only enables faster and more accurate data processing but also augments human decision making with insights that were previ-ously difficult to access or predict in real time (Li et al. 2023).

Evolution of AI in Project Management

The early use of AI in projects was primarily focused on automating repetitive tasks, such as scheduling and document control. Today, AI is evolving into a strategic enabler, capable of driving decision making, optimizing design alternatives, predicting risk events, and improving stakeholder engagement. The transformation has been accelerated by the growing availability of big data, increased computing power, and the mat-uration of AI algorithms.

Key AI Applications in Megaprojects

There is no denying the fact that AI is rapidly transforming how megaproj-ects are conceived, executed, and managed—enabling data-driven precision at a scale once unimaginable. From predictive analytics to sus-tainability optimization, AI applications now touch every dimension of project performance, offering smarter insights, faster decisions, and more resilient outcomes across the entire project life cycle. Here are a few of the many application areas:

1. Predictive Analytics and Forecasting
   ○ AI systems can analyze vast historical project datasets to predict outcomes related to quality, schedule, and cost.

- ○ Machine learning models can identify leading indicators of project slippage or cost escalation, often before they manifest.
- ○ Predictive forecasting helps decision makers plan interventions proactively, rather than reactively.

2. Risk Assessment and Management
   - ○ AI enables continuous risk identification and monitoring by scanning data from project reports, e-mails, sensors, and external sources.
   - ○ Natural language processing (NLP) can interpret unstructured data to uncover hidden risks.
   - ○ Dynamic risk models adjust in real time, providing a constantly evolving risk profile.

3. Design Optimization
   - ○ Generative design tools use AI to propose multiple design alternatives based on parameters such as cost, material availability, and performance criteria.
   - ○ This allows for early-stage optimization, balancing competing objectives like sustainability, cost, and constructability.

4. Resource Allocation and Productivity Tracking
   - ○ AI tools optimize resource deployment by matching availability, skill sets, and project needs.
   - ○ Workforce tracking using AI-driven facial recognition, drones, or Internet of Things (IoT) sensors enhances real-time productivity management.

5. Supply Chain and Logistics Management
   - ○ AI systems forecast demand for materials and equipment, helping prevent shortages and overstocking.
   - ○ Route optimization algorithms support logistics planning by accounting for real-time variables like weather, traffic, and geopolitical risks.

6. Quality Control and Assurance
   - ○ Computer vision systems can inspect construction quality using drone footage and flag deviations from design.
   - ○ AI-driven quality analytics help detect patterns and recommend corrective actions before problems escalate.

7. Safety Management
   ◦ AI can predict safety incidents by analyzing past incident data, site conditions, and behavioral indicators.
   ◦ Wearable sensors integrated with AI systems can alert workers and supervisors to dangerous conditions.

8. Document Management and Decision Support
   ◦ Intelligent document processing tools, such as Kofax, ABBYY FlexiCapture, or Microsoft Syntex, automatically organize and summarize project documents.
   ◦ AI chatbots and decision engines provide immediate answers to project team queries, improving knowledge access.

9. Stakeholder Engagement and Communication
   ◦ Sentiment analysis tools gauge stakeholder perception from social media, e-mails, and community feedback.
   ◦ AI-driven translation and communication platforms help facilitate multicultural collaboration across global teams.

10. Carbon Management and Sustainability
   ◦ AI models simulate environmental impact and suggest more sustainable construction methods.
   ◦ Energy consumption, emissions, and waste generation can be tracked and optimized in real time.

Challenges of Integrating AI in Megaprojects

Despite the substantial promise of AI, integrating it into megaproject environments is not without challenges. These challenges span technical, organizational, cultural, and ethical dimensions.

1. Data Quality and Availability: AI is only as effective as the data it learns from. In many legacy megaproject systems, data is either siloed, incomplete, unstructured, or outdated. This undermines the efficacy of AI tools and can lead to biased or inaccurate outputs. Establishing data governance policies and digitizing legacy systems are often prerequisites for AI integration.

2. Resistance to Change: AI introduces a fundamental shift in how decisions are made and tasks are performed. For some team members, especially those with decades of experience, this shift may feel threatening or dehumanizing. Overcoming this requires deliberate change management, training, and showcasing AI as a support tool, not a replacement.

3. High Implementation Costs: Although the cost of AI technology has declined, the total cost of integration including infrastructure, training, licensing, and maintenance remains high. For many project owners, the ROI is not immediately obvious, especially if the project duration is relatively short. Cost–benefit analysis and Staged implementation strategies can help manage these perceptions.

4. Cybersecurity Risks: Integrating AI and IoT devices into megaprojects increases exposure to cyber threats. A compromised AI system can disrupt operations, leak sensitive data, or even result in safety hazards. Strong cybersecurity protocols, encrypted data pipelines, and regular system audits are essential components of any AI-enabled project.

5. Ethical and Legal Concerns: Questions around data privacy, algorithmic bias, and accountability must be addressed proactively. Who is responsible when an AI system makes an error? What recourse exists for those affected? Project teams must establish clear ethical guidelines and ensure compliance with data protection laws.

Case Examples of AI in Action

Case 1: Predictive Maintenance in LNG Projects

In a large LNG construction project, AI-driven sensors monitored critical equipment such as compressors and heat exchangers. The system predicted potential failures up to three weeks in advance, allowing teams to intervene without impacting the construction schedule. This reduced downtime and prevented cascading delays.

Case 2: AI-Powered Design Optimization in a Mining Expansion

A global mining company used generative design to evaluate over five hundred design permutations for a new processing facility. The AI optimized layouts based on cost, safety, and accessibility. The selected option reduced expected construction time by 14 percent and material costs by 9 percent.

Case 3: Dynamic Risk Monitoring in a Cross-Border Pipeline Project

An AI risk management platform aggregated weather data, geopolitical developments, and supply chain signals in real time. It issued early warnings about potential border crossing delays due to new import regulations. The project team adjusted procurement and avoided what would have been a six-week delay.

Governance and Strategic Alignment

AI adoption should not be an IT initiative, it must be part of a megaproject's strategic governance framework. This includes:

- Appointing an AI integration lead at the governance level
- Including AI-readiness reviews in stage-gated development processes
- Establishing partnerships with technology providers
- Ensuring board-level awareness and endorsement

Furthermore, AI use must be consistent with the project's broader values and business case. AI should enhance, not distort, the project's strategic intent. AI tools should never be forced into a megaproject environment where the business leaders do not approve its deployment.

Skills and Capability Development

As AI becomes more central to project execution, project professionals must upskill. This includes:

- Data literacy: Understanding data sources, quality issues, and interpretation

- Technology fluency: Comfort with AI tools, platforms, and their limitations
- Change leadership: Ability to lead teams through tech-driven transformation

Project managers of the future will not just manage schedule and cost; they will manage digital ecosystems.

Future Outlook

The role of AI in megaprojects is poised to grow exponentially. We are moving toward fully integrated AI ecosystems where planning, monitoring, and reporting are harmonized in real time. AI will become an invisible but omnipresent force shaping decisions, optimizing outcomes, and reducing risk.

In the long run, AI could enable:

- Autonomous construction equipment
- Real-time adaptive project scheduling and meaningful budget at completion forecasting, including ongoing schedule versus cost challenges
- Embedded ethics monitoring for labor and environment
- AI-driven stakeholder consensus forecasting

However, this future must be shaped deliberately. Project leaders must steer AI development toward outcomes that benefit not only the project but society at large.

AI Across the Megaproject Life Cycle

AI's utility is not confined to execution alone. From the earliest Stages of opportunity assessment through final delivery and operational handover, AI can support strategic decisions and enhance productivity:

- Opportunity Identification: AI can analyze market trends, regulatory landscapes, and competitor activities to identify high-value project opportunities.

- Feasibility and Concept Selection: AI models evaluate hundreds of design and planning options against multidimensional criteria such as risk, cost, and stakeholder impact.
- Optimization and Definition: Simulation tools and generative algorithms help refine engineering and financial models, identifying the most viable pathways for development.
- Execution and Construction: As detailed earlier, AI supports real-time tracking, productivity optimization, safety monitoring, and procurement logistics.
- Operations and Handover: AI supports predictive maintenance, performance optimization, and continuous improvement in asset performance post-handover.

Cross-Sector Innovations and Lessons

The energy, metals, and mining sectors stand to benefit uniquely from AI because of their capital intensity, regulatory complexity, and extended life cycles. However, megaproject practitioners can learn valuable lessons from other sectors:

- Health Care: AI in hospital construction is improving space utilization through simulation-based planning.
- Aviation: Airline infrastructure projects leverage AI to predict passenger flows and optimize terminal layouts.
- Urban Development: Smart cities use AI to design adaptive transport networks and sustainable building systems that reduce resource consumption.

These insights suggest that cross-sector collaboration can accelerate innovation in megaprojects.

Integration Best Practices

To effectively integrate AI into megaproject development, organizations should:

- Develop an AI Roadmap: Outline specific objectives, key technologies, and integration timelines

- Start Small and Scale: Begin with pilot projects and scale AI adoption based on results and learning
- Invest in Talent and Training: Build internal capabilities rather than relying solely on external vendors
- Prioritize Ethics and Transparency: Create policies that ensure responsible AI use and data privacy
- Foster an Innovation Culture: Encourage experimentation, agile processes, and collaborative thinking

With these practices in place, AI becomes more than a buzzword; it becomes a core enabler of megaproject success.

When Success Fails: The Illusion of Completion

One of the most critical observations in modern megaproject delivery is that successful execution does not always translate into real success. Projects may tick every box on scope, schedule, and cost yet still fail to deliver meaningful or sustainable outcomes. This phenomenon, often summarized as "the operation was successful, but the patient died" highlights a key gap in how success is defined and measured.

Such misalignment typically arises when project teams are overly focused on delivery metrics, while strategic outcomes and organizational readiness are overlooked. In some documented cases, teams celebrated on-time delivery only to later realize the asset was underutilized, poorly integrated, or misaligned with business needs (Chih and Zwikael 2023).

True project success must be reframed to go beyond delivery excellence. It must encompass:

- **Strategic alignment**: Is the project solving the right problem?
- **Operational readiness**: Can the receiving organization absorb and use the asset?
- **Sustainability**: Will the solution still make sense five years from now?

The Future of Work and the Implications for Megaproject Development

Technological Advancements and Automation

Technologies such as AI, machine learning (ML), robotics, and digital twins are reshaping the landscape of megaproject delivery. These advancements lead to increased automation, reducing human errors, enhancing productivity, and improving the accuracy of project designs and planning.

Pros:

- Efficiency and Precision: AI-powered systems can handle repetitive tasks with greater precision and speed, reducing delays and cost overruns. This makes AI every practitioner's copilot or coworker, as opposed to job displacer, across the board.
- Improved Safety: Automation of dangerous tasks, especially in construction, reduces on-site risks for workers.
- Data-Driven Decision Making: Digital twins, AI, and IoT enable real-time monitoring and predictive analytics, allowing for proactive decision making and risk mitigation.

Cons:

- Job Displacement: Automation may reduce the need for certain roles, leading to concerns about unemployment among traditional project workers.
- Skill Gaps: As advanced technologies become the norm, project professionals need upskilling, which may present challenges for mid-career professionals who struggle with digital transformation.

Remote Work and Collaboration Tools

The COVID-19 pandemic accelerated the adoption of remote work and virtual collaboration platforms like Zoom, Microsoft Teams, and project management tools such as Asana, Trello, and Primavera. These tools have enabled teams to collaborate on megaprojects across geographies.

Pros:

- Cost Reduction: Reducing the need for on-site presence cuts down travel and accommodation costs for professionals, especially in global projects.
- Access to Global Talent: Megaprojects can tap into a larger, more diverse talent pool without being constrained by location.
- Flexibility: Flexible work arrangements can improve employee satisfaction and work–life balance, reducing turnover.

Cons:

- Coordination Challenges: Remote work can lead to miscommunication and delays in decision making, especially in highly complex megaprojects.
- Limited On-Site Interaction: Megaprojects often require hands-on leadership and teamwork on the ground, making remote work less effective for certain tasks.
- Security Risks: Handling sensitive data over digital platforms increases the risk of cyberattacks and data breaches.

Changing Workforce Demographics

The workforce is becoming increasingly diverse, with a growing emphasis on inclusivity and multigenerational collaboration. Younger generations prioritize flexibility, sustainability, and purpose-driven work, while older professionals bring decades of experience but may require digital upskilling.

Pros:

- Innovation through Diversity: A diverse workforce brings fresh perspectives and creative problem-solving approaches.
- Mentorship Opportunities: Experienced professionals can mentor younger workers, passing on critical industry knowledge while adapting to new technologies themselves.

- Increased Focus on Sustainability: Younger generations tend to prioritize environmentally conscious practices, pushing megaprojects to adopt greener technologies and reduce their carbon footprint.

Cons:

- Intergenerational Conflicts: Different work styles and values between older and younger professionals can lead to friction and communication barriers.
- Training and Development Costs: Organizations may need to invest heavily in training programs to help workers adapt to new technologies and work models.

Sustainability and Environmental, Social, and Governance

As sustainability becomes a focal point, megaprojects must align with ESG principles. This trend reflects the global demand for projects that minimize environmental impacts and contribute positively to communities.

Pros:

- Regulatory Compliance and Reputation: Adhering to ESG principles helps companies avoid regulatory penalties and enhances their reputation with investors and stakeholders.
- Attracting Investors: Many investors prioritize projects that meet sustainability standards, making it easier to secure funding.
- Long-Term Savings: Sustainable design choices, such as energy-efficient infrastructure, may result in long-term cost savings for megaprojects.

Cons:

- Higher Upfront Costs: Implementing sustainable practices can increase initial project costs, particularly in terms of green technology and material sourcing.

- Complexity of Compliance: Navigating the global regulatory landscape of ESG standards adds layers of complexity to project planning and execution.

Project Professionals' Employability

With the future of work evolving, the employability of project professionals depends on their adaptability to technological changes, their soft skills, and continuous learning.

Skills in Demand:

- Digital Fluency: Knowledge of project management software, data analytics, and AI tools will be crucial for professionals to remain competitive.
- Soft Skills: Communication, leadership, and collaboration skills will become even more important as teams become more diverse and virtual.
- Specialization in Sustainability: As ESG standards become more central, project professionals with expertise in green technologies and sustainable design will be in high demand.

Challenges:

- Skills Obsolescence: Workers who do not continuously update their skill sets risk falling behind, especially as automation takes over more routine tasks.
- Global Competition: Remote work enables companies to hire talent from around the world, increasing competition for jobs.

Opportunities:

- Hybrid Roles: Professionals who can bridge the gap between technical expertise and managerial skills will be highly sought after.
- Lifelong Learning: Opportunities for continuous education through certifications, online courses, and on-the-job training allow professionals to stay relevant.

The future of work presents both opportunities and challenges for megaproject development. On the one hand, technological advancements and new work models increase effectiveness and efficiency, reduce costs, and expand access to global talent. On the other, they introduce complexities related to employability, project management, and ESG compliance. For project professionals, adaptability, upskilling, and embracing new ways of working are essential for thriving in this evolving landscape.

Embedding Systems Thinking in Evaluation

A recurring issue in post project reviews is the absence of systems thinking. Projects are evaluated in isolation, rather than as part of a wider network of processes, stakeholders, and evolving objectives. This reductionist view blinds leadership to critical interdependencies and unintended consequences.

Applying systems thinking forces project teams to ask broader questions:

- How will this project interact with adjacent systems?
- What organizational capabilities must evolve alongside this asset?
- How might success in one area create failure in another?

Embedding systems thinking into evaluation frameworks helps prevent projects from becoming technically successful but strategically irrelevant. In the next section, we bring together all the insights from this book, offering strategic guidance and actionable recommendations to project managers, practitioners, investors, and executives committed to delivering successful megaproject in an ever-evolving world.

Summary and Recommendations

Introduction

Megaprojects are ambitious, large-scale undertakings that command billions in investment, involve a vast network of stakeholders, and span extended timelines. Their significance is hard to overstate; they shape national economies, transform regional infrastructure, and influence long-term development patterns. Despite their potential to deliver transformational value, megaprojects often encounter pitfalls such as delays, cost overruns, and misalignment with intended outcomes. This section consolidates key insights from the previous chapters, highlighting critical considerations, systemic challenges, best practices, and practical recommendations to guide project professionals toward successful megaproject delivery.

Strategic Perspectives on Megaproject Development

The strategic importance of megaprojects lies in their potential to stimulate economic growth, support national objectives like energy independence and urban resilience, and meet global sustainability targets. These projects typically serve broader policy goals while also navigating intense public scrutiny. As such, their planning and execution demand a robust alignment between long-term vision and short-term deliverables. The involvement of governments, private investors, regulators, and communities amplifies the need for inclusive decision making and transparent stakeholder engagement from the outset.

Megaprojects are inherently complex. They require deep technical knowledge, coordination of diverse supply chains, and management of uncertainties ranging from regulatory delays to geopolitical risks. Successful delivery depends on maintaining organizational agility and investing in scenario planning that considers dynamic external forces such as political upheavals, commodity market shifts, and environmental constraints.

Evaluation Approaches

Robust evaluation is central to megaproject viability. This involves not just assessing financial returns but also social impact, technical feasibility, and risk exposure. Economic viability should be analyzed using both cost–benefit frameworks and broader economic modeling to assess indirect effects such as job creation, trade facilitation, and innovation spillovers.

Equally important is the evaluation of environmental and community impacts, especially under increasing regulatory and societal demands for ESG compliance.

Evaluation techniques such as MCDA, scenario-based modeling, and probabilistic risk assessment help project sponsors and evaluators balance multiple trade-offs. Post completion reviews, coupled with continuous monitoring and real-time performance tracking, are essential to deriving insights and refining future project frameworks.

Decision-Making Models and Enablers

Decision making in megaprojects is multitiered, spanning political, strategic, and operational levels. While some decisions are top-down due to governmental oversight or centralized investment strategies, modern project governance favors a collaborative model. This inclusive approach ensures that stakeholders are more committed to project outcomes and that risks and expectations are better shared.

Critical decisions such as greenlighting the project, choosing contracting structures, managing scope changes, or responding to execution risks must be informed by data and scenario simulations. Predictive analytics and AI are becoming indispensable for modeling potential disruptions and evaluating alternative decisions in near real time.

Challenges in the Field

The persistent challenges facing megaprojects include timeline slippages, budget blowouts, and community opposition. Schedule delays arise from regulatory bottlenecks, under resourced teams, or unforeseen environmental or site-related constraints. Cost overruns are frequently driven by scope creep, inaccurate forecasting, or inflationary pressures. These issues often originate in weak front-end planning or failure to anticipate external shocks.

In addition, growing environmental awareness and social activism have heightened scrutiny on project impacts. Projects that fail to account for ESG criteria early in development may face litigation, reputational damage, or funding withdrawal.

Best Practices for Megaproject Success

Successful megaprojects display a series of common traits:

First, front-end planning is rigorous and holistic. The use of structured frameworks, feasibility studies, and clearly articulated project objectives ensures alignment across teams and decision makers. Early investment in FEED often correlates with smoother downstream execution.

Second, sustained stakeholder collaboration is crucial. Continuous engagement through community consultations, investor briefings, and regulatory alignments reduces uncertainty and builds trust.

Third, an agile approach to project delivery helps manage dynamic environments. This doesn't mean abandoning structure, but rather embedding flexibility into contracts, designs, and execution plans so the project can pivot when necessary without compromising objectives.

Fourth, risk management is proactive rather than reactive. Projects with integrated risk governance models can identify early signals of trouble and take corrective action before risks become disruptions.

Fifth, technology integration transforms how teams operate. Tools like digital twins, AI-assisted planning, and real-time dashboards create transparency and enable evidence-based decisions at scale (Bolpagni et al. 2024).

Sixth, single point accountability for both the business outcome and the project outcome, and continuity of key people.

To ensure alignment between strategic intent and execution, it is critical to designate a clearly accountable individual who is empowered to make decisions and held responsible for overall results. Continuity in leadership, especially among key roles such as project sponsors, project managers, and technical leads, greatly enhances the ability to maintain focus and avoid knowledge loss during transitions.

Seventh, independent peer reviews. A project review is an appraisal conducted by a party external to the project to provide an outside perspective to the project owner and the team on the health of the project. An independent review before a project is authorized is a very important project quality assurance step.

These reviews can identify early warning signs, validate assumptions, and provide unbiased insights into potential risks and blind spots that internal teams may overlook. They also help improve transparency and credibility with stakeholders.

Eighth, early user (i.e., operations) involvement.

Engaging end-users, particularly from operations, from the early stages ensures that practical requirements are captured and that the final deliverables are usable and sustainable. Their input helps shape system design, user interfaces, and handover processes, leading to smoother transitions from project to operations.

Ninth, clear project goals and objectives, and an all-embracing success measures' definition prior to project start.

Success criteria must go beyond just being "on time and on budget." They should include operational performance, stakeholder satisfaction, sustainability, and long-term value creation. Establishing and documenting these from the outset enables objective tracking and reinforces accountability throughout the project life cycle.

Strategic Recommendations

To institutionalize these best practices, several actionable recommendations are proposed:

1. Implement IPD Models: These models bring all stakeholders such as engineers, contractors, clients, and financiers into a shared framework, fostering aligned incentives, reducing friction, and enhancing accountability across the project life cycle.
2. Prioritize Front-End Planning and FEED: Early investments in scope clarity, risk planning, and scenario testing prevent major missteps downstream.
3. Adopt Data Analytics and AI: These tools should be used not only for planning and monitoring but also for dynamic decision making during execution. Predictive analytics helps teams stay ahead of disruptions.
4. Embed ESG from Day One: Sustainable practices must be embedded in design, procurement, and operational strategies, not tacked on as compliance requirements.

5. Foster a Culture of Continuous Learning: Establish structured feed-back loops, knowledge transfers protocols, and postmortem reviews to carry insights into future initiatives.

Insights

Megaprojects are not just engineering endeavors; they are vehicles of transformation. Delivering them successfully requires more than capital and technical know-how. It demands visionary leadership, robust systems thinking, and a deep understanding of both human dynamics and technological potential. With disciplined planning, stakeholder alignment, and a commitment to innovation, megaprojects can transcend their historical reputation for failure and become benchmarks of sustainable development.

Case Study: Thames Tideway Tunnel

One of the best illustrations of these principles in practice is the Thames Tideway Tunnel in London. A £4.9 billion effort to overhaul the city's sewer system, the project exemplifies how digital tools and ESG alignment can redefine megaproject delivery.

The use of a real-time digital twin allowed engineers and planners to simulate stress conditions, track progress with precision, and identify risks before they materialized. Predictive analytics supported proactive scheduling, resource optimization, and coordination across multiple teams. As a result, the project remained largely on track despite its complexity and urban constraints. The integration of environmental safeguards and community transparency reinforced public support and regulatory compliance.

This case study demonstrates that the right combination of technology, strategy, and leadership can convert complexity into opportunity and set new standards for how the world's most ambitious projects are delivered.

Call to Action

As we conclude this exploration of megaproject development, evaluation, and decision making, the need for decisive action has never been more urgent. The global stakes are high, megaprojects shape nations, industries, and societies. Their failures leave scars; their successes leave legacies. This final section is a direct call to project leaders, business executives, investors, policymakers, engineers, and planners to step beyond theoretical best practices and commit to transformative action.

Embrace Comprehensive Integrated Planning and Stakeholder Engagement

Every successful megaproject begins with vision but thrives on detail. Leaders must prioritize rigorous front-end planning to anticipate challenges, model uncertainties, and establish clear objectives. This stage should not be rushed or bypassed. It forms the foundation for everything that follows. Equally important is intensive stakeholder engagement. True stakeholder integration, across government, private sector, community representatives, and environmental regulators ensures legitimacy, social license, and shared ownership of outcomes. When stakeholders are heard early and often, resistance gives way to collaboration.

Implement Rigorous Evaluation Frameworks

Megaprojects must be evaluated not only for their economic impact but also for their social, environmental, and strategic alignment. This demands a consistent evaluation framework, combining cost–benefit analysis with performance metrics and environmental assessments. Real-time dashboards and feedback mechanisms should enable ongoing evaluation, not just postcompletion review. Projects that embed evaluation into their DNA create a culture of accountability and transparency, where performance is continuously optimized and insights are captured.

Foster Innovation and Adaptability

The world is evolving and megaprojects must evolve with it. Innovation is no longer a luxury; it's a prerequisite. From AI-assisted planning to autonomous equipment and digital twin technology, the toolkit for innovation is expanding. But adopting technology alone is not enough. Teams must also embrace adaptability, an ability to change course when data signals new risks or opportunities. In an age of volatility, rigid project models fail. Agile governance, scenario planning, and iterative delivery models are essential to resilience.

Strengthen Decision-Making Processes

Better decisions yield better outcomes. Yet too many projects suffer from indecision, opaque reasoning, or politically driven interference. Decision-making frameworks must be transparent, evidence-based, and inclusive. Decisions should be made at the right levels, by people equipped with the right data, context, and authority. The use of predictive analytics and AI can supplement human judgment with real-time forecasts, while digital governance platforms can track accountability and rationale. Trust is built when decisions are made and communicated clearly.

Promote Sustainability and Long-Term Value

No megaproject should be seen in isolation from its impact on the planet and people. Sustainability must be embedded from design through decommissioning. Environmental stewardship, social equity, and governance transparency must guide procurement, construction, and operations. Projects that prioritize ESG considerations attract investor confidence, public support, and regulatory favor. But more importantly, they generate enduring value, leaving behind not just infrastructure but societal advancement (Srivastava and Narayan 2024).

Invest in Capacity Building and Knowledge Sharing

The future of megaprojects lies in the hands of those who lead and execute them. Investing in people is therefore paramount. Capacity building must go beyond technical training to include leadership development, cross-disciplinary education, and cultural competence. Organizations should also foster open knowledge ecosystems, where lessons learned, case studies, and performance data are shared across projects and organizations. The creation of institutional memory is vital to breaking cycles of repeated mistakes.

A Final Word: The Moment Is Now

Megaprojects are more than construction efforts; they are commitments to the future. They reflect our ambition, our values, and our ability to collaborate across divides. The world today faces complex challenges from climate change and digital disruption to urbanization and resource scarcity. Megaprojects can be tools of progress or symbols of waste. The difference lies in leadership, discipline, and the willingness to act boldly and wisely.

Let this be a call to project sponsors to fund what matters and walk away from what doesn't. Let it be a call to engineers to demand integrity in design. Let it be a call to communities to raise their voices and shape what is built around them. Let it be a call to governments to align infrastructure with the common good. And above all, let it be a call to every project practitioner to build not just structures but legacies.

The time to transform megaproject management is not tomorrow; it is NOW.

This book began with a simple premise: that megaprojects, despite their complexity and risk, can be delivered successfully with the right mindset, processes, and tools. Along the way, we've explored each critical stage from opportunity assessment to the FID, dissected best practices, exposed pitfalls, and illuminated pathways to more resilient and impactful project outcomes.

However, the journey does not end here. Megaprojects will continue to evolve, shaped by innovation, climate imperatives, shifting geopolitics, and societal expectations. What remains constant is the responsibility of those who frame, plan, fund, lead, and execute these monumental endeavors. This book is both a guide and a challenge: to approach each megaproject not just as a task to complete but as an opportunity to shape a better, smarter, and more equitable future.

Let us not simply manage megaprojects; let us lead them with foresight, integrity, and purpose.

Reflection Questions

1. How can megaproject teams maintain alignment with strategic business goals throughout the execution phase, especially when facing dynamic external changes?
2. What are the potential ethical, operational, and organizational challenges of integrating AI into megaproject environments, and how should these be addressed during project planning?
3. In what ways does the future of work—including technological change, remote collaboration, and demographic shifts—reshape how megaprojects are staffed, managed, and delivered?

APPENDIXES

Appendix I: Basis of Schedule Template

1. *Project Overview*
   - Project Name:
   - Project ID:
   - Location:
   - Project Stage:
   - Prepared By/Date:
2. *Schedule Objective*
   - Describe the purpose of the schedule (e.g., planning, baseline, control).
   - Clarify what the schedule is intended to represent (e.g., full project life cycle, execution Stage only).
3. *Schedule Scope and Level*
   - Define the scope covered (e.g., engineering, procurement, construction, commissioning).
   - Detail the work breakdown structure (WBS) levels included.
   - Indicate the level of detail used (e.g., activity durations, resource-loaded or not).
4. *Assumptions*
   - Highlight critical assumptions (e.g., labor availability, site access, regulatory approvals).
   - Note any assumed start and finish dates for major Stages.

5. *Key Milestones*

Milestone name	Target date	Notes
Final Investment Decision (FID)	[Date]	Executive approval required
Construction Start	[Date]	Subject to permit readiness
Mechanical Completion	[Date]	Commissioning readiness
Commercial Operation	[Date]	Start of revenue generation

6. *Schedule Constraints*
   - External constraints (e.g., permit dates, seasonal impacts, third-party dependencies)
   - Internal constraints (e.g., budget limits, workforce caps)
7. *Methodology and Tools*
   - Software used (e.g., Primavera P6, MS Project)
   - Critical path methodology, rolling wave planning, and so on
   - Update frequency and control processes
8. *Productivity and Duration Basis*
   - Basis of activity durations (historical data, vendor input, benchmarks)
   - Crew productivity assumptions and labor productivity metrics
9. *Risk and Contingency*
   - Summary of risk-adjusted durations (if applicable)
   - Inclusion of float, buffer times, or contingency logic
10. *Interfaces and Integration*
    - Description of how interfaces with other schedules (e.g., contractors, vendors, operations) are managed and synchronized.
11. *Approval and Change Control*
    - Sign-off responsibilities for schedule versions
    - Process for schedule changes and baseline resets

Appendix II: Sample Basis of Cost Estimate Template

Section	Details
Project Name	[Insert Project Title]
Project Description	[Brief overview of project scope and objectives]
Estimate Class and Accuracy Range	[Class 2/Class 3] per AACE or industry classification
Date of Estimate	[MM/DD/YYYY]
Currency	[e.g., USD]
Exchange Rate Assumptions	[If applicable]
Scope Basis	[Reference to scope documents and drawings used]
Key Assumptions	• Project start date • Market conditions • Labor productivity
Exclusions	[List any costs intentionally excluded from the estimate]
Methodology Used	[Bottom-up, parametric, analogous, vendor quotes, etc.]
Contingency	[e.g., 10% based on Monte Carlo simulation or risk assessment]
Escalation Factors and Methodology	[Annual escalation rates and how applied]
Benchmarking/Validation	[Any comparisons done with past similar projects or industry standards]
Risks Considered	[Reference to risk register or sensitivity analyses performed]
Estimate Prepared By	[Name/Role/Department]
Estimate Reviewed By	[Name/Date/Role]

Appendix III: Sample Terms of Reference for Independent Evaluation

Section	Details
Project Name	[Insert Project Title]
Project Stage	[e.g., Pre-FEED, FEED, Execution Readiness, Final Investment Decision]
Review Title	[e.g., Independent Evaluation for FID Readiness]
Date of Review	[Planned date or review period]
Review Sponsor	[Name of sponsoring organization or individual]
Purpose of the Review	[Clearly define the objective: e.g., to evaluate technical completeness, strategic alignment, financial robustness, etc.]
Scope of Review	• Technical Readiness • Cost Estimate Validity • Schedule Maturity • Risk Management Strategy • Governance and Decision Protocols
Review Criteria/ Questions	• Does the project align with strategic priorities? • Are key risks identified and mitigated? • Is the cost estimate credible? • Is the team organizationally and technically prepared?
Review Team Composition	[List of subject matter experts and roles, internal–external mix if applicable]
Methodology	• Document review • Interviews with project team • Site visits (if required) • Benchmarking against similar projects
Deliverables	• Final Evaluation Report • Summary of Findings • Recommendations • Presentation to executive leadership
Timeline and Milestones	[Key dates from kickoff to final report delivery]
Confidentiality Requirements	[Disclosure restrictions, if applicable]
Points of Contact	[Names and contact info of coordinators and leads]

Appendix IV: Minimum Requirements of the Project Execution Plan

The Project Execution Plan (PEP) is the master document that defines how a megaproject will be executed, monitored, and controlled. It integrates the strategic, technical, commercial, and operational dimensions of project delivery into a unified framework. To be effective, the PEP must meet a set of minimum content requirements that ensure clarity, alignment, and readiness across all functions. The following outlines the essential components that a comprehensive PEP should address:

1. Executive Summary
   - Overview of the project objectives, scope, and critical success factors
   - Summary of execution strategy and major milestones
2. Project Scope Definition
   - Clearly defined boundaries, deliverables, exclusions, and interface points
   - Breakdown of scope by work packages, systems, or components
3. Organizational Structure and Governance
   - Detailed project organization chart with roles and responsibilities
   - Governance framework including reporting lines, decision rights, and approval protocols
4. Execution Strategy and Methodology
   - Contracting and procurement strategy
   - Construction philosophy (modularization, site works, SIMOPS, etc.)
   - Logistics and supply chain strategy

5. Integrated Project Schedule
   - Detailed Level 2 or 3 schedule with milestones and critical path
   - Schedule control approach and progress measurement system
   - Linkages to long-lead items, permitting, and commissioning
6. Cost and Budget Control
   - Approved budget baseline with contingency allocation
   - Cost control methodology and change management framework
   - Basis of Estimate (BoE) and cost reporting structure
7. Risk Management Plan
   - Risk register summary with quantified impact assessments
   - Risk mitigation plans and assigned ownership
   - Integration with contingency planning and decision gates
8. Quality Management Framework
   - Quality objectives, assurance strategy, and inspection/testing plans
   - Compliance requirements with standards, specifications, and certifications
9. Health, Safety, and Environmental (HSE) Plan
   - HSE strategy, KPIs, hazard identification, and control measures
   - Emergency response protocols and site safety culture programs
10. Resource and Workforce Planning
    - Manpower curve by discipline
    - Key resource availability and mobilization strategy
    - Labor relations and training requirements
11. Interface and Stakeholder Management
    - Identification and management of technical and organizational interfaces
    - Stakeholder engagement strategy and communication protocols
12. Project Controls and Reporting
    - Integrated cost-schedule-performance management approach
    - Earned Value Management System (EVMS), KPIs, and dashboard reporting
13. Commissioning and Start-Up Strategy
    - Systemization plan, turnover philosophy, and readiness criteria
    - Interface with operations and transition to steady state

14. Information and Document Management
    ○ Control of project documentation, revision control, and digital platforms
    ○ Data handover protocols and archiving standards
15. Lessons Learned and Continuous Improvement
    ○ Feedback mechanisms, review cycles, and integration of lessons learned
    ○ Planned knowledge capture and transfer initiatives

Note: The PEP should be a living document updated through the project life cycle. It must be tailored to the specific project context, stakeholder expectations, and prevailing external conditions. Adherence to these minimum requirements ensures that the execution plan is not just a document but a disciplined roadmap for delivery.

Appendix V: Scope of Work and Estimate Summary Template

Project Title:
    Project Name:
    Project Manager:
    Prepared by:
    Date:

Version History

Version	Date	Comments
1.0		

1. Context

Provide brief background information, business environment, or need that gave rise to the project.

2. Key Business Objective Addressed by the Project

Summarize the strategic or operational business objectives this project aims to fulfill.

3. Project Objectives

Overall:
    [What is the overarching aim of the project?]
    Specific:
    [List specific goals.]
    Excludes:
    [Clarify what is NOT part of the project.]

4. Project Deliverables

List all major deliverables the project is expected to produce.

5. Project Budget

Specify the requested budget and include projected cash flow if needed.

6. Business Value

Explain how the project contributes to business value—financial, operational, strategic.

7. Completion and Success Criteria

Define what "success" looks like and how project completion is determined.

8. Schedule and Milestones

Schedule:
    [Outline project timeline.]
    Milestones:
    [List critical checkpoints or delivery points.]

9. Assumptions

Note key technical, operational, or stakeholder assumptions.

10. External Dependencies and Constraints

List key factors that are external to the project but critical to its success.

11. Statutory, Regulatory, HR, and HSEC Considerations

Identify any legal, safety, HR, or regulatory requirements.

12. Communication Plan

Describe how updates, risks, and changes will be communicated across stakeholders.

13. Change Management Plan

Specify how project scope or execution changes will be tracked and approved.

14. IP Considerations

State intellectual property ownership, licenses, or confidentiality expectations.

15. Authorization and Approval

Name | Role | Date | Signature
    Project Manager
    Project Sponsor
    VP/GM (if needed)
The above signatures confirm alignment and formal approval of the scope and execution plan.

Appendix VI: Change Management Template

1. Change Overview and Tracking

Project Name	
Change ID	
Date Logged	
Change Title/Description	
Initiator Name/Role	
Change Category (Scope/Schedule/Budget/Other)	

2. Impact Assessment

Impact on Budget (original versus revised)	
Impact on Timeline (milestones affected)	
Impact on Resources (manpower, tools, tech)	
Impact on Risk Profile (new or changed risks)	
Impact on Stakeholders (internal/external)	
Impact on Regulatory/Compliance Issues	

3. Stakeholder Communication Plan

Stakeholder Group	
Communication Method (e-mail, meetings, etc.)	
Communication Frequency	
Responsible Party for Communication	

4. Change Action Plan

Action Steps	
Assigned To	
Start Date	
End Date	
Resources Required	

5. Approval and Authorization

Name	Role	Approval Date	Signature

6. Monitoring and Post change Review

Has the Change Been Implemented? (Y/N)	
Was the Change Effective? (Qualitative Review)	
Lessons Learned	
Follow-Up Actions Required	
Reviewed By/Date	

Appendix VII: Risk Register Template with Descriptions

Field	Description	Input
Risk ID	Unique identifier for each risk.	
Risk Classification	Categorize the risk (e.g., Financial, Technical, Legal, Environmental).	
Risk Description	A concise summary of the risk being identified.	
Causes	Describe the underlying reasons or triggers for this risk.	
Consequences	Outline the potential impact if the risk materializes.	
Risk Owner	Person or role responsible for monitoring and managing the risk.	
Inherent Risk (Likelihood/ Consequence)	Risk level before any controls are applied.	
Residual Risk (Likelihood/ Consequence)	Expected risk level after control measures are applied.	
Response Strategy	Selected approach (e.g., Avoid, Mitigate, Transfer, Accept).	
Control Measures	Actions or controls implemented to manage the risk.	
Status	Current state of the risk (e.g., Open, Monitoring, Closed).	
Review Date	Next scheduled review or update for this risk.	

Appendix VIII: Procedure Template

TABLE OF CONTENTS

1. Purpose

State the reason this procedure exists. What objective does it aim to achieve?

2. Scope

Define the scope: where, when, and to whom this procedure applies.

3. Definitions

List and define any terms or acronyms used in this document.

4. Requirements

Specify the requirements to be met before or during the procedure.

5. Responsibilities

Outline who is responsible for each part of the process.

6. Instructions

Detail the steps required to execute this procedure, divided into subsections.

6.1 Change Requests

Describe how to initiate and submit a change request.

6.2 Evaluation of Schedule and Cost Impact

Explain the method for analyzing schedule and cost implications.

6.3 Review and Approval

Define the process for reviewing and approving the proposed changes.

6.4 Control Documentation

Explain how documentation is to be maintained and updated.

7. Attachments

List any forms, templates, or supporting documentation attached to this procedure.

Appendix IX: Board Investment Request Template

1. Investment Title

Provide the formal title of the investment, including location and type (e.g., commodity, asset class).

2. Summary of Investment

Briefly describe the investment opportunity, what it delivers, and the reason for this request.

3. Strategic Alignment

Explain how the investment aligns with the overall company strategy or growth areas. Discuss the "Why invest and why now?" question.

4. Investment Stages and Approval Sought

Specify the Stage (e.g., Optimization to Definition, Definition to Execution) and exact approval being requested.

5. Investment Amount

Total amount requested and any Stage breakdown.

6. Milestones and Timelines

List key milestones, expected completion date, and steady-state operations timing.

7. Valuation Summary

Include Net Present Value (NPV), IRR, Payback Period, and sensitivity summary.

8. Risk Summary

Highlight key risks (operational, market, SHSEC) and proposed mitigations.

9. Expected Returns and Payback

Summarize the expected financial returns, ROI, and timeframe for payback.

10. Key Partners/Operators

List all major partners and their ownership shares post-investment.

11. Portfolio Financial Impact (if applicable)

Outline any material impact to overall earnings, gearing, or financial ratios.

12. Attachments

Reference any supporting documents such as cost curves, market studies, or financial models.

Appendix X: Schedule and Cost Assurance Review (SCAR) Template

1. Project Overview

Project Name:	
Stage:	
Reason for Review:	
Date of Review:	

2. Documents Reviewed

List all documents reviewed during the SCAR process:

3. Summary of Key Findings

Summarize major findings and opportunities discovered during the SCAR.

4. Schedule Summary

Work Area/ Package	Previous Schedule	Current Schedule	Review Team Summary

5. Cost Summary

Work Area/ Package	Previous Estimate	Current Estimate	Review Team Summary

6. Schedule and Cost Risk Events and Uncertainties

Risk/Uncertainty	Probability of Occurrence	Impacted Area

7. Schedule and Cost Performance Opportunities

List identified opportunities that could improve schedule or cost performance.

8. Recommendations

State recommended Schedule and Cost KPIs, along with any qualifying conditions.

9. Inclusion to the Work Plan

List key activities to be added or emphasized based on review findings. Note disagreements, if any.

10. Approval

Reviewer Name and Signature:	
Date:	

Appendix XI: Project Dashboard Template

1. Project Snapshot

Project Name:	
Stage:	
Review Date:	
Overall Status:	
Project Manager:	

2. Key Risks and Issues

Risk/Issue	Impact	Mitigation/Action

3. Schedule Overview

Planned Completion Date:	
Actual/Forecast Completion Date:	
Schedule Variance:	

4. Financial Overview

Item	Planned (US$M)	Actual/Forecast (US$M)
Total Budget		
Cost to Date		
Forecast at Completion		

5. Key Milestones (Planned Versus Actual)

Milestone	Planned Date	Actual Date

6. Performance KPIs

KPI	Threshold	Target	Current

7. Endorsements/Sign-Offs

Reviewer Name and Signature:	
Date:	

Appendix XII: Project Initiation Template

1. Project Overview

Project Name:
   Project Stage:
   Project Manager:
   Start Date:
   End Date:
   Project Sponsor:

2. Objectives

Summarize the key objectives of the project. What is this project trying to achieve?

3. Business Case Summary

Briefly explain the rationale for the project. Why is this investment being made?

4. Project Scope

Describe the scope of work, what is included and what is excluded.

5. Stakeholders and Governance

List key stakeholders and governance structure.

- Executive Sponsor:
- Steering Committee:
- Key Departments or Partners:

6. Timeline and Key Milestones

List key milestones and their planned dates.

7. Budget Overview

Total Estimated Budget:
Funding Source:
Initial Budget Breakdown (if available):

8. Assumptions and Constraints

Identify critical assumptions and known constraints impacting the project.

9. Risks and Dependencies

Summarize initial risks and project dependencies.

10. Project Team

List core team members and their roles.

- Name—Role
- Name—Role

11. Approvals

Provide signature fields for formal approval.

Project Manager:

Signature: _____ Date: _____

Project Sponsor:

Signature: _____ Date: _____

Appendix XIII: Project Planning Template

1. Project Summary

Provide a concise summary of the project, its background, and purpose.

2. Planning Objectives

Define the key planning goals (e.g., schedule adherence, cost control, scope clarity).

3. Scope Statement

Detail the in-scope and out-of-scope elements of the project.

4. Work Breakdown Structure (WBS)

Describe the high-level WBS or reference an appendix where it is detailed.

5. Schedule Management Plan

Summarize the key Stages, deliverables, and timeline. Include Gantt reference if available.

6. Cost Management Plan

Provide budget planning, baseline estimates, and cost control measures.

7. Risk Management Plan

Summarize the approach to identifying, analyzing, and managing risks.

8. Resource Plan

Outline human and material resources, roles, and responsibilities, and years of relevant experience.

9. Quality Management Plan

Define quality targets and how compliance will be ensured.

10. Communication Plan

Specify how information will be shared among stakeholders and frequency.

11. Procurement Plan

Describe procurement strategy if applicable (materials, vendors, contracts).

12. Change Management Approach

Define how project scope/schedule/cost changes will be evaluated and approved.

13. Project Control and Reporting

Explain how progress will be monitored and reported, including KPIs.

14. Approvals

Project Manager:

    Signature: _____ Date: _____

    Project Sponsor:

    Signature: _____ Date: _____

Appendix XIV: Gate Requirements Template

1. Concept Stage

List the required deliverables for this Stage and their current status.

Deliverable Name	Owner/Responsible Party	Status	Notes

2. Optimization Stage

List the required deliverables for this Stage and their current status.

Deliverable Name	Owner/Responsible Party	Status	Notes

3. Definition Stage

List the required deliverables for this Stage and their current status.

Deliverable Name	Owner/Responsible Party	Status	Notes

4. Execution Stage

List the required deliverables for this Stage and their current status.

Deliverable Name	Owner/Responsible Party	Status	Notes

5. Commissioning and Handover/Transition to Operations

List the required deliverables for this Stage and their current status, including pre-start-up safety review (PSSR) timing, regulatory reviews/approvals status, and so on.

Deliverable Name	Owner/Responsible Party	Status	Notes

Appendix XV: Lesson Learned Template

Project Information

Project Name:	
Team/Category:	
Session Date and Location:	

Attendees

List all attendees including company and job title.

Lessons Learned

Item	Comment	+/Δ	Impact	Impact Level (H/M/L)	Recommendation	Action by and Date

Notes and Guidelines

- The symbol + indicates something done well and worth repeating.
- The symbol Δ indicates an opportunity area for improvement.
- Impact level should reflect how critical the issue was to project outcome (high, medium, or low).
- Be objective, constructive, and specific in all entries.
- This session is for learning and improvement, not for assigning blame.

Appendix XVI: Monthly Report Template

1. Executive Summary

Subsection	Details/Input
Highlights and Overall Perspective	
Issues Summary/Resolution	

2. SHSEC (Security, Health, Safety, Environment, and Community)

Subsection	Details/Input
Statistics and Incidents	
Improvements	

3. Schedule and Progress

Subsection	Details/Input
General	
Schedule	
Progress Performance Summary Report	
Issues Summary/Resolution	

4. Cost Performance

Subsection	Details/Input
General	
Cost Performance Summary Report	
Change Management	
Contingency Drawdown Status	
Issues Summary/Resolution	

5. Engineering

Subsection	Details/Input
Work Accomplished This Month	
Work Planned for Next Month	
Issues Summary/Resolution	

6. Procurement (Contracts and Supply Services)

Subsection	Details/Input
Work Accomplished This Month	
Work Planned for Next Month	
Issues Summary/Resolution	

7. Construction and Commissioning

Subsection	Details/Input
Work Accomplished this Month	
Work Planned for Next Month	
Issues Summary/Resolution	

8. Owner's Activities

Subsection	Details/Input
Consulting Services	
Staffing	

9. Current Site Photographs

Subsection	Details/Input
[Attach visuals or paste images here]	

References

Acqirc Research Group. 2024. *The Future of Megaproject Management: Execution Readiness and Gate Assurance.* Technical Report. Acqirc Research Group. https://acqirc.org/publications/research/the-future-of-megaproject-management/.

Alavi, Maryam, and Dorothy E. Leidner. 2001. "Review: Knowledge Management and Knowledge Management Systems: Conceptual Foundations and Research Issues." *MIS Quarterly* 25 (1): 107–136.

Alotaibi, Fahad S., and Subir Ghosh. 2023. "Strategic Execution Alignment in Complex Projects: A Case-Based Analysis." *Journal of Management in Engineering* 39 (5): 04023076.

Alqershy, Mohammad T., Qian Shi, and Feng Zhang. 2024. "Exploring Governance Mechanisms in Megaprojects: A Mixed-Methods Systematic Review." *Engineering Management Journal* 37 (1): 1–24.

Argote, Linda, and Ella Miron-Spektor. 2011. "Organizational Learning: From Experience to Knowledge." *Organization Science* 22 (5): 1123–1137.

Bakke, Christina, and Anders Johansen. 2025. "Integrating Target Value Delivery and Front-End Planning in Industrial Megaprojects." *IOP Conference Series: Earth and Environmental Science* 1172 (1): 012019.

Baroudi, Bassem, and Claire Jackson. 2023. "Independent Project Evaluations as Governance Instruments in Megaprojects." *International Journal of Managing Projects in Business* 16 (4): 870–890.

Bolpagni, Matteo, Angelo Luigi Camillo Ciribini, and Alessandro Bruttini. 2024. "Digital Twins and Decision-Making in Infrastructure Megaprojects." *Journal of Construction Engineering and Management* 150 (3): 04023105.

Brookes, Naomi J., and Giorgio Locatelli. 2015. "Power Plants as Megaprojects: Using Empirics to Shape Policy, Planning, and Construction Management." *Utilities Policy* 36: 57–66.

Chen, Liang, and Qiang Zhang. 2024. "Front-End Engineering Design and Project Success in Large-Scale EPC Projects." *Engineering Management Journal* 36 (1): 22–34.

Cheng, Jackson W., and Mohan M. Kumaraswamy. 2024. "Schedule Integration and Control Strategies in Large-Scale Infrastructure Projects." *Construction Management and Economics* 42 (1): 25–40.

Chih, Ying-Yi, and Ofer Zwikael. 2023. "Reframing Project Success: Beyond the Iron Triangle." *International Journal of Managing Projects in Business* 16 (2): 212–229.

Cottafava, D., Corazza, L., Shams Esfandabadi, Z., & Torchia, D. (2024). "Megaprojects from the Lens of Business and Management Studies: A Systematic Literature Review." *Journal of Public Affairs*, 24(3), e2937

Davenport, Thomas H., and Laurence Prusak. 1998. *Working Knowledge: How Organizations Manage What They Know.* Harvard Business Press.

Davis, Kevin. 2023. "Effective Stakeholder Engagement in Major Projects: Learning from Failure." *International Journal of Project Management* 41 (2): 145–158.

Denicol, Juliano, Andrew Davies, and Ilias Krystallis. 2023. "What Are the Causes and Cures of Poor Megaproject Performance?" *Project Management Journal* 54 (1): 27–45.

Esposito, Giovanni, and Andrea Terlizzi. 2023. "Governing Wickedness in Megaprojects." *Policy & Society* 42 (2): 131–147.

Flyvbjerg, Bent. 2023. *The Power of Strategic Misrepresentation in Megaproject Decision Making.* Oxford University Press.

Garemo, Nils, Magnus Hjerpe, and Jan Mischke. 2023. *A Value Assurance Framework for Megaprojects.* McKinsey Global Infrastructure Report.

Ghazali, Norhayati H., and Shazlin M. Hassan. 2023. "Quantitative Risk Mitigation in Construction Megaprojects: A Review of Simulation Practices." *Journal of Construction Engineering and Management* 149 (10): 04023080.

Haiyirete, Xuekelaiti, Xiaochang Gan, and Jian Wang. 2024. "Research on Safety Decision-Making Behavior in Megaprojects." *Systems* 12 (8): 315.

Hosseini, Amin, and Ahmed M. Farid. 2025. "A Hetero-Functional Graph Theory Perspective of Engineering Management of Mega-Projects." *arXiv.* https://arxiv.org/abs/2505.24045.

Ika, Lavagnon A., Peter E. Love, and Jeffrey K. Pinto. 2024. "Before You Start Managing That Major Project: What You Should Know About Cost Overruns and Benefit Shortfalls." In *Mastering Project Leadership*, edited by Lavagnon A. Ika and Jeffrey K. Pinto. Routledge.

Jefferies, Marcus, and Steve Rowlinson. 2024. "Embedding ESG Principles in Megaproject Delivery: Strategies for Social Responsibility." *Journal of Cleaner Production* 432: 138945.

Kwak, Young Hoon, Jin Park, and Biswajit Y. Chung. 2023. "Governance and Strategic Discipline in Megaproject Execution: Empirical Insights from Public-Private Partnerships." *Engineering, Construction and Architectural Management* 30 (8): 2754–2771.

Kwak, Young Hoon, Jin Park, Biswajit Y. Chung, and Subir Ghosh. 2024. "Strategic Alignment in Megaproject Mergers: A Systems Integration Perspective." *International Journal of Project Management* 42 (1): 25–39.

Lehtonen, Markku, and Martin de Jong. 2024. "Regulatory Dynamics and Megaproject Adaptation." *Policy and Society* 43 (1): 88–103.

Levitt, Raymond E. 2012. "Innovation in Megaprojects: Systems Integration at the Boundary." *Engineering Project Organization Journal* 2 (1–2): 1–12.

Lewis, James P. 2001. *Project Planning, Scheduling, & Control: A Hands-On Guide to Bringing Projects in on Time and on Budget.* 3rd ed. McGraw-Hill.

Li, Qi, Xiaodong Zhang, and Yan Wang. 2023. "Artificial Intelligence in Construction Project Management: Trends, Applications, and Challenges." *Automation in Construction* 154: 105004.

Li, Yongkui, Mengqi Wang, Giorgio Locatelli, and Yueran Zhang. 2024. "Navigating the Future of Megaprojects Sustainability: A Comprehensive Framework and Research Agendas." *International Journal of Managing Projects in Business* 17 (3): 533–561.

Lindner, Felix, and Georg Schreyögg. 2024. "Organizational Culture Clashes in Post-Merger Infrastructure Integration." *International Review of Administrative Sciences* 90 (1): 88–106.

Liu, Shiyuan, Ruoyu Jin, Yifan Zhang, and Chen Wang. 2023. "A Lifecycle Approach to Digital Integration in Megaproject Planning." *International Journal of Project Management* 41 (3): 211–226.

Locatelli, Giorgio, Giulio Mariani, Tiziano Sainati, and Marco Greco. 2017. "Corruption in Public Projects and Megaprojects: There Is an Elephant in the Room!" *International Journal of Project Management* 35 (3): 191–204.

Love, Peter E. D., Deepak Mistry, and Jane Matthews. 2023. "Opportunity Management in Complex Megaprojects." *Engineering, Construction and Architectural Management* 30 (2): 400–418.

Malekpour, Shirin, Warren E. Walker, Franziska J. de Haan, Niki Frantzeskaki, and Vincent A. W. J. Marchau. 2020. "Bridging Decision Making Under Deep Uncertainty (DMDU) and Transition Management to Improve Strategic Planning for Sustainable Development." *Environmental Science & Policy* 108: 1–12.

Marques, Guilherme, and António Monteiro. 2024. "Scheduling Maturity and Integrated Control in Industrial EPC Delivery." *International Journal of Project Organisation and Management* 16 (1): 47–61.

Martins, João P., and Filipe T. da Silva. 2024. "Integrative Frameworks for Megaproject Planning: Bridging Strategy and Operations." *Journal of Construction Engineering and Management* 150 (1): 04023091.

Meredith, Jack R., and Samuel J. Mantel. 2000. *Project Management: A Managerial Approach.* John Wiley & Sons.

Merrow, E. W. (2024). *Industrial megaprojects* (2nd ed.). Wiley. ISBN 978-1-394-22223-1

Miller, Roger, and Brian Hobbs. 2024. "Execution Strategies in Large Infrastructure Projects: A Lifecycle Governance Perspective." *International Journal of Project Management* 42 (1): 35–49.

Miller, Roger, and Christopher Waller. 2024. "Mapping Systemic Risks in Infrastructure Megaprojects." *Journal of Risk Analysis and Management* 36 (2): 143–160.

Müller, Ralf, and Rodney Turner. 2023. "Governance Frameworks for Large-Scale Projects: Comparative Insights." *Project Management Journal* 54 (1): 30–44.

National Audit Office. 2025. *Lessons Learned: Governance and Decision-Making on Megaprojects.* UK Government Press.

Nguyen, Thanh H., and Le-Hoai Luu. 2024. "Collaborative Practices in Megaproject Execution Planning: Lessons from Infrastructure Development in Southeast Asia." *International Journal of Project Organisation and Management* 16 (2): 112–129.

Nonaka, Ikujiro, and Hirotaka Takeuchi. 1995. *The Knowledge-Creating Company: How Japanese Companies Create the Dynamics of Innovation.* Oxford University Press.

Odeck, James, and Morten Welde. 2023. "Macroeconomic Variability and Its Effect on Infrastructure Investment Decisions." *Transport Reviews* 43 (2): 205–221.

Okafor, Tochukwu, and Adriaan van der Merwe. 2024. "Stakeholder Alignment and Social License in Energy Infrastructure Delivery." *Project Management Journal* 55 (2): 79–92.

Papadonikolaki, Eleni, and Zhen Liu. 2023. "Integrating Digital Innovation in Infrastructure Megaprojects." *Automation in Construction* 153: 104775.

Patel, Sanjay, and Andrew Davies. 2023. "Financial Modeling Under Uncertainty in Capital-Intensive M&A Deals." *Journal of Corporate Finance* 78: 102620.

Priemus, Hugo, and Bert van Wee. 2022. "Strategic Decision Making in Complex Infrastructure Projects." *Transport Policy* 120: 78–86.

Rahman, Faisal, and Dominique Thibault. 2023. "Better Decisions Through Evidence-Based Evaluation in Project Governance." *Project Decision Analytics* 3 (2): 101–118.

Schindler, Markus, and Klaus Lüthje. 2024. "Evaluation Transparency and Board Accountability in Complex Capital Projects." *Journal of Strategic Infrastructure Studies* 12 (1): 33–48.

Senge, Peter M. 2006. *The Fifth Discipline: The Art & Practice of the Learning Organization.* Rev. ed. Currency/Doubleday.

Smith, James, and Hannah Lee. 2025. "The Dark Legacy of Megaprojects: A Case of Local Disengagement." *Environmental Impact Assessment Review* 98: 106958.

Srivastava, Pranav, and Sandeep Narayan. 2024. "Sustainability Integration in Megaproject Governance: A Stakeholder-Centric Model." *Sustainable Development* 32 (1): 89–105.

Sullivan, David R. 2023. "Project Execution Planning in Capital-Intensive Industries: A Systems Approach." *International Journal of Project Management* 41 (2): 103–119.

Turner, Mark, and Srinivas Kalidindi. 2021. "Innovation in Megaproject Delivery: A Systematic Review." *International Journal of Innovation Management* 25 (2): 2150016.

Turner, Rodney, and Steve Simister. 2023. "Integrating Technical Due Diligence in Energy Sector M&A Transactions." *Project Leadership and Society* 5: 100119.

van Marrewijk, Alfons, and Kathelijne Smits. 2023. "Megaprojects and the Legacy Challenge: Long-Term Thinking in Project Governance." *Journal of Management in Engineering* 39 (3): 05023001.

Ward, Stephen, and Chris Chapman. 2024. "Risk and Uncertainty in Megaprojects: Conceptual Frameworks and Practical Tools." *Project Risk Journal* 18 (1): 25–39.

Wenger, Etienne, Richard A. McDermott, and William M. Snyder. 2002. *Cultivating Communities of Practice: A Guide to Managing Knowledge.* Harvard Business School Press.

Wong, Kai T., and Jason Y. Lee. 2023. "Cost Estimation Integrity in Large-Scale Infrastructure: Benchmarking and Contingency Modeling." *Construction Economics and Building* 23 (2): 42–58.

Yescombe, E. R. 2022. *Public-Private Partnerships in Infrastructure: Principles of Policy and Finance.* 3rd ed. Academic Press.

Zhang, Yifan, and Liang Chen. 2023. "Megaproject Governance in China: A Review and Visual Analysis." *Buildings* 13 (6): 1443.

AI Usage Disclosure

During the preparation of this work, the author employed generative AI tools such as ChatGPT (OpenAI) to support the development process of certain elements, especially the Learning Outcomes and Reflection Questions. These tools were used in accordance with academic and ethical standards. All outputs were carefully reviewed and edited by the author, who assumes full responsibility for the final content.

About the Author

Akin Oni is a megaproject executive, thought leader, and mentor whose career spans more than three decades across continents, industries, and cultures. From the oilfields of West Africa to the mining hubs of Australia and Latin America, the frozen frontiers of Canada, and the energy corridors of the United States, UK and Japan, he has led or advised on some of the world's most complex and consequential projects.

With project leadership roles at some of the world's asset-intensive companies, Akin has been entrusted with stewarding billions of dollars in capital investments. His expertise lies not just in the disciplines of engineering, contracts, project controls, governance, and execution but in what truly makes or breaks megaprojects: ethics, decisions, leadership, and integrity.

Driven by a passion to see capital deployed wisely and responsibly, Akin challenges prevailing norms in project development and champions approaches that align vision with discipline, and ambition with accountability. His voice is both inspirational and practical, shaped by real-world experience where the costs of poor decisions are counted in billions—and the rewards of wisdom are measured in generations.

Beyond boardrooms and project sites, Akin is a mentor, speaker, and builder of communities of practice. He has served with distinction in professional associations such as AACE International, Toastmasters International, and PMI, and he actively invests in raising the next generation of project professionals worldwide. His calling is to not only build infrastructure that fuels economies but also to build people who will lead with courage, clarity, and conviction.

In *Megaproject Development and Decision Making*, Akin distills decades of experience into insights that are both sobering and empowering. He reminds us that megaprojects are more than engineering feats; they are reflections of our values, our choices, and our willingness to shoulder responsibility for the future.

Through his writing, Akin invites leaders, investors, policymakers, and practitioners alike to embrace a higher standard of excellence—because in megaprojects, as in life, decisions shape destiny. His weekly newsletter on his authoring activities is now being viewed by thousands on various platforms across all continents.

Learn more at *www.akinoni.com* and follow the journey.

Index

www.ingramcontent.com/pod-product-compliance
Lightning Source LLC
Chambersburg PA
CBHW061503180526
45171CB00001B/15